EDUCATION NETWORKS

"This book is a revelation of the emerging intersection between the global power elite, information technology, and schools. Spring opens our eyes to tensions taking place at this intersection and the future of schooling."

Paul E. Pitre, Washington State University

"A timely and critical analysis of the impact of information and communication technology on learners as well as a well-researched articulation of the for-profit network behind this industry. As with his other work, Spring is able to weave together the sociocultural/political/economic in fascinating ways. ... He pushes readers to think in different ways about themselves, their learning, and the influences on that learning from a global political perspective."

Kathleen deMarrais, University of Georgia

"Provides a comprehensive and enlightening picture of whom and what is pushing the ICT agenda for the schools, as well as a compelling and convincing explanation for the national obsession with data-driven 'accountability' systems."

Bess Altwerger, Towson University

Education Networks is a critical analysis of the emerging intersection among the global power elite, information and communication technology, and schools. Joel Spring documents and examines the economic and political interests and forces—including elite networks, the for-profit education industry, data managers, and professional educators—that are pushing the use of ICT for online instruction, test preparation and tutoring, data management, instructional software packages, and more, and looks closely at the impact this is having on schools, students, and learning.

Making a distinction between "mind" (as socially constructed) and "brain" (as a physiological entity), Spring draws on recent findings from comparative psychology on the possible effects of ICT on the social construction of the minds of students and school managers, and from neuroscience regarding its effect on students' brains. Throughout, the influence of elite networks and powerful interest groups is linked to what is happening to children in classrooms. In conclusion Spring offers bold suggestions to change the course of the looming technological triumph of ICT in the "brave new world" of schooling.

Joel Spring is Professor of Education, Queens College and the Graduate Center of the City University of New York. His acclaimed work in Educational Policy Studies involves the application of history, sociology, economics, political science, and philosophy to the analysis of national and global school programs. He is the author of over twenty scholarly books and textbooks on these topics.

Sociocultural, Political, and Historical Studies in Education
Joel Spring, Editor

For additional information on titles in the Sociocultural, Political, and Historical Studies in Education series visit **www.routledge.com/education**

EDUCATION NETWORKS

Power, Wealth, Cyberspace, and the Digital Mind

Joel Spring

QUEENS COLLEGE AND THE GRADUATE CENTER,
THE CITY UNIVERSITY OF NEW YORK

Routledge
Taylor & Francis Group

NEW YORK AND LONDON

First published 2012
by Routledge
711 Third Avenue, New York, NY 10017

Simultaneously published in the UK
by Routledge
2 Park Square, Milton Park, Abingdon, Oxon OX14 4RN

Routledge is an imprint of the Taylor & Francis Group, an informa business

© 2012 Taylor & Francis

The right of Joel Spring to be identified as author of this work has been asserted by him in accordance with sections 77 and 78 of the Copyright, Designs and Patents Act 1988.

Library of Congress Cataloging in Publication Data
Spring, Joel H.
Education networks : power, wealth, cyberspace, and the digital
mind / Joel Spring.
p. cm. -- (Sociocultural, political, and historical studies in education)
1. Educational technology--Economic aspects. 2. Information
technology--Economic aspects. 3. Educational technology--Political
aspects. 4. Information technology--Political aspects. 5. Educational technology
industries. 6. Education--Effect of technological innovations on. I. Title.
LB1028.3.S637 2012
371.33--dc23
2011037053

ISBN13: 978-0-415-89983-3 (hbk)
ISBN13: 978-0-415-89984-0 (pbk)
ISBN13: 978-0-203-15680-3 (ebk)

Typeset in Bembo
by Taylor & Francis Books

Printed and bound in the United States of America by
Walsworth Publishing Company, Marceline, MO.

CONTENTS

PREFACE

I started this book wondering why school districts were investing in information and communications technology (ICT) while facing reduced budgets and the possibility of laying off teachers. Who were the political and economic groups calling for expanded use of ICT in education? Would the increased use of ICT improve the quality of schooling? What about claims that multitasking on computers was inhibiting the ability of students to concentrate and creating a generation with attention deficit disorder? Were people becoming addicted to digital games and social media? Was ICT increasing student access to global knowledge or did students primarily use the Internet for shopping and social contacts? Would more authoritarian school systems result from the increasing ability of governments to use ICT for disseminating propaganda, censoring online communications, maintaining surveillance of users, and keeping massive data files on students and graduates?

In Chapter 1, I begin answering these questions by studying global elite networks which support the expansion of ICT in education. For-profit ICT companies producing educational software, games, and hardware have an obvious stake in convincing government officials and the public to buy their products. New York City provided me with a good example because two ICT powerhouses and members of the global superclass, Mayor Michael Bloomberg and media mogul Rupert Murdoch, were involved in expanding online instruction and the use of ICT in New York public schools. These two members of the global elite are networked with other companies and individuals calling for the expansion of ICT in education.

Important players, called the "shadow elite" in this book, advocate for ICT while moving between for-profit ICT companies, foundations, and government. For-profit ICT companies want government agencies to spend more money buying their products even if it means laying off teachers.

In Chapter 2, I explore the role of the shadow elite as they try to convince government agencies to spend more money on educational technology.

In Chapter 3, I examine the resulting government policies which include the United States' National Education Technology Plan. These government policies are also influenced by private foundations advocating for more ICT in schools, such as the Bill and Melinda Gates Foundation and the Foundation for Excellence in Education. One of the more interesting network relationships is the funding by the Gates Foundation of the publisher Pearson to create online courses to be sold to schools.

Some educators feel that students will be more motivated to learn if learning is made fun through "edutainment" provided by learning games. In Chapter 4, I discuss the development of the edutainment industry and its backers in government and universities. Edutainment software appeared in the early days of personal computers. Today, digital gaming is big business with certain companies dominating the field. With the development of smart phones and iPad-like devices, thousands of educational apps are being sold for every age group including toddlers. Those interested in making a profit selling learning games to schools claim that they are an educational panacea because they make learning fun.

What is the effect of ICT on the brains and minds of students? There exists, as I review in Chapter 5, a great deal of contradictory literature claiming either ICT improves brain functions or ICT reduces the ability of students to concentrate and remember. In addition, there are debates about the impact of social media on youth. Some argue that social media lack the nonverbal communications of face-to-face relations which can leave the user feeling lonely while networked to thousands.

In Chapter 6, I explore attempts to use social media in schools to reduce political and religious conflicts along with the general role of ICT in political and civic education. Some educators hope that ICT will result in increased involvement of youth in political and civic activities. Others argue that ICT is primarily used by youth for shopping, social networking, and entertainment with political usage confined to youth already interested in politics. However, there is a more ominous side to concerns about the political usage of ICT, namely the ability of government to use ICT to propagandize students, censor Internet work, and maintain lifelong surveillance of students. For-profit companies are selling to governments software and technology that filters and reports user action on the Internet. The Great Firewall of China is a model for this type of ideological management of Internet users. Consequently, a potential result of expansion of ICT in schools is enhancing what is called the Trinity of Authority, namely propaganda, censorship, and surveillance.

In Chapter 7, the final chapter of the book, I review proposed scenarios for global schools and the use of ICT. For this discussion, I use scenarios from the Schooling for Tomorrow project of the Organization for Economic Cooperation and Development. Also, I compare a school for the children of the global elite with the government-operated Florida Virtual Global School. I also examine the future growth of ICT resulting from the combination of technological evolution and consumerism. The book ends on the question: is online schooling part of a steady march to an authoritarian society?

1

THE DIGITAL MIND, SUPERCLASS NETWORKS, AND EDUCATION

"Data Mining Gets Traction in Education," proclaimed the *Education Week* headline, "Researchers Sift 'Data Exhaust' for Clues to Improve Learning."[1] Are students now merely seen as data by school and government officials, and researchers? Is the school viewed as a "mine of student data" with heavy duty mining machinery expelling "exhaust" that other machinery can sift through to discover how students really learn? Do metaphorical terms like "data mining," "traction," and "data exhaust" reflect how school administrators, educational officials, and researchers view public education? *Education Week* reporter Sarah Sparks describes the process of "data mining":

> Educational data mining uses some of the typical data included in state long-itudinal databases, such as test scores and attendance, but researchers often spend more time analyzing ancillary data, such as student interactions in a chat log or the length of responses to homework assignments—information that researchers call "data exhaust."[2]

Why has global school politics been reduced to discussions of data, such as test scores, graduation rates, and the gender, ethnicity, and family income of students? Why do global leaders primarily think about education as a potential contribution to economic growth and stability? What is the relationship between information and communication technologies (ICT) and the digital mind, the politics and economics of schooling, and students as data? The answer to these questions can be found in a complex interrelationship between ICT businesses, the concerns of the global elite, the effect of the digital world on the social construction of the mind, and global networks of educators and business elites.

Corporatism and Education

Corporatism, the marriage of business and government, is now more pervasive in education with the use of ICT to collect student data and provide online instruction and virtual classrooms. It is also global in scope. By corporatism I mean an intertwining of government and business with business being in control. In education this phenomenon began in the late 19th century and was consolidated after World War II.[3] With the advent of the digital age in the 1990s, corporatism made new inroads in schools with businesses marketing their digital equipment and software to schools; a growing reliance on data to measure the worth of teachers and schools; and the growth of online instruction and virtual classrooms. Data analysis is now the primary tool of corporate management including school management.

In some cases, as I discuss in this book, there are proponents of online instruction who would replace traditional classrooms and teacher roles with virtual classrooms with teachers replaced by facilitators or online instruction in the home. One reason is that online instruction is cheaper. Consider the case of Florida when during the 2010–2011 school year some local schools could not afford to hire new teachers to meet the requirements of Florida's 2002 Class Size Reduction Amendment that limits high school classrooms in core subjects like English and math to 25 students, fourth- through eighth-grade classes to 22 students, and kindergarten through third-grade classes to 18 students. The amendment does not limit the class size of virtual classrooms. According to *New York Times* reporter Laura Herrera 7,000 Miami-Dade County high school students were placed in virtual classrooms because the school system did not have enough teachers for core subjects. The online courses are provided by the state's Florida Virtual School. Jodi Robins, the assistant principal of curriculum at Miami Beach High, said that even if students struggled in certain subjects, the virtual labs were necessary because "there's no way to beat the class-size mandate without it."[4] Reporter Herrera asked Chris Kirchner, an English teacher at Coral Reef Senior High School in Miami, about forcing students into virtual classes. He replied, "The way our state is dealing with class size is nearly criminal. They're standardizing in the worst possible way, which is evident in virtual classes."[5]

Another reason for virtual classrooms, more technology in the classroom, and online instruction is the profits gained through the sale of hardware and software, and consultations about data analysis with local and state education authorities. Educational corporatism is driven by a desire for profits by ICT companies and educational entrepreneurs, and those wanting to standardize the curriculum to ensure that schools do not teach anything that threatens the power of multinational corporations. For instance, Florida Virtual School provides standardized online courses in subjects to virtual classrooms around the state. Online instruction comes prepackaged and standardized and it does not benefit from teachers who might introduce critical comments or question the content of courses. Online instruction from Florida Virtual School promises reduced costs by not requiring certified teachers for virtual classrooms or even school buildings for at-home online instruction.

ICT: Shaping and Controlling Knowledge and Expanding Educational Corporatism

The politics and economics of ICT exemplify the continued growth of corporatism in education. I will use the New York City school system as an example of the interplay between global elites, ICT companies, and school systems. The New York City example provides an opportunity to define the digital mind and its social construction as related to ICT managers and schools. It also highlights the power of social networking in influencing school policies with two of the New York City players being identified as among the most powerful people in the world. As further examples of the interplay between elite social networks, ICT, and school politics I will discuss the World Economic Forum and Boao Forum for Asia.

A theme in this book is the effect of ICT on the knowledge disseminated by education to students. This section will establish a framework for discussing this theme which I will elaborate on later in this chapter regarding the social structure of the digital mind and in later chapters regarding the influence of ICT companies on school policies and student learning. Today, ICT dominates discussions about the goals and methods of instruction of global school systems. The major educational ICT players are media; the Internet; educational institutions; and education companies, including publishers, and software producers and other producers of learning materials. For the purpose of this chapter I am defining information as textual content and visual images, including how these texts and visuals are organized. For instance, the Google search engine retrieves information using a particular and ever changing method. The method of retrieval by the Google search engine organizes the information distributed to the public including information used by students, teachers, and educational institutions.

In addition, Google, about which the company's cofounder Sergey Brin said, "We want to make Google the third half of your brain,"[6] opened in 2010 its website Culturomics (http://www.culturomics.org/) which allows the user to search a digital storehouse of 500 billion words contained in books published between 1500 and 2008 in English, French, Spanish, German, Chinese, and Russian. This will, according to the announcement of the project by *New York Times* reporter Patricia Cohen, be "the first time a data set of this magnitude and searching tools are at the disposal of Ph.D.'s, middle school students and anyone else who likes to spend time in front of a small screen."[7] Erez Lieberman Aiden, a junior fellow at the Society of Fellows at Harvard, said about the project, "The goal is to give an 8-year-old the ability to browse cultural trends throughout history, as recorded in books."[8]

I am defining "politics of ICT" as the exercise of power to try and control the information distributed through media, the Internet, and educational institutions. For instance, consider ICT politics regarding the presence of the Google search engine in the People's Republic of China. The Chinese government insisted on censoring Google's search engine, forcing the company to move to Hong Kong in 2010. In its place, the government promoted the use of the Chinese search engine

Baidu. Interestingly, Baidu reacted to the cost of government censorship. Kaiser Kuo, the director of international communications for Baidu, argues that it is wrong to suggest that censorship was helping his company: "Google no longer incurs the costs of censorship that we continue to incur; those costs include not only hardware, software and manpower but most importantly the time of our very senior managers. We should not labor under the illusion that censorship is some sort of competitive advantage to Baidu."[9]

Today, Google influences the learning of students and the public who use it to search the Internet. As I will explain in more detail later in the book, the struggle over censorship of Google has spilled over into the global arena with the company invoking the rules of the World Trade Organization to protect the supposed freedom of its search engine.

The politics of ICT also includes its effect on the mind and brain. Prior to this century, the primary concern was the relationship between knowledge and the mind, with the mind being considered a product of the interaction between a person and society. In the 21st century, neuroscience and evolutionary biology have complicated this scenario through findings that the organic brain physically changes when learning and it is disposed to react in certain ways to the world outside of itself. For instance, as I will describe in more detail later, Nicholas Carr reports brain research which demonstrates that the actual use of Google and the Internet physically changes the organic brain.[10]

Therefore, ICT politics, as I use the concept, refers to power struggles to control media, the Internet, and educational institutions which in turn shape a socially constructed mind and result in physical changes in the organic brain. Also, I argue, the media, the Internet, and educational institutions are interrelated, particularly with the growth of online instruction and research and an increased emphasis in educational systems on the collection and analysis of data. In a broader sense, the media often, but not always, serves the interests of power and is often the source of public ideas about learning and educational institutions. There are many reasons for wanting to control ICT, including maintaining political and economic power and the desire by education companies, including publishers, and software producers and other producers of learning materials, to sell their products.

ICT Politics: The Superclass and Public Schools

Before discussing the effect of ICT on the social construction of the mind, I would like to provide an example of the interplay between the global superclass and ICT; for-profit ICT education companies; and an interrelated network of global leaders and workers. My goal is to weave these themes through my analysis of global education politics.

In this example I will be using the term "superclass" as defined by David Rothkopf in *Superclass: The Global Power Elite and the World They Are Making*.[11] The major players in my educational example are members of the superclass. Rothkopf estimates that about 6,000 people belong to the global superclass, which includes all the world's billionaires, heads of major global corporations and financial companies, political and military leaders of globally influential countries, and major religious leaders. Obviously, the members of the superclass are constantly changing as personal fortunes rise and fall, corporations and financial institutions change leaders, national political and military leaders are replaced, and religious leadership shifts.

My example involves two members of the global superclass, who built their fortunes in ICT, and the schools of the world class city of New York. Also involved is a for-profit education company Wireless Generation. The story begins in 2001 when billionaire and superclass ICT mogul Michael Bloomberg was elected mayor of New York City. *Forbes* lists Bloomberg as the 10th wealthiest man in the United States and 23rd among world billionaires.[12] *Forbes* also lists him as 23rd on the list of the world's most powerful people.[13] *Forbes* magazine used the following four criteria to identify the world's most powerful:

- Does a person have influence over a lot of people?
- Do they have significant financial resources relative to their peers?
- Are they powerful in multiple spheres?
- Do they actively wield their power?[14]

Bloomberg's fortune is built on an ICT company that provides financial data and news. The company, Bloomberg L.P., describes itself:

> In 1981 Bloomberg started out with one core belief: that bringing transparency to capital markets through access to information could increase capital flows, produce economic growth and jobs, and significantly reduce the cost of doing business. Today's Bloomberg builds on that foundation – *everything we do connects decision makers in business, finance and government to a broad and dynamic network of information, news, people and ideas that enables faster, more effective decisions* [author's emphasis].[15]

Enhancing his power as head of the city and expressing a desire to improve the city's schools, Mayor Bloomberg lobbied the New York state legislature to pass a law creating mayoral control of the schools. After gaining control, Bloomberg appointed as school Chancellor Joel Klein, a lawyer from another ICT conglomerate, Bertelsmann. Bertelsmann, which identifies itself as "media worldwide," is composed of six corporate divisions including media groups RTL, Aravato, DirectGroup, and BMG. It also owns Random House book publishers and a magazine and newspaper conglomerate called G+J.[16]

Technically, Klein, along with his future replacement, ICT executive Cathleen Black appointed Chancellor in 2010, had no professional educational background and lacked the legal requirements to head the New York City schools. New York state law requires substantial education credentials and experience. Without this educational background, the appointment requires a waiver by the state Commissioner of Education. Bloomberg received the waiver to appoint Klein.

Because of either his personal management style, the influence of educational companies wanting to promote student testing and data collection, or the global discourse on improving schools by measuring student achievement, Klein initiated changes that centered on student testing and data collection. Also, Mayor Bloomberg, looking through the eyes of his company, might see data collection as the key to good management. Bloomberg's company's website declares: "Bloomberg keeps the financial and business worlds humming by providing the highest quality data, news and analytics. That's why influential decision makers turn to us every day."[17]

Klein was not unique in this approach to school change since testing and data collection were, as I will explain later, being echoed in education ministries around the world. To aid in this endeavor Chancellor Klein contracted with the company Wireless Generation to use their data collection and analysis program Achievement Reporting and Innovation System (ARIS). Wireless Generation states on its website: "Wireless Generation ... builds large-scale data systems that centralize student data and give educators and parents unprecedented visibility into learning."[18]

The reader might be wondering why testing and data collection are considered the key to global school improvement. The Bloomberg–Klein emphasis on data collection could, in part, be a product of both of them being attuned to the dissemination of public information through their media. Data related to test scores is the easiest and simplest educational finding to distribute by media companies. Certainly, discussions of the validity and problems related to educational policy or teaching methods cannot be reduced to a one-minute sound bite. Of course, this is not the only reason for the increasing global reliance on educational data systems. Other factors that will be discussed later in this book are the influence of for-profit companies like Wireless Generation, the influence of computer systems on how the mind perceives schooling, and the general global discourse about how education can contribute to economic growth and solve economic problems.

Joel Klein left his position as Chancellor to become an executive vice president at News Corporation which bought 90 percent of Wireless Generation for $360 million. The founder and head of News Corporation is another member of the superclass, billionaire and ICT mogul Rupert Murdoch. At the time of purchase, Murdoch expressed his belief in the potential of the education market: "We see a $500 billion sector in the U.S. alone," he said, "that is waiting desperately to be transformed by big breakthroughs that extend the reach of great teaching."[19] Similar to Bloomberg, *Forbes* lists Murdoch among the richest and most powerful. He is listed ahead of Bloomberg as the 13th most powerful person in the world and behind Bloomberg as 117th among global billionaires.[20] The global ICT reach of Murdoch's News Corporation includes publishers, television broadcasting, newspapers, and information services.[21]

In announcing the hiring of Klein, News Corporation issued a press release stating, "Mr. Klein will act as a senior advisor to Mr. Murdoch on a wide range of initiatives, including *developing business strategies for the emerging educational marketplace* [author's emphasis]."[22] In the same press release Rupert Murdoch is quoted as saying, "His record of achievement leading one of the country's toughest school systems has given him a unique perspective that will be particularly important as we look into a sector that has long been in need of innovation."[23]

Leaving office to assume a position in charge of business strategies for the education market for News Corporation with direct connections to his previously contracted service provider Wireless Generation, Klein described his goal as getting private investors interested in the education sector.

> I'll be looking at how to stimulate private investment in what I think are instructional platforms and other technologies I think will change the way K-12 education is delivered. I've got a lot to do before I tell you the details, but that's the basic concept. I think it's going to take substantial private capital to be able to generate the kind of technological advancement I think is absolutely essential. New York City is so far ahead in this discussion, but we're still in the earliest phases of that discussion.[24]

While Klein was Chancellor, Murdoch's *New York Post* supported Klein's successful effort to raise the state limits on the number of charter schools. And, according to *New York Times* reporters Jeremy W. Peters, Michael Barbaro, and Javier C. Hernandez, "they [Murdoch and Klein] agreed on a core set of education principles: that charter schools needed to expand; poor instructors should be weeded out; and the power of the teachers union must be curtailed ... he [Murdoch] quietly donated $1 million to an advocacy group, Education Reform Now, run by Mr. Klein, bankrolling a continuing campaign to overturn a state law protecting older teachers."[25]

Murdoch and Klein's close relationship became news in 2011 when Murdoch's newspapers in Great Britain came under police investigation for hacking phones for news stories. Murdoch appointed Klein to head an investigation within the company. Klein became Murdoch's de facto chief of internal affairs of News Corporation. Klein could be seen sitting behind Murdoch during televised testimony given before an investigative committee of the British Parliament.[26]

Another twist in the Wireless Generation and New York City schools story occurred the year after Klein left office to join Rupert Murdoch's group that bought the company. In early 2011, the amount of money spent on educational technology by New York public schools was criticized because of budget shortfalls that would require eliminating 6,100 teaching positions. A *New York Times* article specifically raised concerns about the amount of money being paid to Wireless Generation's Achievement Reporting and Innovation System. Reporter Sharon Otterman wrote, "The city comptroller, John C. Liu, announced audits last week of spending on online learning and of the Achievement Reporting and Innovation System, or ARIS, an $80 million school information database that cost more than projected and has been criticized for not living up to its promise of helping schools track student progress effectively."[27]

Consequently, the company Klein contracted with as New York City School Chancellor and later worked with after being hired by Rupert Murdoch not only cost more but proved not to be effective. In addition, the school administration was spending on other ICT projects during the fiscal crises. Criticism by the City Comptroller and the Manhattan borough president was directed at not only the $542 million to be spent on wiring schools for ICT but also the $50 million contracts to be spent on an online course-management system. There were also expenses for hiring Rosetta Stone and Pearson for training and software use. Some schools were using Rosetta Stone to teach foreign languages—used as a substitute for foreign language teachers.[28]

When the schools were asked to justify the high cost of wiring schools, the justification was contradicted by city officials. Otterman reported:

> City officials said the most crucial reason for the new spending was to prepare for computerized standardized English and math tests being developed by a national consortium that may replace the existing state assessments in the 2014–15 school year. But the state Department of Education said last week that those exams, at least at first, would also be available in pencil-and-paper format to give districts time to make the transition. In response, the city said it wanted to be ahead of the curve, because the scoring of online tests would be faster and more accurate.[29]

ICT Leaders and New York Schools

There is another twist in the relationship between the media and Wireless Generation. The Chief Executive Officer of the company, Larry Berger, who retains 10 percent of the ownership after the Murdoch purchase, serves on the board of trustees of Editorial Projects in Education, the nonprofit corporation that publishes *Education Week*. *Education Week* is the major national newspaper in the United States and promotes the increasing use of technology in schools through its series "Digital Directions" which is billed as "Tracking news, trends and ideas in educational technology."[30]

The network connections of News Corporation, Wireless Generation, *Education Week*, and Joel Klein's promotion of educational technology all seemed to come together in a Wireless Generation full page advertisement appearing in the March 27, 2011, issue of *Education Week*'s special supplement *Technology Counts*, along with many other ads for for-profit ICT companies. The ad features Wireless Generation's technology Burst Reading which is presented as a "Sophisticated technology [that] analyzes formative assessment data to form skills-based groups and generate 10-day sequences of … engaging lesson plans."[31] Among the technological solutions offered to schools by Wireless Generation are: Instructional Improvement Systems; Differentiated Curriculum & Instruction; Assessment & Analysis Tools; Consulting & Professional Services; and Open Source Initiatives.

When Joel Klein resigned in 2010, Mayor Bloomberg appointed ICT executive Cathleen Black as the new Chancellor. The appointment set off a furor because

Black lacked any experience as a professional educator and she and her children never attended a public school. An official New York City press release on the appointment stressed Black's background as a global ICT leader:

> For eight years beginning in 1983, Black served as President and Publisher of USA Today, and then Executive Vice President of the paper's parent company, helping personnel from Gannett publications coast to coast and from across the publishing industry build a nationwide newspaper that few expected to last ... as President, and then as Chairman of Hearst Magazines, Black led a team of some 2,000 employees producing more than 200 local editions of 14 magazines in more than 100 countries. Under her leadership, Hearst had record-breaking years they built on decades of success with titles like Cosmopolitan, Esquire, Good Housekeeping, Harper's Bazaar, Marie Claire, Popular Mechanics, Redbook, and Town & Country, introduced highly-acclaimed new titles like O, The Oprah Magazine.[32]

Mayor Bloomberg justified his appointment with a statement reflecting how his mind thought about public schools: "Cathie Black is a superstar manager who has succeeded spectacularly in the private sector. She is brilliant, she is innovative, she is driven—and there is virtually nobody who knows more about the needs of the 21st century workforce for which we need to prepare our kids."[33] Bloomberg apparently didn't distinguish in his mind between the abilities needed to manage USA Today and Cosmopolitan and those needed to teach history, math, science, and other school subjects.

There are two important things to note about Bloomberg's justification for appointing Black. First, Bloomberg doesn't give any evidence of his mind differentiating between operation of an ICT company and public schools teaching a diversity of students. Both, apparently in Bloomberg's mind, involve the same management skills involving transmitting information. Second, Bloomberg seems to believe from the above quote that the primary mission of schooling is preparing a "21st century workforce." As a corporate leader, Bloomberg's mind would appear to see the world through the eyes of a manager interested in hiring well educated workers. Like any media company, schools transmit information. In turn, schools supply workers to businesses.

Also, the City's press release emphasized Black's management of digital systems, which was congruent with Klein's emphasis on testing and data collection. The press release stated that Black "created digital platforms that were inconceivable in 1995. As the media industry has tackled digital changes, Hearst Magazines has been widely-regarded as being at the forefront of that evolution."[34]

Bloomberg's appointment was greeted with a wall of protest by politicians and educators concerned with Black's lack of school experience. At first the New York State Commissioner of Education David Steiner was hesitant about granting Bloomberg another waiver to appoint a school's Chancellor who did not meet the legal requirements of substantial education credentials and experience. A compromise was quickly reached between the Mayor's office and the state to appoint a second in command with an educational background that would complement Black's skills as a media manager.

Black's appointed second in command Shael Polakow-Suransky was, like the previous Chancellor Klein, a person devoted to testing and data collection. *The New York Times* headlined Polakow-Suransky's appointment: "Shael Polakow-Suransky Is Believer in (More) Testing / New No. 2 at City Schools Believes in More and Better Testing."[35] *The Times* provided this description of his background, "Polakow-Suransky is the chief accountability officer of the New York City Department of Education, a job that is as institutional as they come. He traffics in hard numbers, overseeing a system that assigns grades to schools based on complex and fixed formulas, in which success depends largely on how students score on a single test."[36]

ICT, the Digital Mind, and Schools

The above example of New York City exemplifies the effect of one aspect of what I will call the "digital mind" on schools involving two of the richest and most powerful men in the world (Bloomberg and Murdoch) who built their fortunes on ICT; a lesser power (Cathleen Black) but still an important global ICT player; two that I will call servants of power to the ICT world (Klein and Polakow-Suransky); and a fresh entrepreneur to the ICT field (Berger). I refer to "one aspect" of the digital mind because there are variations in the digital mind depending on differing social contexts and circumstances. In this example, the social context is organizers and owners of ICT companies and implementers within a school system.

First, it should be noted that all of the above people have an economic interest and/or disposition to favor global schools adopting ICT for managing student data, producing and scoring tests, and online instruction. Both ICT owners and managers within school systems have an economic interest in selling products and/or ensuring the importance of their jobs.

Second, owners and managers of ICT companies and those whose jobs in institutions like schools involve managing ICT have a disposition to see the world through the lens of data processed by computers. I am using the phrase "disposition to see the world" to indicate one aspect of what I am calling the "digital mind."

Suggesting that the owners and managers being discussed might have digital minds that are a reflection of their work follows in a tradition from the 19th century when Western thinkers began to grapple with the issue of the social construction of the mind or, in other words, the social construction of how people see the world and how their knowledge is organized within their organic brains. The most prominent names in this tradition include Karl Marx, George Herbert Mead, Emile Durkheim, Karl Mannheim, Claude Levi-Strauss, and Michel Foucault.[37] I don't have space in this book to review the range of complex discussions generated by these Western thinkers. However, in keeping with this tradition, I am going to assert that work and the social relations related to work have an impact on the social construction of a person's mind.

What is important for a manager in the digital age, particularly an owner or manager of an ICT company? Data! The computer allows for the rapid computation of a wide range of business tasks to produce daily, weekly, or monthly spreadsheets including profitability of particular products, the work of employees, and various branches of a company. Today, a corporate manager might look at a computer-generated spreadsheet and determine whether or not a worker or branch of the company has met his production and profitability goals, which are broken down into categories according to the company's work; for instance, a global publisher might use weekly computer- and software-generated spreadsheets to determine if an editor has achieved her signing goals for acquiring new books, whether or not she has put enough books into production, and whether she is achieving her revenue goals.

ICT has made it possible to easily manage and expand global corporations. Obviously, global companies existed before the digital age such as the British East Indian Company which, after being granted a Royal Charter by Elizabeth I in December of 1600, expanded the British Empire across India and surrounding countries. Communicating with messages sent on sailing ships with accounting and records kept by hand, the Company operated at a snail's pace compared to the instant messaging of the Internet and number crunching power of the computer. In comparison, 21st century global managers can be in continuous contact with branches around the world, hop on a plane and be flown almost any place within a day, and turn on their computers and gain instant access to spreadsheets indicating how well the various parts of the global corporation are functioning.

Digital management requires data which in most cases involves numbers that can be processed through software programs. Is this the management world of global superclass members Bloomberg and Murdoch? Staring at a computer screen that opens the door to management by numbers, I would hypothesize that the digital manager's mind begins to be structured in a similar fashion in keeping with the argument that the social relations of work contribute to the social construction of the way a person sees the world. The digital manager's mind might begin to see the world as data that can be made understandable by entering it in a software program.

The digital mind of the school manager might look for data that will help her understand how well her school or schools are functioning. What information about schools can be reduced to numbers that can be processed by software? The answer is test scores, dropout rates, attendance, and numbers regarding student ethnic background, gender, and family income and other quantifiable data. In the digital manager's mind, the goal of student achievement is similar to the goal of profitability in a global corporation. For the digital manager's mind, student achievement is seen as quantifiable data in the form of test scores that allows software programs, such as those sold by Wireless Generation to the New York City schools, to compare students and schools, rate schools (this is similar to a corporate manager rating an employee according to her profitability), and establish quantifiable goals based on raising student test scores (increased profitability).

Digital managers use data to monitor their employees, which in the case of schools is particularly directed at teachers and school administrators. Again, the digital manager needs numerical data to do this monitoring. The source of this data, as exemplified by the actions of superclass members Bloomberg, Murdoch, and their hired help, is student test scores. Test scores become the measure of the profitability of schools. In the case of teachers, their profitability (student achievement) to the system can be determined by data from student test scores.

Seeing the World Through Data

Psychological studies provide another opportunity to explore the digital mind of managers using ICT. Psychologists, along with sociologists, have tackled the problem of the social construction of knowledge. An important example of how psychologists deal with this issue is Richard Nisbett's *The Geography of Thought: How Asians and Westerners Think Differently ... and Why* (2003) in which he conducted and gathered psychological studies of how people think in Confucian-based cultures (such as China, Korea, and Japan) and Socratic and Aristotelian-based cultures (such as Europe, North America, and Australia).[38] With globalization these differences are rapidly disappearing or they are, according to Nisbett, resulting in possible biculturalism and hybridity of thought.

The title, *The Geography of Thought,* indicates Nisbett's basic argument that geographical conditions fostered different forms of agricultural production which, in turn, affected how people saw the world. Basically the difference—I am over-simplifying Nisbett's argument—in agricultural production was the individual farming methods of the West versus the collective agricultural production of rice farming in Confucian-based countries. Supported by psychological studies by scholars in Western and Confucian-based countries, Nisbett argues that these differences in geographical conditions and agricultural production resulted in Socratic-Aristotelian-based societies seeing the world as broken up into categories of objects without a consideration of their context and Confucian-based societies seeing a complex holistic world. Again I want to emphasize that while I am presenting a simple description of Nisbett's argument, he backs it up with over two hundred pages of discussions of international comparative psychological studies. Nisbett summarizes the differences in how minds generate differing world views:

> Thus, to the Asian, the world is a complex place, composed of continuous substances, understandable in terms of the parts, and subject more to collective than to personal control. To the Westerner, the world is a relatively simple place, composed of discrete objects that can be understood without undue attention to context, and highly subject to personal control. Very different worlds indeed.[39]

These world views result in differences in interpretation of human action. Based on a series of international psychological studies, Nisbett argues that Confucian-based societies tend to see human action as a product of the environment while Western societies look more at the internal state of the individual. Nisbett writes regarding studies done by Chinese and American psychologists:

> It should come as no surprise that Chinese people are inclined to attribute behavior to context and Americans tend to attribute the same behavior to the actor. We saw in the last chapter that East Asians attend more to context than do Americans. And what captures one's attention is what one is likely to regard as causally important. The converse seems equally plausible: *If one thinks something is causally important one is likely to attend to it. So a cycle gets established whereby theories about causality and focus of attention reinforce each other* [author's emphasis].[40]

The above quote is illustrated by an experiment in Hong Kong where participants were presented with a story about a young man who is told by his doctor that he must lose weight. He attends a lavish banquet with a huge and tempting display of desserts and promptly overeats. The response to the story by participants depends on their thinking from the perspective of a Confucian-based or Western culture. It is important to note that Hong Kong was an important British colony until being returned to China in the 1990s and its population is noted for its biculturalism. Reponses to the scenario from a Confucian-based perspective placed the blame for the overeating on the tempting displays of the banquet. Those seeing the incident from a Western perspective placed the blame on a failure of the overeater's character.[41]

In other words, if a people see the world as a complex whole then they more readily link causes for human action to the environment while those seeing the world as separate and discrete categories are more likely see the causes of human action in the character of the person.

What does the above mean for interpreting the mind of the Western digital manager? This digital manager looks at a computer screen or spreadsheet printout that is composed of numerical data processed by some form of software. If the data shows a decline in student achievement then the digital manager, according to Nisbett's framework, would look for the cause in the source of the data, namely the school. Looking for the cause in the school could lead to the neglect of a more holistic approach that would link a decline in test scores to a complex world. For instance, rather than focus on school change as a source for raising test scores a more holistic approach might look for causality in the conditions in which the child lives, such as the quality of the child's neighborhood, family income, peer groups, family structure, immigrant status, and language issues. Changing the school will not change the effect of many of these outside conditions.

In summary, digital managers' minds often see their company and/or school through the lens of data organized by a particular software program. As a result, there is a constant demand by the digital manager for more and better data. The student is seen as data and a source of data, such as attendance, test scores, race, family income, and other characteristics. If there is a problem, such as data showing low test scores, then the digital manager tends to look for solutions within the institution providing the data rather than having a more holistic view that might see causes in environmental conditions that, in fact, cannot be changed by just changing the school. The student becomes data and the school becomes a data source.

The Brain, Data Overload, Multitasking, and Bucket Drool

What happens to the brain when faced with an overload of data? Can the brain adjust to the digital mind's encounter with an overload of data requiring multi-tasking? All studies of the digital generation (roughly defined as those who grew up with the Web and computers since the 1990s) emphasize that the brains of the digital generation have changed to handle the requirements of computer multitasking. The military recognizes the existence of the multitasking mind of the digital generation, as expressed by Lt. Gen. Mark P. Hertling, who oversees initial training for every soldier: "It's the way this generation learns. It's a multitasking generation. So if they're multitasking and combining things, that's the way we should be training."[42] In this chapter I will begin discussing the effect of ICT on the brain in the context of the digital mind. I will expand on these effects in Chapter 4.

As noted at the beginning of this chapter, educational researchers are now talking about "mining" data by sifting through "data exhaust." This represents one aspect of the digital mind that sees an unending collection of data and subsequent analysis. How does the brain handle the vast amount of data presented to the digital mind? The U.S. military has contracted with a number of research institutions to help train the brains of its personnel to handle multitasking and data overload. The use of Drones in Afghanistan to kill militants resulted in many civilian deaths because Drone operators were often overwhelmed by the amount of data that appears on their computer screens and the requirements of multitasking data from Drones and other surveillance devices. In fighter jets, pilots receive so much information on their screens that they refer to them as "drool buckets" because they can get lost staring at them. Art Kramer, a neuroscientist and director of the Beckman Institute, a research lab at the University of Illinois, expressed this concern, "There is information overload at every level of the military—from the general to the soldier on the ground."[43]

How is the military trying to train the brain to react to the digital mind's encounter with multitasking through digital overload? At George Mason University researchers are having subjects simulate the data overload experienced by military Drone operators. Subjects wear a cap with electrodes that measure brain waves as they are exposed to increasing levels of data. As the amount of data increases, the subject's brains shows sharp spikes in theta waves indicating an inability to con-centrate. This sharp spike in theta waves, explained researcher Raja Parasuraman, is "usually an index of extreme overload."[44]

Michael Barnes of the Army Research Laboratory is trying to improve the neurological response of military personnel to multitasking and data overload. The Army found that soldiers operating tanks when receiving data and videos on their tank's computer screens are often unable to concentrate and actually miss targets that are near them. Consequently, the military is developing training programs that will change the brains of soldiers so that they can concentrate in a world of multitasking and data overload. "The whole question we're asking is whether we can rewire the functioning of the attention system through mindfulness," said one of the researchers, Elizabeth A. Stanley, an assistant professor of security studies at Georgetown University.[45]

As previously noted, the military's attempt to educate the brains of soldiers to concentrate when the digital mind encounters data overload and multitasking is based on current knowledge of the brain's plasticity. The brain's plasticity can be related to the difficulty of concentrating on a single object. Multitasking and data overload change the brain and make it difficult to concentrate.[46] On the other hand, the assumption of neuroscientists working for the military is that the brain can be changed so that concentration is possible.

What do these concerns and research mean for the digital minds of school managers? Does it lead to an inability to concentrate? Do the brains of school managers become unable to focus on any particular data set? Does a lack of concentration lead to a demand for more data sets which results in compounding the concentration problems? Is the almost insatiable demand by school managers for more data a result of the brain's difficulty in focusing when multitasking and receiving vast amounts of data? Do school managers suffer from "bucket drool?"

The Digital Mind, Networking, and Global Schools

Increasing participation in virtual communities has shaped the way we see human relations. I use "we" because I feel that I am influenced by the ability of the Internet to create networks of communities and, consequently, I am applying network analysis to my discussion of global school politics. In our ongoing discussion of the superclass involvement in the New York Public Schools, Bloomberg, Murdoch, Klein, Black, Berger, and Polakow-Suransky form a network of relationships leading from the New York schools to the global elite. However, this network reflects what Nicholas Christakis and James Fowler call "positional inequality."[47] In *Connected: The Surprising Power of Our Social Networks and How They Shape Our Lives*, they define positional inequality as occurring "not because of who we are but because of who we are connected to."[48] For instance, Bloomberg and Murdoch hold pivotal positions in the global network of power as compared to Berger and Polakow-Suransky.

John Guare's 1990 play *Six Degrees of Separation* ushered in an era of virtual communities which created a mindset that sees everyone linked through their connections with others. According to David Knoke and Song Yang, social science publications using social networks as a key concept increased rapidly with the advent of the World Wide Web and the creation of social network websites such as My Space and Facebook and many other sites that linked members of a variety of interest groups.[49]

Like Google, social networking is a political concern in China. In December 2010, Facebook founder Mark Zuckerberg visited the offices of the Chinese search engine Baidu to explore business opportunities in what the Associated Press calls the "world's largest Internet market."[50] According to the Associated Press's report on Internet censorship in China: "China censors Internet content it deems politically sensitive and blocks many websites, including Facebook, Twitter and YouTube."[51] Censorship of the Internet in China is done through what is called the "Great Firewall" created by computer scientist Fang Binxing. The "Great Firewall" has created a group of dissidents about Internet censorship:

> China's nervousness about the power of social networking was on display Monday, when the computer scientist seen as the father of China's "Great Firewall" of Internet controls apparently was forced offline by angry comments within a few hours of opening a microblog. Anonymous posters peppered the microblog of Fang Binxing with hundreds of caustic or sarcastic comments, and eventually all of Fang's posts and the responses were taken down.[52]

The major Chinese alternative to Facebook's social networking is Renren (http://renren.com/).

In the New York City example being used in this chapter, our key players seem to be linked to the rich and powerful of the world. While the New York City school Chancellor Cathleen Black does not make the *Forbes* list of the world's most powerful, *Forbes* did rank her as 67th among the world's most powerful women.[53] This means that all the major players in the New York City schools are linked in varying degrees to the world's richest and most powerful people. Certainly, when a person shakes the hand of the head of the New York City schools, Mayor Michael Bloomberg, they are indirectly touching the hands of the global elite—of course this does not mean that they will actually talk face-to-face to the world's most rich and powerful.

The social network directly linked to Cathleen Black is depicted in a 2007 *Forbes Magazine* article by James Brady who attended her holiday season party at her Park Avenue apartment in New York City. The roster of guests included *Reader's Digest* editor Jackie Leo, *Town & Country*'s Pam Fiori, Tom and Meredith Brokaw, Atoosa Rubenstein of *Seventeen* magazine, Helen Gurley Brown (the woman who originally saved *Cosmo*), Tim Zagat of dining guide fame, Phil Donahue, and David Granger, editor of *Esquire*. Writer Brady described the social networking at the party:

> I attempted to scribble a few notes while balancing a glass of very decent wine and exchanging trade chat and gossip with editors, publishers, writers

and more or less famous Manhattan folk … A guy I knew from the old Murdoch days discussed with me the O.J. Simpson mess. "Rupert is the smartest man in town. How could he let this happen?" I inquired. "He was in Tokyo and Australia at the time," he replied.[54]

The casual mention of Rupert Murdoch's name suggests that some, if not many, in attendance had direct or indirect connections with him.

Chancellor Joel Klein is indirectly associated with these elites through Bloomberg and Larry Berger, Chief Executive Officer of Wireless Generation, who has indirect connections to the global elite through both Bloomberg and Murdoch. In turn, all of these people are indirectly connected to the United States' most important education newspaper *Education Week*, where Berger, as previously mentioned, sits on the Board of Trustees of Editorial Projects and its promotion of ICT through its project "Digital Directions."

Christakis and Fowler's concept of "positional inequality" suggests that one's position in the above network will determine one's influence over educational policy in New York City and, maybe, the world. Consider how this network operated in 2010 when New Jersey's Governor Chris Christie appointed Christopher D. Cerf as the state's education commissioner. Cerf served as New York City's deputy schools chancellor from 2006 to 2009 and is reported to be one of "Chancellor Joel I. Klein's closest confidants and a stalwart advocate of Mr. Klein's most controversial education reforms: opening more charter schools; closing failing schools; using student test scores to evaluate and compensate teachers; and restricting some traditional benefits in teachers' contracts."[55] He also worked on Bloomberg's reelection campaign.

Cerf became part of Joel Klein's network in the 1980s when he joined Klein's law firm, Onek, Klein, and Farr. Cerf networked through political contacts working in the White House counsel's office from 1993 to 1996. He entered the education world in the late 1990s working for the Edison Schools (now EdisonLearning and EdisonLearning International) described as "one of the world's largest for-profit operators of public schools."[56] Cerf is also chief executive officer and president of the for-profit Sangari Global Education.

The Cerf–Klein–Bloomberg connections lead us into another world of for-profit education. EdisonLearning focuses its work in the United States while EdisonLearning International works with schools in the United Kingdom and Abu Dhabi. EdisonLearning claims it "serves more than 450,000 students in 25 states, the United Kingdom, and the Middle East."[57] In the United States, EdisonLearning claims to be "the country's largest provider of charter school management and school district support services to the K-12 market."[58] It should be noted that the Cerf–Klein–Bloomberg–Christie network supports the expansion of charter schools for which EdisonLearning provides for-profit management services.

Like others in this network, Jeff Wahl, President and Chief Executive Officer of EdisonLearning entered the for-profit education business without any background in education. The Edison Learning website describes Wahl's qualifications:

> When he joined the organization in 2007, Jeff brought an extensive background and experience in strategy development and operational/financial management. Jeff spent 15 years with General Electric (GE) in a variety of operational and P&L assignments, including senior leadership positions with GE Capital. Specifically, he served as president of GE Capital's Great Lakes Bureau in Buffalo, NY. Jeff began his career as a supervising senior accountant at KPMG-Peat Marwick.[59]

Sangari Global Education, where Cerf is chief executive officer and president, describes itself:

> *Sangari* is a mission-driven company that believes quality, investigation-centered science education is the key to sustained prosperity. For more than 40 years, we have successfully provided high-quality science and engineering materials to universities in 16 countries, including Argentina, Brazil, Egypt, England, Greece, Pakistan, Portugal, Romania, South Africa, and Spain … *Sangari* offers the world's leading investigation-centered integrated science program and currently serves over 500,000 students in North and South America.[60]

Sangari's Vice President and Chief Technology Officer Rajeev Bajaj is also networked with the New York City school system. His biography on Sangari's 2010 website states:

> Rajeev most recently served as a Managing Director in the Office of Accountability of the New York City Department of Education where he was responsible for spearheading the efforts to develop the first district-wide comprehensive accountability and data management system. Rajeev has held multiple policy and operations roles within the New York City Department of Education including Chief of Staff for the Office of Accountability, Director of New School Facilities and Real Estate and Development, and Special Assistant to the Deputy Chancellor for Teaching and Learning.[61]

All of the above involve a dizzying number of network connections. Figure 1.1 provides an illustration of these connections.

Network Ideology

Within the network portrayed in Figure 1.1 there is a shared set of economic interests and educational values as outlined below:

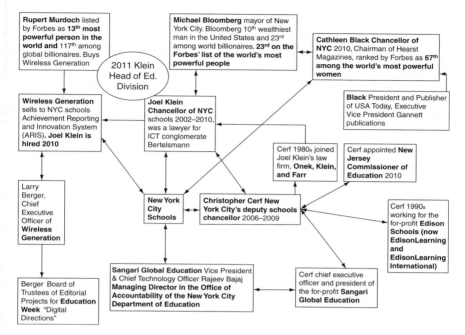

FIGURE 1.1

Shared economic interests:

- Information and Communication Technologies
- The selling of online instruction and educational software packages
- For-profit education
- For-profit global education companies
- For-profit charter management companies

Shared education values:

- Educational success measured by standardized test scores
- Online instruction
- Charter schools
- For-profit education companies improve schools

Superclass, Social Networking, and World Economic Forum Education Initiative

Not all members of the global superclass necessarily share the network ideology illustrated in Figure 1.1. As previously mentioned, I am using two sources for identifying these important players in global education. One is the already mentioned book *Superclass* by David Rothkopf and the other *Forbes'* annual list of the most wealthy and powerful global citizens. Unlike *Forbes'* list, Rothkopf does not provide a list of names because, he argues, the list keeps changing with the rise and fall of individual wealth and changing political positions.

As mentioned previously, Rothkopf identifies the superclass as those exercising power by their wealth, as heads of major global corporations and financial companies, as political and military leaders, and as major religious leaders. He lists the following characteristics of the 6,000+ included in the superclass:

Male 93.7%
Median Age 58
All of the world's approximately 1,000 billionaires
Reside (Approximate Percentage)
United States 17%
Europe 33%
United States, China, Britain, India, Brazil, Russia, Germany, Japan, and Mexico combined 57%
Asia and Pacific Region 33%
Occupation
Business 50%
Finance 13%
Government 18%
Military 7%
Religious 4%
Other 2%
Education
Attended Top 20 Elite Universities 30%
Postgraduate Degree 47%
Undergraduate Degree 91%
No High School Diploma 2%[62]

Rothkopf begins his book discussing the social networking of the superclass and others at the World Economic Forum in Davos, Switzerland. Social networking at Davos involves face-to-face meetings, as contrasted with virtual social networking which will be discussed later in this book. *New York Times* columnist Andrew Ross Sorkin offered this description of networking at Davos: "Of course, much of the week is really about one thing: networking. As the 'Black Swan' author Nassim N. Taleb described it to Tom Keene of Bloomberg Television, the event is 'chasing successful people who want to be seen with other successful people. That's the game.'"[63]

The Economic Policy Institute's Jeff Faux, as quoted by Rothkopf, agrees with Sorkin but recognizes the economic and political impact of networking at Davos: "It is more like a political convention, where elites get to sniff one another out, *identify which ideas and people are 'sound'* and come away with increased chances that their phone calls will be returned by those one notch above them in the global pecking order [author's emphasis]."[64]

"Identify which ideas and people are 'sound'" identifies an important aspect of networking and the dissemination of educational ideas. What are the major educational ideas that floated through the World Economic Forum network? Not surprisingly they were about how education could benefit global economies as exemplified by the World Economic Forum's Global Education Initiative and the concerns of its organizational subgroup the New Champions. The New Champions' meetings are described thus: "At the Annual Meeting of the New Champions, the World Economic Forum brings together emerging global leaders and Mentors willing to share the knowledge and perception that only come with experience. It is this powerful mix of questioning, insight and resilience that makes the Summer Davos unique."[65] At its 2009 annual meeting in Dalian, People's Republic of China, the following economic objectives were expressed for education:

How can educational systems become more aligned with the skills required by industry?

Key Points:

- The private sector needs to partner with the public sector in curriculum development.
- Creating classes of entrepreneurs will ultimately help students go from being employees to employers.
- Soft skills are required more than hard skills for students to make relevant employees.
- Greater competition among universities will ensure that they provide better services.
- For education to remain relevant, it must be based on values, real-life experiences and discovery.[66]

Economic goals for education were expressed at the World Economic Forum's MENA (Middle East and North Africa) Roundtable on Entrepreneurship Education, Global Education Initiative, held in Marrakech, Morocco, in October 2010. The meeting's "Manifesto" declared:

The gap between skills and jobs is widening further in the MENA region and many countries lag behind other countries around the world in terms of competitiveness. The region must invest in developing entrepreneurial and innovative skills to build sustainable economic development, create jobs and generate renewed economic growth.[67]

The World Economic Forum's MENA meeting placed emphasis on schools teaching entrepreneurial skills for the global economic system.

Educational institutions, from the earliest levels up, need to adopt 21st century methods and tools to develop the appropriate learning environment to encourage creativity, innovation and the ability to think "out of the box" to solve problems. Entrepreneurship enables the development of leadership and life skills and has become increasingly recognized as a key competency.[68]

In summary, it appears that network discussions within the World Education Forum are about how education can contribute to economic growth and stability along with training innovative entrepreneurs.

World Economic Forum and ICT: The Modern Savior

How might ICT be discussed in the World Economic Forum network? One possibility is reflected in the Forum's upbeat title for its report on technology, *Empowering People and Transforming Society: The World Economic Forum's Technology Pioneers 2011*.[69] The Report's Foreword opens with the suggestion that technology is the panacea for many of the world's problems:

How will the world cope with the crucial issue of water management and treatment? How can individuals and corporations benefit even more from the 24/7, ubiquitous connection to the Internet – and prevent the resulting reputation and security risks? What new approaches to treating rare and neglected diseases will emerge and save lives in the coming years? How can technology help modify behaviors to optimize energy use and bring us closer to a low-carbon economy? The 31 start-ups selected as the World Economic Forum's Technology Pioneers of 2011 innovatively address these and other challenges of our rapidly evolving society.[70]

The Report opens with a story of how Twitter helped save the day shortly after the 2010 earthquake in Haiti when a Medecins Sans Frontières' (Doctors Without Borders) cargo plane was blocked from landing by the U.S. military. U.S. television journalist Ann Curry sent out a Twitter message: "To the US military running Haiti's airport, find a way to let the doctors without borders plane land."[71] Then, according to the World Economic Forum's report, the magic of modern ICT was demonstrated:

Curry's message was spotted a moment later by Jeff Pulver, a technology entrepreneur credited with a pioneering voice over Internet protocol technology, who happened to be sitting in front of his computer screen at his home in New Jersey. Pulver, a social networking enthusiast who has some 360,000 followers on Twitter, "re-tweeted" Curry's message. Within moments Pulver and others who relayed Curry's message, got a direct response from the US military via Twitter saying "we are on it." In addition, Curry shared Medecins Sans Frontières tweet with her contacts in the military. As a result of Curry's efforts and the attention from Twitter users from around the world, the situation received significant attention and the plane was allowed to land a short time later.[72]

World Forum's list of technological pioneers is divided into the categories of Clean Tech, Information Technology and New Media, and Life Sciences and Health. The Report identifies 13 pioneers of Information Technology and New Media for 2011. Knewton, one of these 2011 pioneers, claims to be bringing analytical tools to teachers and students as textbooks become digital and are delivered through e-readers.[73] These analytical tools will identify parts of the e-textbooks by structure and level of difficulty and link them to the digital profile of each student. Knewton's website provides the following description of its pioneering work:

> Knewton is developing the industry's most powerful Adaptive Learning Platform, customizing educational content to meet the needs of each student. Whereas traditional classrooms and textbooks provide the same material to every student, Knewton will dynamically match lessons, videos, and practice problems to each student's ideal learning arc.
>
> Knewton works by tagging all content down to the atomic concept level. The system further tags the resulting content by structure, difficulty level, and media format. Then we can dynamically generate for each student, each day, the perfect bundle of content based on exactly which concepts she knows and how she learns best.[74]

Knewton also provides Web-based test preparation courses for GMAT, LSAT, and SAT test preparation courses.

Another World Economic Forum report suggesting that its network discusses ICT as the answer to global problems is *The Global Information Technology Report 2009–2010: ICT for Sustainability*. The Report's Preface, written by Robert Greenhill, Chief Business Officer of the World Economic Forum, promotes ICT as a remedy for global ills:

> As the world economy begins to recover from one of the worst economic crises in decades, information and communication technologies (ICT) is bound to play an increasingly prominent role as a key enabler of renewed and sustainable growth, given that it has become an essential element of the infrastructure underpinning competitive economies. *ICT will continue spreading its revolutionary power to modernize economies and societies and improve living conditions and opportunities around the world* [author's emphasis].[75]

In summary, social networking at the World Economic Forum might identify for participants "which ideas and people are 'sound'" for global and national education policies. These educational ideas are naturally linked to the overall economic concerns of the Forum. Primarily concerned with economic growth and stable global economic systems, the Forum's membership is logically focused on how education can contribute to these ends. In addition, the network seems attuned to the idea that ICT is a panacea for global problems including education.

Boao Forum for Asia: Asia Searching for Win-Win

The Boao Forum for Asia is similar to the World Economic Forum in bringing together the politically powerful and rich to discuss regional economic issues. It was initiated in 1998 by Fidel V. Ramos, former President of the Philippines, Bob Hawke, former Prime Minister of Australia, and Morihiro Hosokawa, former Prime Minister of Japan. Similar to the idea of the World Economic Forum meeting in a particular place like Davos, the permanent site of Boao is on an island off the southernmost part of China.[76]

The 14 member Board of Directors of the Boao Forum is composed of major government officials and heads of corporations, including the former prime ministers of Malaysia, Japan, and France; the corporate leaders of SABIC, the Ericsson Group, SK Group, and Mitsubishi Corporation; the Secretary General of the Federation of Indian Chambers of Commerce and Industry; a former Secretary of the Treasury of the United States; a senior minister in the Singapore government; the Chairman of the International Chamber of Commerce; and a former member of the Political Bureau of the Central Committee of the Chinese Communist Party.[77]

The Boao Forum focuses on Asian economic development and integration with the slogan "Asia Searching for Win-Win." Social networking is an important aspect of the Forum's meeting as exemplified by the plans for the 2011 gathering for a day devoted to golf at the BFA "New Fortune Cup" Golf Invitational.[78]

"Which ideas and people are 'sound'" regarding education in the Boao Forum network? Similar to the World Economic Forum one could readily hypothesize network conversations about how education could contribute to economic development. *The Boao Forum for Asia: The Development of Emerging Economies Annual Report 2009* confirms this hypothesis. The emerging economies focused on in the report are labeled the "E11" which includes a powerful player at the Boao Forum, the People's Republic of China, along with Argentina, Brazil, India, Indonesia, Republic of Korea, Mexico, Russia, Saudi Arabia, South Africa, and Turkey. The Annual Report defines an emerging economy as:

- Having relatively high economic growth rate
- Having significant economic scale and population
- Having middle-level or below per capita income
- Having relatively high economic openness
- Having relatively broad representativeness
- Having relatively insignificant controversy [meaning political and social stability][79]

The educational ideas promoted by the Annual Report for the E11 nations are focused on helping emergent nations join the ranks of developed countries. The Report declares: "Promoting education is the most important pump priming task for the E11 in order to bring out their late-mover advantage and accelerate economic development."[80] The Report suggests that E11 countries spend more on education, "because it is the basis for providing more specialized and high-caliber professionals and guaranteeing competitiveness of the E11."[81]

Conclusion: Digital Mind, Superclass, and Networks of Power

Our discussion of the digital mind has so far been limited to owners and executives of ICT companies who either manage school systems or sell education products. Missing from this picture are the digital minds of students, something that will be discussed in later chapters. ICT managers and producers have an economic interest and/or disposition to see schools' success as the proper management of student data, the collection of numerical test results, and the use of instructional software or online instruction. They have a disposition to see the world through the lens of data processed by computers.

Consequently, the digital mind of ICT managers tends to see schools as institutions composed of data while not seeing the holistic context of students' lives such as their families, neighborhoods, and income levels. If data shows a decline in test scores, the data manager sees it as a school and individual student problem and might not blame the social world of the student. This is similar to the previously discussed psychological experiment in Hong Kong where participants were asked to react to overeating by a person attending a banquet. Some respondents saw it as a failure of individual character while others blamed the environment of tempting food. If a child from a low-income family scores poorly on a test, the data manager might see it as a problem related to the influence of classroom instruction and school administration on the individual student and might propose improved instruction or school reorganization. A holistic approach might call for improving the child's social conditions including raising family income and improving neighborhood conditions.

Networks of power, as exemplified by social networks at the World Economic Forum and Boao Forum for Asia, tend to judge education according to its contribution to economic growth and stability. Networks also create the situation of network inequality, with some people having access to the global superclass while others remain distant. Today, these networks of power tend to see technology as the panacea for world problems and the solution for classroom instruction.

So what do we need to study to broaden this picture of the digital mind and the networks of educational power? First are the workings of the education industry and its "shadow elites."[82] Shadow elites representing the for-profit education industry are interested in having schools and students using taxpayer money to buy their products to replace teacher-made lesson plans and tests and, in some cases, restructure teachers' roles to favor the use of digital educational products. Second, these shadow elites have connections to networks of power planning educational policies that favor the use of ICT in schools. And third, these digital education products have an effect on the social construction of the students' minds and, as I will discuss regarding the findings of neuroscience, on the actual functioning of their brains.

2

SHADOW ELITES, GLOBAL NETWORKS, AND THE EDUCATION INDUSTRY

The conceptual framework of this chapter is borrowed from Janine Wedel's *Shadow Elite: How the World's New Power Brokers Undermine Democracy, Government, and the Free Market* (2009). I will use this conceptual framework for analyzing the networks between governments and the education industry, or as I am calling it educational corporatism. Wedel's shadow elite is an example of corporatism in action. She uses the term "performance state" to describe modern states which act like businesses and depend on data to analyze their successes.

In this chapter, I will use a variety of examples of for-profit companies seeking funding from the world's governments, including in the United States for-profits lobbying for more benefits from government funding of No Child Left Behind legislation and the efforts of Michael Golden, Corporate Vice President of Microsoft's Education Products Group, to sell his company's products to global higher education systems. I will discuss for-profit education companies and schools that are nonprofit in their own countries but begin acting like for-profits when establishing branch campuses in other countries. Corporatism is highlighted in this chapter's four government educational examples, namely Korea, Qatar, Abu Dhabi, and Singapore. In all four countries businesses and governments work hand-in-hand in educational planning.

Wedel argues that a global trend is for governments to outsource to private firms what might be considered traditional government functions. She calls the bureaucracies of these governments "Swiss-cheese" to symbolize the holes left in government as services are turned over to private companies. In some cases, government hiring of outside services is the result of new ventures such as the example used in this chapter of Korea, Qatar, Abu Dhabi, and Singapore's financial support of branch campuses of foreign universities in their countries. Thus we are dealing with two categories of "Swiss-cheese" governments. The first involves governments turning over services that they provided in the past to for-profit industries. The second involves governments initiating new services by first hiring outside agencies.

The holes in Swiss-cheese government bureaucracies also represent the reduction in government staff, making it difficult to regulate government services. Wedel writes:

> Because the number of government contracts and contractors has risen, while the number of civil servants available to supervise them has proportionately fallen, thus decreasing the government's capacity to oversee the process, even when government officials sign on the dotted line, they are sometimes merely rubber stamping the work of contractors.[1]

The concept of a Swiss-cheese bureaucracy relates directly to education, with more and more school services being privatized. In the United States, the federal legislation No Child Left Behind (2001) specifically provides for the hiring of for-profit companies. For instance, the section of the legislation dealing with failing schools provides for technical assistance which "shall include assistance in analyzing data … [which] may be provided … by … a private not-for-profit organization or *for-profit organization*, an educational service agency, or another entity with experience in helping schools improve academic achievement [author's emphasis]."[2] For schools requiring improvement the legislation requires the hiring of outside instructional help for students in these schools with the provision for contracting with:

> a *for-profit entity*, or a local educational agency that—(i) has a demonstrated record of effectiveness in increasing student academic achievement; (ii) is capable of providing supplemental educational … the term "supplemental educational services" means tutoring and other supplemental academic enrichment services that are—(i) in addition to instruction provided during the school day; and (ii) are of high quality, research-based, and specifically designed to increase the academic achievement of eligible children [author's emphasis].[3]

As noted in the above quotes, NCLB opens the door for schools to hire at government expense for-profit companies to analyze data and test scores and provide tutoring and enrichment programs.

Falling under these provisions are companies such as the Wireless Generation discussed in Chapter 1 which was contracted by New York City schools to analyze test score data. The for-profit Sylvan Learning, which provides tutoring and test preparation services, recognizes on its website the importance of NCLB for its business:

No Child Left Behind (NCLB)
No Child Left Behind (NCLB) is a sweeping, landmark educational reform that was passed into law in 2001. There are numerous components to the

NCLB act. *One that Sylvan Learning is involved with is Supplemental Educational Services or SES.* The supplemental services of NCLB provide low-income students in struggling schools with the opportunity to obtain tutoring services at no cost to parents. Importantly, NCLB grants parents the right to choose a supplemental services provider for their child. Parents may choose providers from a list approved by their state and made available by their school district [author's emphasis].[4]

Kaplan, Newton Learning, and Princeton are other for-profit beneficiaries of NCLB. One outraged Blog, Schools Matter, offers this critical assessment of government purchases of tutoring and test preparation services:

> Kaplan Gets Fat on School Money for Poor Kids
> The flood of federal, state, and local education dollars into the coffers of corporations like Kaplan, Newton Learning, and Princeton Review remains unchecked, even though there is no evidence, scientifically based or otherwise, that these corporate interventions are doing any good for anything other than corporate bottom lines. In fact, there is growing evidence from insider accounts like this one in the September *Harper's* that the spread of Kaplan's influence into scripted curriculum writing is further undercutting efforts to bring real teaching and learning to urban students who are being left further behind as corporate bosses get richer on money intended for education – not exploitation.[5]

Hiring for-profit companies for tutoring and test preparation replaces the work that teachers could fulfill after school hours. In other words, according to the image of the Swiss-cheese government, a hole is created in school government when a teacher is replaced by an outside for-profit company. In keeping with the Swiss-cheese concept of bureaucracy there is no provision under NCLB on how these for-profit supplementary education services will be regulated or who will have responsibility for evaluating their services. The legislation does specify that these for-profit school services should have "a demonstrated record of effectiveness in increasing student academic achievement" but it's not clear if cash strapped state and local school governments have the personnel and/or time to regulate companies like Sylvan Learning, Kaplan, Newton, and Princeton.

Swiss-cheese Government: Flexians and Flex Nets

Corporatism is embedded in Janine Wedel's labeling of the shadow elite working between business and Swiss-cheese governments as "flexians" who are linked through "flex nets." Flexians, as she defines them, have easy movement between government and for-profit companies. For instance, Joel Klein, as discussed in Chapter 1, moved from a private ICT company to the Chancellorship of the New

York City Schools, and from there to Rupert Murdoch's NewsCorp and the for-profit company contracted to handle data analysis for New York schools, Wireless Generation. The network of relationships shown in Figure 1.1 in Chapter 1 illustrates a flex net for these shadow elite.

Wedel argues that the shadow elite maintain personal relations with government officials as they move between government and the private sector. Often flexians represent multiple private and public organizations. Consider the example in Chapter 1 of New Jersey's Education Commissioner Christopher D. Cerf who served as New York City's deputy schools chancellor from 2006 to 2009; was part of Chancellor Joel Klein's personal network after working at Klein's law firm in the 1980s; worked in the White House counsel's office from 1993 to 1996; and worked for the for-profit education companies Edison Schools and Sangari Global Education. With this easy movement between government positions and the private sector, Cerf exemplifies Wedel's concept of the flexian and flex net. The flexian operates within what Wedel calls the "performance state" in which effectiveness is measured by data collection and analysis is exemplified by the increasing demand for data to measure school performance.

Wedel quotes Barry C. Lynn, a political economy analyst, regarding the functioning of the shadow elite: "Our political economy is run by a compact elite able to fuse the power of our public government with the power of private corporate governments in ways that enable them not merely to offload their risk onto us but also to determine with almost complete freedom who wins, who loses, who pays."[6]

The performance state, according to Wedel, is also characterized by the use of public relations to influence a media that is primarily providing news as a form of entertainment. News as entertainment results in the rise of what is called "truthiness" which is defined by the American Dialect Society as "the quality of preferring concepts or facts one wishes to be true, rather than concepts or facts known to be true."[7] Consider as a truthiness the example of the brand name of the 2001 education legislation No Child Left Behind. There was no research evidence that the legislation's requirements would in fact achieve its goal of providing students with equality of educational opportunity as promised in its preamble and represented by its title. Without research to back up the provisions of No Child Left Behind the legislative name is more of a wish than a reality. Using the brand name No Child Left Behind, the media in reporting any news about the legislation is engaging in truthiness by just naming the legislation.

Governments Pay For-Profit Education Industry

The growth of Swiss-cheese public schools is exemplified by government funding of for-profit schools and the importation of foreign schools. This process has turned some schools, which in their home countries are considered non profits, into enterprises that seek to profit to their home institutions by the sale of their products in a foreign country. For example, consider the decision by leaders in the South

Korean government to turn the honeymoon retreat and fruit growing Jeju Island into a site for foreign schools. Concerned about the number of South Korean parents who send their children abroad to attend school and wanting to improve the learning of English for participation in the global economy, government officials envision an island dotted with Western-type schools where residents are only allowed to speak English. On the island the government has funded the 940 acre Jeju Global Education City which by 2015 will have 12 prestigious Western schools.

Allowing foreign schools to take profits from their Jeju Global Education City schools was key to enticing them to locate on the island. When the first plans were made, an unnamed South Korean official said, "Many foreign education institutes hesitate to invest in the city mainly due to the regulation banning them from taking profits generated here out of the country." *Korea Times* reporter Park Si-soo explained, "To attract renowned foreign education institutes, the local government has also eased regulations to help foreign investors take benefits generated here out of the country."[8]

Government developers believe, according to the *Korea Times,* that the education city will help the local economy by attracting not only students from mainland Korea but also foreign students wanting to learn English. The same unnamed government official told reporter Si-soo, "We believe the town will serve as an essential and strong growth engine that will lead to balanced national development, a pivotal move to transform Jeju into an international city."[9]

How is Swiss-cheese government reflected in foreign investment in education in South Korea? An editorial comment in the *Korea Times* noted the absence of regulation of the funds provided to foreign schools to locate in South Korea: "The government has made efforts to set up more foreign schools as a means to construct an environment friendly to foreign investors. However, these schools' accounting and other operations have not been supervised by the authorities."[10] This editorial comment preceded an article dealing with possible corruption in government financing of a franchise of England's Dulwich College, a private London School in Seoul. The following report by *Korea Times* staff writer Kang Shin-who describes the problems facing Swiss-cheese governments:

> Dulwich College Seoul has been accused of having bribed district office staffers in exchange for favors to attract funding for the construction of a basement parking lot under the school building.
>
> The school is suspected of having inflated the cost for the parking lot, which was paid for with taxpayer money, to use the gap to finance the construction of the rest of the school building.
>
> The London-based school opened its branch in Banpo-dong, southern Seoul, last month. It needed a total of 13.7 billion won ($12 million) budget for the construction of the three-story school building with a parking lot. According to the Seocho District Office, the parking place is open to the public and can accommodate about 160 cars.

Sources from the school and construction firms, who are familiar with the deal, say the actual cost for building the parking lot was about 4 billion won but the Seocho office allocated 6.5 billion won in taxpayer money in what they called a three-way collusion among the school, the office and builders.[11]

The Chadwick school of California is another private school seeking to make money in South Korea by opening a branch in the Incheon Free Economic Zone city of Songdo. Forming a new entity called Chadwick International, it provides this description on its website:

> Chadwick International (CI) is an independent coeducational non-denominational K-12 international school located in the newly created Incheon Free Economic Zone, named International Business District (IBD), in Songdo, South Korea. The school is the first of its kind in Korea to offer a world-class international school program that Korean students can attend together with expatriate and dual citizenship holders. CI is an integral part of the master-planned city of Songdo.[12]

The Incheon Free Economic Zone is part of a series of Free Economic Zones being created by the government to attract foreign businesses with regulations allowing foreign investors to take money out of the country. *Korea Times* reporter Do Je-hae provides this definition of a free economic zone: "A Free Economic Zone (FEZ) is an area specially designated to provide companies with the optimal environment to engage in global business activities. Ultimately, FEZs are aimed at building world-class cities based on policies of global standards and catering to multinational and multicultural communities."[13] It is planned that English will be the major spoken language in the Incheon Free Economic zone and it will be wired as a global U-City: "A U-City has all its major information systems—including residential, medical, business and governmental—interconnected. Virtually everything is linked to an overall system through technologies such as wireless networking and RFID tags."[14]

The first school to locate in Jeju Global Education City was the prestigious private girls school North London Collegiate.[15] Founded in 1850 by Frances Mary Buss with support from her family, including her brother Septimus and her father, R.W. Buss, who illustrated Dickens' novels, the school gained academic acclaim.[16] While tuition is high in England, the school claims "Central to the ethos at North London Collegiate School is the provision of bursary places to allow bright girls to benefit from the world class education on offer, irrespective of their social or financial circumstances."[17]

Making money, North London Collegiate School asserts, is the primary reason it is establishing a branch campus on Jeju Island. In its official announcement of the enterprise, the school announced that it "has been investigating possible franchising opportunities abroad over the last 18 months, *primarily to raise additional funds* to support bursary places at the School but also to provide a range of cultural and educational links for pupils and staff [author's emphasis]."[18] The news release continued "NLCS, Jeju will be the first school to open in the Education City and will eventually educate up to 1400 students in a co-educational boarding and day school. This is a tremendously exciting moment in the history of the School and the first time since 1871 that the NLCS family of schools has increased."[19]

Swiss-cheese Education in the United States

The United States provides another example of Swiss-cheese education government. Flexians, flex nets, the performance state, entertainment media, and truthiness represent the current dynamics between for-profit education industries and governments. A common economic and political goal of the shadow elite is to lobby governments for more privatization of government services and for more public money to be spent on these privatized services. One example, which I discuss in another book, *The Politics of American Education*, involves the Education Industry Association (EIA) which represents 450 global for-profits including online education providers, school improvement and management services, charter school operators, alternative education and special education services, professional development providers, after-school tutoring providers, and educational content providers.[20] Obviously, this trade association has a stake in increased federal funding of for-profit education through the No Child Left Behind legislation. In a document titled "Education Industry Association & ESEA [No Child Left Behind] Organizing Principles," the organization asserts, "Funding education research and innovation ... requires focused investment that must include an equal role for the *private sector*. ... The ability of our nation to educate over 55 million students and achieve the President's ambitious education goals is not possible without the active participation and support of the *private sector* [author's emphasis]."[21]

Worried that funding would be reduced, the EIA produced a PowerPoint for its members in which the first slides reflect the organization's dependence on public money. The reference to "SES" refers to supplementary education services funded under No Child Left Behind.

> PowerPoint: Educational Industry Association[22]
> *Weather Report for SES* [supplementary education services]: *Storm Warnings are Posted!!!*
> Slide 3
> Overview
> - *Current Threats to SES and Why*
> - *USED Actions to Date*
> - *Congressional Actions/Timeline*
> - *Forecast*
> - *What You Can Do to Preserve SES*

Slide 4

No Child Left Behind (NCLB) Created/Expanded Markets for Private Sector

- Supplemental Educational Services (SES)
- Professional development
- Assessment and curricula
- Comprehensive school reform/restructuring
- Special/Alternative Education
- Drop-out prevention/recovery
- Technology
- Data and student information systems

WILL ESEA BE AS OPEN TO PRIVATE SECTOR?

The final slide announced the lobbying campaign to increase government funding of for-profit education industries: "EIA has launched $1.5 million Campaign to preserve and improve SES thru Tutor Our Children, Inc. (TOC) to position fight as civil rights issue for low-income students. Join the Campaign to Save SES TODAY."[23]

Business Flexians: Michael Golden and Microsoft

A global example of the workings of the shadow elites is Michael Golden, Corporate Vice President of Microsoft's Education Products Group, who represents a company that sees major profits from sales of its education products. Golden exemplifies how some business people network between the education world and government to sell their company's products. In an interview by Emil Protalinski for Arstechnica, Golden described his role as carrying "out Microsoft Corp.'s vision of enabling access to quality education experiences for all through technology … [and being] responsible for leading Microsoft's education strategy execution, driving education product development, business development, and go-to-market efforts."[24] During the course of the interview Golden makes this idealistic statement about the role of Microsoft in bringing ICT to the world's students:

> Now I have the chance, in this global role, to work with 1.4 billion students. So again, it's a little bit removed, but the breadth is really pushing it. And so that's the reason I took the job: the chance to take to scale, across the world, some of these solutions that we know are successful in certain places. We have to create the conditions, and the interests, and the knowledge, to make them successful across the world.[25]

Selling Microsoft products to 1.4 billion students is a rich source of revenue for the company. In taking on this task, Michael Golden links Microsoft to a network of governments, educational systems, and other education businesses. At Microsoft,

Golden extended his network to global education leaders and organizations setting the stage for the sale of Microsoft products.

Golden's biography exemplifies a flexian at home in government and business. Before being appointed Corporate Vice President of the Education Products Group at Microsoft Corp, he was deputy secretary of the Pennsylvania Department of Education's Office of Information and Educational Technology. While working for the Pennsylvania government he introduced changes in schools that are dear to heart of ICT entrepreneurs, including connected classrooms and one-to-one computing environments.[26]

As a flexian moving between government and for-profit businesses, he also worked as senior vice president of marketing and strategic planning at Pearson School. Pearson School advertises itself: "Pearson is the world's leading PreK-20 educational publishing company, dedicated to working with educators to change the way America thinks."[27] Prior to Pearson, Golden acted as private consultant on "business development, strategic planning, marketing and corporate finance to education, media and consumer products companies."[28]

From his position at Microsoft in 2008, Golden expanded his networks to other promoters of ICT and global educational systems. For instance, in 2009 Golden appeared as a speaker at Milken Institute Global Conference 2009 which had the obviously appealing theme for those wanting to sell ICT products to schools systems: "Infusing Technology into Education for Economic Competitiveness." The other speakers at the Milken conference were Glenn Kleiman, Executive Director, Friday Institute for Educational Innovation and Professor, Department of Educational Leadership and Policy Studies, North Carolina State University; Keith Krueger, CEO, Consortium on School Networking; and Bette Manchester, Executive Director, Maine International Center for Digital Learning and former Director of Special Projects, Maine Learning Technology Initiative. Glenn Kleiman's Friday Institute for Educational Innovation promotes the use of ICT in schools, as highlighted by the Institute's description: "We are developing, evaluating, and disseminating innovative approaches to teaching and learning that are made possible by multi-media and networked technologies."[29]

Probably the most important network connection for Golden at the Milken conference was Keith Krueger, CEO, Consortium on School Networking. Founded in 1992, the Consortium is the major professional organization for technology administrators in local U.S. school districts. The Consortium provides an excellent network to sell Microsoft products. Also, the Consortium is a major promoter for the expanded use of ICT in schools. Consider the Consortium's Core Beliefs which call upon the use of ICT to transform learning and to make it ubiquitous in U.S. public schools:

Core Beliefs

- The primary challenge we face in using technology effectively is human.
- Technology is a critical tool to personalize learning and overcome barriers of time and space for each learner.

- Equitable and ubiquitous access to technology is a necessity.
- The effective use of technology for the systemic transformation of learning cannot occur without strong organization, leadership, and vision.
- Technological fluency allows our children to be prepared for the world of today and tomorrow.
- Technology enables innovation in our educational systems, resulting in greater efficiencies and productivity.
- To maximize the benefits of technology solutions the district technology leader should be part of the executive leadership team (CTO, CIO, etc.) of the education organization.
- Global connections are vital to transforming the education process and improving learning.[30]

The Consortium's stated strategies fit those of Microsoft in wanting to expand the use of ICT in education. Two of its strategic goals for 2009–12 are:

- Enabling educational leaders, including superintendents and other executive team members, to understand the strategic benefit of technology and demonstrate the value of having a CTO at the cabinet level.
- Advocating for a vision and necessary resources in support of the role of technology in advancing 21st century learning.

The other speaker at the Milken forum, Bette Manchester, Executive Director, Maine International Center for Digital Learning, represents a nongovernment organization that developed out of Maine's 2000 Learning Technology Initiative. Founded in 2008 by former Maine Governor Angus King and Bette Manchester, the International Center "identifies, uses, conducts, and disseminates collaborative action research and formal research, and supports the development of local, state, national and international policies and practices in the field of digital learning and teaching."[31] The network connection with the Center provides another opportunity to promote Microsoft products and ICT.

In 2009, Microsoft and Michael Golden managed to network with the United Nations Educational, Scientific and Cultural Organization (UNESCO) to form the UNESCO-Microsoft Task Force on Higher Education and Information and Communication Technology (ICT) at the 2009 meeting of the UNESCO Conference on Higher Education. According to Microsoft "the task force will be responsible for putting together a strategic plan tailored to higher education institutions across the globe to prepare students for the growing challenge associated with economic stimulus efforts but also for the workforce needs of 21st century companies."[32] It should be noted that former Microsoft head Bill Gates suggested in his 2010 newsletter to the Bill and Melinda Gates Foundation regarding ICT and higher education, "We should focus on having at least one great course online for each subject [university level] rather than lots of mediocre courses."[33] This approach would make Microsoft type products central to the functioning of global universities plus increase the standardization of knowledge.

It is important to note regarding Golden and Microsoft's networks that present at the meeting which resulted in the UNESCO-Microsoft agreement were, as announced by UNESCO, "150 ministers of education, senior education officials and policy advisors [who] are discussing how governments and universities can take full advantage of e-technology's potential to address the current knowledge and skills challenges facing higher education."[34]

When the announcement was made about the creation of the Microsoft-UNESCO agreement, Golden made clear Microsoft's position on the importance of ICT in education along with promoting the company's products. The unquestioning belief of those who were present in an important role for ICT in education, even though it meant more profits for Microsoft, meant that no one questioned Golden's comments about the agreement:

> We believe that technology has a vital role to play in building up 21st-century skills, broadening access to education and personalizing the learning experience to adapt teaching to the unique needs of each learner. This program makes technology resources more accessible than ever before to governments and students across the world. We will continue to support UNESCO and our newly formed UNESCO-Microsoft Task Force on Higher Education and ICT in every way we can.[35]

Also at the ceremony, Nicholas Burnett, UNESCO Assistant Director-General for Education, also indicated the importance of relationships with global governments: "Through the creation of the UNESCO-Microsoft Task Force on Higher Education and ICT we will help mobilize critical strategic resources to better assist ministries of education worldwide."[36]

How will Microsoft profit from an alliance with UNESCO particularly for higher education? The for-profit answer can be found in Microsoft's Academic Alliance which the company advertises as "the easiest and most inexpensive way for academic departments to make the latest Microsoft software available in labs, class-rooms, and on student PCs." The program, which is available in more than 160 countries worldwide, has two primary goals:

- To make it easier and less expensive for academic institutions to obtain Microsoft developer tools, platforms, and servers for instructional and research purposes.
- To build a community of instructors who can share curriculum and other learning resources to support the use of these technologies.[37]

In addition, Microsoft promotes Microsoft Partners in Learning Alliance Agreement which supports government use of its products:

Agreement provides the framework for a comprehensive joint public/private implementation plan that supports your vision for transformational change ... Alliance Agreements establish firm commitments from all stakeholders to help ensure that common goals are achieved and to form the basis of long-term, ongoing education partnerships.[38]

The UNESCO-Microsoft agreement allowed Microsoft to make major inroads into national systems of higher education. UNESCO Assistant Director-General for Education, Nicholas Burnett, claimed that the agreement would allow the "innovative application of technology [which] has the potential to impact broad change in higher education in terms of learning, teaching and research."[39] In the context of the relations between for-profit companies and governments, Burnett pointed out how the agreement allowed for Microsoft influence over national higher education policies: "It is the mandate of the UNESCO-Microsoft Task Force on Higher Education and ICT to offer guidance to governments on the use of information and communication technology (ICT) in education and programs that facilitate increased access and solutions that will scale to address challenges globally."[40]

Similar to the example in Chapter 1 of virtual classrooms taking the place of teachers in Florida during the state's economic crisis, Microsoft viewed the economic downturn at the time of the agreement with UNESCO as an opportunity to sell its products. In fact, at the time of the UNESCO agreement Microsoft offered seed money which was greeted with the revealing headline, "Microsoft Commits $50 Million in Higher Education Resources, Training and Certifications to Drive Economic Recovery."[41] The announcement provided the following economic justification for expanding ICT and Microsoft's role in higher education:

Given the current economic crisis, governments are faced with designing and funding enhancements to higher education in order to support and spur economic recovery. With its commitment of resources and tools, available through the Microsoft Education Alliance Program agreement, Microsoft aims to make it easier for governments and the public education sector to bring ICT access and skills to the next generation of students and teachers.[42]

Self-serving might be the best way to describe the $50 million offered by Microsoft as part of the UNESCO-Microsoft agreement. The $50 million was in the form of free software and certifications which would lead to future purchases of Microsoft products by the world's higher education systems. These $50 million worth of freebees from Microsoft consisted of:

- **Microsoft DreamSpark.** A technology that enables students to download Microsoft developer and design tools at no charge, as well as additional science, technology, engineering, math and design (STEM-D) resources. More than 70 countries have high schools enrolled in DreamSpark programs.

- **Microsoft Live@edu.** A program providing a suite of communication and collaboration tools for students, faculty, staff, and alumni in K–12 schools and on college campuses worldwide. With Live@edu, schools gain access to Microsoft Office Outlook Live for e-mail, Microsoft Office Live Workspace to share documents and collaborate, Windows Live Messenger for instant messaging, and Windows Live SkyDrive for 25 GB of online data storage space. Thousands of schools across 86 countries currently use Live@edu to enhance the learning experience.
- **Digital Literacy Curriculum.** An online curriculum that adult learners new to computing can access in 30 languages to gain the basic skills to perform everyday tasks as well as a general awareness of the benefits of computing. To date, the Digital Literacy Curriculum reaches 5.8 million people worldwide.
- **Microsoft IT Academy Program.** A world-class digital literacy and technology curriculum that enables faculty and students to earn industry-recognized professional certifications—one of the most effective means of improving student employability. Nearly three-quarters of IT Academy Program members surveyed report that program resources and benefits improve student employability and earning potential. More than 6,000 academic institutions worldwide are members, reaching more than 360,000 students and 8,000 faculty.
- **Microsoft Students to Business.** A program available in 69 countries that connects businesses with universities to provide students with skills training, industry insight and job placement services. To date, 100,000 students have been trained and 5,000 companies are registered to find students with practical technology skills.
- **Microsoft Certification.** A program available on Microsoft Office applications for IT professionals, developers and technical specialists. Microsoft Certification provides recognized credentials that help students get and keep the skills needed for employment, and that measure and validate the ability to solve real-world problems. More than 2.6 million IT professionals and 2.2 million information workers are certified on technologies used by organizations and individuals.[43]

Michael Golden is representative of the new global educational entrepreneur who works global networks to sell their company's products. In contrast, the following examples of Qatar and Abu Dhabi illustrate what happens when governments use their riches to purchase educational institutions and turn nonprofit schools into ones acting like for-profits.

Branch Campuses: Buying Schools with Gulf Oil Money and Joining a Global Network

Corporatism is the defining characteristic of Qatar and the United Arab Emirates' (UAE) Abu Dhabi where oil revenues allow the government extensive involvement and expenditures to attract businesses and branch campuses of foreign universities.

Similar to Korean examples, university branches locating in Qatar's Education City and Abu Dhabi's downtown center and later in 2014 in its new cultural center on Saadiyat Island are being transformed from being nonprofits in their home countries to acting like for-profits in marketing their branch campuses. In *The Great Brain Race: How Global Universities are Reshaping the World*, Ben Wildavsky writes about the franchising of Western universities by the establishment of branch campuses in other countries. He argues that these universities are behaving "like for-profit firms in seeking new markets."[44] James Reardon-Anderson, dean of Georgetown University's branch in Education City, told Wildavsky, "It would be disingenuous to say that anybody in Education City, whatever role they're playing, is not here in part because of material rewards."[45] Drawing on a theory of multinationalization developed by Nigel Thrift of the University of Nottingham, Wildavsky writes, "the first international activity is trade with overseas partners, which in the case of universities might involve exchanges of students and professors. Next ... companies start producing subsidiaries in other countries. ... While some in higher education may deplore this rhetoric of consumerism, when customers want what universities have to offer, universities will find a way to reach those customers."[46]

Funded by the Qatar Foundation, Education City provides classroom buildings and supports faculty salaries, housing, and transportation for branch campuses of Virginia Commonwealth, Weill Cornell Medical College, Texas A&M University, Georgetown University School of Foreign Service, and Northwestern University. According to *New York Times* reporter Tamar Lewin, "For the Cornell medical school alone, the Qatar Foundation promised $750 million over 11 years."[47] Mark Weichold, dean of Texas A&M in Qatar said, "Had the Qatar Foundation not been willing to provide the level of support it did, we wouldn't have considered going beyond a study-abroad site."[48]

Thinking like any business, higher education becomes a product to be marketed. The marketing of higher education was highlighted in a 2008 interview with Charles E. Thorpe, the dean of Carnegie Mellon in Qatar. In response to the question, "How will this globalization of US Universities effect the funding available to the universities on US soil?"[49] Thorpe answered in the language of consumerism, "To a large extent, the overseas campuses that are described here are tapping into new markets, bringing education to new students."[50]

Thorpe was asked whether or not the establishment of branch campuses in Qatar was a form of American academic imperialism. Thorpe answered somewhat defensively: "First of all, we are here at the invitation of the Qatar Foundation, so we're responding to what our hosts ask for; we're not pushing our favorite US-centric agenda."[51] In addition, Thorpe moved the question away from American academic imperialism by pointing out expansion of other universities: "Second, the Qatar Foundation is actively courting Universities from around the world. We know there are many fine universities in the US, but there are other fine schools around the world that should also contribute. In fact, in the Emirates there are already institutions from Australia and Europe, so this is a world-wide phenomenon."[52]

Virginia Commonwealth University Qatar's website indicates the rich support it receives from various Qatar agencies:

> VCUQatar benefits from a funding situation that allows it to be driven by innovative programmatic needs rather than typical fiscal constraints. Externally funded student and faculty research opportunities are expanding with the rapid development of Qatar, now among the wealthiest countries in the world based upon per capita GDP. The VCUQatar Center for Research in Design has research funding from the Qatar Science and Technology Park to develop portable, sustainable architecture for labor housing and is expanding collaborations with faculty and external partners. The school is the center for design education in the country by emphasizing design entrepreneurship and design awareness through lectures, exhibitions, and conferences.[53]

Global networking in Education City is promised to those attending one of the Education City's universities. Their website proclaims:

> INTERNATIONAL NETWORKS
> Students, faculty, and staff are from over 60 nations around the world. This rich mix of nationalities, experiences, and cultures represents an educational resource in itself. Learning for the 21st century will be defined by the need for global citizens who can engage comfortably and confidently across all forms of diversity. Education City is a perfect environment in which to gain these skills.[54]

Besides promising to put students in contact with a global network, which according to my previous discussions of networks will enhance the student's ability to succeed in global employment, Education City promises to educate global citizens who will be able to "adopt different perspectives and exhibit characteristics not widely found among 20th century workers. ... Because of the power of the Education City experience, graduates will be the 21st century global citizens that are so in demand around the world."[55]

Global Connections: New York University Abu Dhabi and the Global Superclass

An example of the workings of the shadow elite in establishing branch campuses is New York University (NYU) president John Sexton. Wildavsky describes Sexton as "widely credited with an entrepreneurial zeal."[56] Under Sexton's leadership from 1988 to 2001 NYU's law school joined the nation's top ten in ratings which, in part, resulted in him being named the school's president in 2002. "Even before NYU agreed to launch its Abu Dhabi campus," writes Wildavsky, "Sexton insisted on receiving a $50 million gift from the Emirates that he termed 'earnest money' to demonstrate UAE's seriousness about the project."[57] In addition, the UAE agreed to pay for all facilities and provide generous faculty salaries. Sexton asserted that he is intent on creating a "global network university."[58] As part of the global network university, NYU has also established a branch of its Tisch School of the Arts in Singapore—TischAsia. TischAsia opened in Singapore in 2007 as a branch of NYU's Tisch School of the Arts. The contacts made in establishing both campuses have networked John Sexton into elite networks of the Gulf oil states and Asia.

Essentially, Sexton plans to use money earned from foreign branches to increase its endowment and to finance its New York campus. Terry W. Hartle, senior vice-president of the Washington-based American Council on Education which represents 1,600 college presidents, said, "Sexton's use of foreign money to raise NYU's academic sights may become a model for other ambitious leaders. If he succeeds, John Sexton will have transformed not only NYU but American higher education." In general Sexton is considered a "master fundraiser" ranked 11th in donations to U.S. colleges in 2009 as compared to 27th in 2008.[59]

Not only is NYU Abu Dhabi globally networked but it also sees its mission in that framework. The school's official website indicates the importance given to global networking:

> NYU has embarked on the project of becoming a Global Network University, a university that challenges the idea that a university can only deliver education at a single home campus. Instead, we have created a structure that allows students and faculty to gather in a set of key locales around the globe to forge new ideas, advance the questions we ask about the world, and create solutions for the problems that beset us all.[60]

Abu Dhabi is only one of the sites that Sexton is trying to make part of a globally networked university. Other locations include the previously mentioned TischAsia in Singapore, NYU Law in Singapore, and 10 academic sites in Accra, Ghana; Berlin, Germany; Buenos Aires, Argentina; Florence, Italy; London, England; Madrid, Spain; Paris, France; Prague, the Czech Republic; Shanghai, China; and Tel Aviv, Israel.

Therefore, a network representation of John Sexton's connections would create a graph filled with so many connecting lines that it would be difficult to read. He has myriad contacts within New York City, the American legal system (he was NYU's law school dean), and the government officials and global educators associated with his vision of a globally networked university. As a member of the global shadow elite, Sexton has, as represented above regarding NYU Abu Dhabi, sought financial support from these world governments.

As an example of Sexton's connections I will use NYU's Board of Trustees member Khaldoon Khalifa Al Mubarak, Chairman of the Executive Affairs Authority, Government of Abu Dhabi. Al Mubarak's Mubadala Development Company is developing the NYU's eventual permanent home in Abu Dhabi on Saadiyat Island.[61]

Al Mubarak works closely, as I will describe below, with Abu Dhabi's Crown Prince Mohammed bin Zayed Al Nahyan. According to a *Business Week* article, Sexton cultivated in Abu Dhabi "a friendship with Crown Prince Mohammed bin Zayed Al Nahyan, whom he first met four years ago when the two men shared a meal of dates and coffee in the royal court."[62]

Al Mubarak can be called a member of Abu Dhabi's shadow elite with his connection to the country's royal family and their ownership of global properties. For instance, the *Manchester Evening News* (United Kingdom) reported in 2008 on the purchase of the famous Manchester City Football Club (The Blues) by "one of the richest men on the planet ... Sheikh Mansour Bin Zayed Al Nahyan ... the estimated wealth of the Al Nahyan family is a huge £560billion."[63] Abu Dhabi itself has been declared the richest city in the world by *Fortune* magazine: "Welcome to Abu Dhabi, the capital of the United Arab Emirates and the richest city in the world. The emirate's 420,000 citizens, who sit on one-tenth of the planet's oil and have almost $1 trillion invested abroad, are worth about $17 million apiece (A million foreign workers don't share in the wealth)."[64]

Reflecting Al Mubarak's role in the shadow elite, the *Manchester Evening News* reported his appointment to chair the Manchester City Football Club: "Sheikhs are keen that they have the respect of the English football hierarchy and public, and are not seen as merely acquiring the club as a plaything. That is why one of Sheikh Mansour's most trusted friends and colleague HE Khaldoon Al Mubarak has been asked to be the new chairman."[65] In the news article, Al Mubarak is described: "United States-educated Al Mubarak has been running the Abu Dhabi government-owned investment and development firm Mubadala Development Company for two years."[66]

Khaldoon Khalifa Al Mubarak's close relationship with his government's political leaders was captured in a *Fortune* magazine article:

> Khaldoon's cellphone rings. "Hello, boss," he says, then whispers, "When the crown prince is on the phone, you answer." The 46-year-old crown prince, Mohammed bin Zayed al Nahyan, has been calling a lot lately. With three dozen construction projects planned in Abu Dhabi, plus infrastructure investments in Algeria, Pakistan, and other countries, there's plenty to talk about. "He's like a CEO running a major corporation," Khaldoon says. "He wants results, and he wants them now."[67]

Mubadala Development, chaired by Al Mubarak, the *Manchester Evening News* article asserts, "has investments in more than 50 different companies worldwide and has assets of around £6billion under management, including an 8.1 percent stake in microchip manufacturer AMD and a five percent stake in Ferrari. Al Mubarak is chairman of Abu Dhabi Motorsports Management and the man responsible for the Emirate's inaugural Formula One Grand Prix in 2009 and beyond."[68]

Exemplifying his global connections, *Bloombergbusiness* provides this executive profile of Al Mubarak's many global connections:

> Mr. Khaldoon Khalifa Al Mubarak is the Chief Executive Officer, Managing Director, Member of Investment Committee, and Director at Mubadala Development Company. In this role, Mr. Al Mubarak oversees the delivery of an aggressive investment strategy, generating significant financial returns, and driving sustainable economic development in the U.A.E. He is also responsible for ensuring that the company's business strategy is aligned with its efforts to diversify the economy of Abu Dhabi. He is the General Manager at Dolphin Investment Company LLC. Previously, Mr. Al Mubarak served as an Executive Vice President of Dolphin Energy and played a pivotal role in the Dolphin gas project by successfully leading the negotiations from concept through to the implementation stage. He is a Director of ALDAR Properties and Dolphin Energy Limited. Mr. Al Mubarak was also employed at UAE Offsets Group. He began his career at the Abu Dhabi National Oil Company and holds a number of other key positions within the public sector. Mr. Al Mubarak is the Vice Chairman of the Supervisory Board of LeasePlan Corporation and Vice Chairman of Piaggio Aero. He is a Board Member at First Gulf Bank, Aldar, and Ferrari. Mr. Al Mubarak is a Director of General Investments FZE, the Chairman of Emirates Aluminum Company Limited PJSC, and the Chairman of The Specialist Diabetes and Research Centre LLC. He served as the Chairman of the Board of Oasis International Leasing Company PJSC, from March 2006 to April 2006. Mr. Al Mubarak also served as the Vice Chairman of Oasis International Leasing Company PJSC. He is a Member of the Abu Dhabi Executive Council and the Chairman of the Executive Affairs Authority of the Government of Abu Dhabi; he is responsible for overseeing the provision of strategic policy advice to the Chairman of Abu Dhabi's Executive Council. Mr. Al Mubarak is a Director of Emirates Foundation. He is the Chairman of The Imperial College London Diabetes Center. He is the Chairman of the Emirates Nuclear Energy Corporation, the Abu Dhabi Media Zone Authority and Abu Dhabi Motorsports Management, Deputy Chairman of the Abu Dhabi Urban Planning Council and a member of both the Abu Dhabi Education Council and the Abu Dhabi Council for Economic Development. Mr. Al Mubarak holds a Bachelor of Science degree in Economics and Finance from Tufts University.[69]

Within Abu Dhabi government, Al Mubarak serves as Chairman of the Executive Affairs Authority which has direct responsibility for NYU's branch campus. The Abu Dhabi government's Executive Affairs Authority website describes one aspect of his work:

> Education and healthcare are two key government policy areas in which Khaldoon (Al Mubarak) also has significant involvement. He is a member of

Abu Dhabi Education Council which is mandated to monitor and deliver international standards of education in the Emirate. He is also overseeing the establishment of a 2,000 student New York University campus in Abu Dhabi, and is a member of the New York University Board of Trustees. NYU announced its decision to establish a campus in an agreement it reached with the Executive Affairs Authority in 2007.[70]

Therefore, through NYU's Board of Trustees member Khaldoon Khalifa Al Mubarak, who is also developing the home for Abu Dhabi NYU, NYU's president John Sexton is connected to Abu Dhabi's royal government and their global business holdings. As I discuss in the next section, NYU's TischAsia located in Singapore links Sexton to an Asian network of elites.

Marketing Singapore Education to the World: Global Schoolhouse and Networks

Corporatism or the corporate state is an apt description of Singapore, where there is a close relationship between business and the government in economic development and educational planning.[71] The major difference between the global education approaches of Qatar and Abu Dhabi and Singapore is that the former countries are spending their oil revenues to become global education centers, while Singapore hopes to earn money by becoming a regional education hub through its "Global Schoolhouse" initiative. A World Bank blog asks, "Is it possible to buy oneself a place at the forefront of the knowledge economy? That is the question that Singapore's Global Schoolhouse policy aims to answer."[72]

Trying to stimulate economic growth, Singapore's government decided to invest in making the country the "Global Schoolhouse" by attracting schools and students from other countries. Like Qatar's Education City, Singapore hopes to become the center of world education networks. The Singapore Economic Development Board and the Education Services Division of the Singapore Tourism Board provide a very candid view of their economic objectives for education in their report "Singapore: The Global Schoolhouse":

> Reputable local and foreign education institutions are enjoying brisk business in Singapore, because of a national initiative to muscle in on the global education market, estimated to be worth S$3.7 trillion (US$2.2 trillion). These education institutions are capitalizing on Singapore's proximity to expanding Asian economies and cosmopolitan yet safe living environment to market the city-state as a choice destination for high quality education.[73]

The report is very candid about its belief that attracting foreign students and schools is an economic enterprise in contrast to some lofty educational ideal. The report refers to "mature education exporters from the United States, the United Kingdom, and Australia" who are interested in selling their products in a global marketplace with an estimated demand for international education to increase from 1.8 million students in 2002 to 7.2 million by 2025.[74]

Regarding education as a for-profit enterprise for Singapore it is important to note the role of the Singapore Tourist Board. The Singapore Tourist Board's role is revealed in "Singapore: The Global Schoolhouse" report in a subtitle, "Marketing Singapore Education to the World." The Tourist Board is mandated "to undertake international marketing efforts to promote and raise awareness of the Singapore Education *brand* [author's emphasis]."[75] The international offices of the Singapore Tourist Board are to attract international students to Singapore. The goal of the Tourist Board's work is to make Singapore a "regional hub for education" and a "magnet for global talent."[76]

The use of the term "Singapore Education brand" highlights the consumerist approach to education by the government. Education in this framework becomes a consumer item provided by Singapore to be consumed by foreign students. This marketing approach to selling the Singapore's Global Schoolhouse initiative is captured in the following quote from the report:

> Singapore Tourism Board markets and collaborates with its industry partners to attract school groups from overseas to undertake enrichment trips to Singapore for sports, cultural and language immersion, and other learning objectives. STB also ensures the integration of its international student population, ensuring their stay in Singapore is productive and memorable.[77]

It is in this environment of educational entrepreneurship that NYU's president John Sexton agreed to establish a branch campus of its Tisch School of the Arts. In 2007, TischAsia opened its doors alongside the branch campuses of four other foreign universities. The four other branches of foreign universities included in Singapore's Economic Development Board's Global Schoolhouse are business schools, including branches of INSEAD; the University of Chicago Graduate School of Business; the University of Nevada, Las Vegas, William F. Harrah College of Hotel Administration; and S.P. Jain Institute of Management and Research Center of Management.

At first glance TischAsia seems out of place next to branches of three business and one hotel management school. How does TischAsia fit into Singapore's corporate plans? One indication is the hiring of film director Oliver Stone as its Artistic Director. Singapore's Minister of State for Trade and Industry Lee Yi Shyan explained that Singapore "has a shot at becoming the Hollywood of the East."[78] Also, the school was seen as balancing the technological and science emphasis in government planning: "We realized many of the economies at this stage of their development require something else – creativity and the understanding of the human. It is this expression of ideas and aspiration where there is room for Singapore to develop."[79]

The increasing global network linked to NYU's president John Sexton and others of the university's administrators by the opening of TischAsia can, in part, be represented by its Board of Directors and Board of Trustees. Four of the seven members of the school's Board of Directors are officials of NYU and one is the Singapore filmmaker Eric Khoo. The other two are Meileen Choo, Executive Director, Cathay Organization Pte Ltd and Jennie Chua, President and CEO, The Ascott Group, Ltd. Two of the four members of TischAsia's Board of Trustees are NYU officials and the other two are Fang Ai Lian, Chairman, Great Eastern Holdings Limited and Gerard Ee, Company Director, Great Eastern Life Assurance Company Limited.[80]

Extensive Asian networks can be linked to Board of Trustees members Fang Ai Lian and Gerard Ee who are both executives in Great Eastern, a Singapore-based insurance company that is part of a larger multinational corporation Oversea-Chinese Banking Corporation Limited. Founded in 1908, Great Eastern describes itself as "an investment holding company, provides various insurance products and services primarily in Singapore, Malaysia, and other Asian countries."[81] Its parent company, Oversea-Chinese Banking Corporation, had revenues of U.S. $5.8 billion. The company provides the following description of its activities:

> We are one of Asia's leading financial services groups and one of the largest financial institutions in the combined Singapore-Malaysia market with total assets of S$224 billion. We have an extensive network of 530 branches and representative offices in 15 countries and territories including Singapore, Malaysia, Indonesia, Vietnam, China, Hong Kong SAR, Brunei, Japan, Australia, UK and USA. This network includes 411 branches and offices in Indonesia operated by OCBC Bank's subsidiary, PT Bank NISP.[82]

TischAsia's Board of Directors member Jennie Chua, President and CEO, The Ascott Group, links NYU administrators to a global real estate enterprise. The Ascott Group owns and operates serviced residence units in the Asia Pacific, Europe, and the Gulf region. It offers its services in London, Paris, Brussels, Berlin, Barcelona, Singapore, Bangkok, Hanoi, Kuala Lumpur, Tokyo, Seoul, Shanghai, Beijing, Hong Kong, Melbourne, Perth, Sydney, Doha, Dubai, and Manama, as well as in China.[83] The Ascott Group is owned by a global multinational conglomerate Capitaland Ltd which is composed of 15 subsidiaries including the Ascott Group. Capitaland advertises itself as one of Asia's largest real estate companies, "The Company's real estate … spans more than 110 cities in over 20 countries."[84] The other non–NYU administrator member of TischAsia's Board of Directors Meileen Choo, Executive Director, Cathay Organization Pte Ltd, represents Singapore's film industry. Cathay Organization Pte Ltd has 14 subsidiaries involved in film production, movie houses, and hotels.[85]

Therefore, NYU's president John Sexton has networked himself into the government and private wealth in the oil-rich Gulf States and Asia. He has also networked himself into a global academic elite as spokesperson for the new "global network university." In 2010, Sexton gave a keynote address at the UK's International Education Conference: Going Global 4 on the topic "World potential; making education meet the challenge" along with other speakers and discussants including

Professor Simon Marginson, Professor of Higher Education, University of Melbourne, Australia; Dr Gwang-Jo Kim, Director, UNESCO Asia-Pacific Regional Bureau for Education; Professor Isak Froumin, Lead Education Specialist, Europe and Central Asia Region, World Bank Russia and Senior Advisor, Higher School of Economics, Moscow, Russia; Professor Leandro Tessler, Director of Foreign Relations, UNI-CAMP, Brazil; and Professor Xie Weihe, Vice-President, Tsinghua University, China.[86] At the same conference, Sexton participated in a panel discussion on the topic "What Makes A Truly Global University" along with John R. Mallea, Former Vice-Chancellor and President Emeritus, Brandon University, Canada; Eric Thomas, Vice-Chancellor, University of Bristol, UK; and Professor Timothy W. Tong, President, The Hong Kong Polytechnic University, Hong Kong.[87]

In conclusion, John Sexton's activities since rising from dean of NYU's law school to its presidency have turned him into a true flexian linked through a global flex net to world governments, corporations, and academics. He has become adept at cajoling governments into funding NYU branches which, in turn, economically benefits his school. Sexton's dream of a "global network university" complements his real world experience in connecting with the global rich and powerful.

Conclusion

Racing around the world trying to cajole governments into buying their latest educational products or funding their campus expansions, flexians like Michael Golden and John Sexton find themselves enmeshed in global networks. A characteristic of these two flexians is a belief in the value of their products either in the form of ICT usages in education or in creating a global networked university. In other words, Golden and Sexton are not cynical exploiters of people's wishes for greater educational opportunities or of government educational funds. They, like most flexians, believe in their products while at the same time they seek ways of expanding consumption. From the foreign school branches in South Korea's Jeju Global Education City and Incheon Free Economic Zone, Qatar's Education City, Abu Dhabi's Saadiyat Island, and Singapore's Global Schoolhouse to Microsoft's global reach, the shadow elite are trying to fill a global demand for more education.

For those governments with limited funds, ICT promises a global education at reduced costs. Consider the report of the 2009 UNESCO World Conference on Higher Education which resulted in the UNESCO-Microsoft Task Force on Higher Education and Information and Communication Technology. The report painted a bleak picture of the global masses demanding quality higher education that governments cannot afford to deliver. Woven through the UNESCO report were statements that promoted ICT as the answer to accessibility and solving the teacher shortage problem. Below are examples of the reliance on ICT in the UNESCO report:

> Higher education must scale up teacher education, both pre-service and in-service, with curricula that equip teachers to provide individuals with the

knowledge and skills they need in the twenty-first century. This will require new approaches, including open and distance learning (ODL) and information and communications technologies (ICTs).

Preparing education planners and conducting research to ODL approaches and ICTs present opportunities to widen access to quality education, particularly when Open Educational Resources are readily shared by many countries and higher education institutions.

The application of ICTs to teaching and learning has great potential to increase access, quality and success. In order to ensure that the introduction of ICTs adds value, institutions and governments should work together to pool experience, develop policies and strengthen infrastructure, especially bandwidth.

The results of scientific research should be made more available through ICTs in addition to open access to scientific literature.[88]

In other words, the global network established by Microsoft through UNESCO contains within it a message that governments should purchase more ICT products to meet consumer demand. Cisco is another example of a company dedicated to creating educational networks. Cisco promotes its products with the motto "Together We Are the Human Network" and ad campaigns which suggest that ICT, by connecting people, will create a global consciousness. Their ads provide a utopian view of a world that learns together and might result in world peace because the "Human Network" crosses the boundaries of culture and wealth.[89]

Cisco packages its education technology as meeting the needs of a "learning society" which its videos suggest involve almost constant Internet access to update skills for the knowledge economy. Cisco's lead education ad states:

> The Learning Society: At Cisco, we believe that all societies need to be learning societies. Through our innovative solutions and partnerships we connect, engage, and empower learners, educators, and leaders to improve learning, accelerate economic growth, and strengthen social well-being.[90]

Cisco ads also promote ICT in education as an inexpensive response to world demand: "Demand for learning is increasing from all sectors of society. See why and how our education systems should respond."[91] A video on Cisco's website is titled "Foster Learning, Growth, and Social Change: Connect, engage, and empower students to improve learning, accelerate economic growth, and strengthen social well-being."[92] After reviewing the world's education needs, the video states that "We need to think Beyond the School."[93] Beyond the school in this case means learning from the "Human Network."

In summary, we are in the new age not only of ICT in education but also of human networks that connect business and government. Wedel's shadow elite are now central for the way educational systems are supported and also for the expansion of ICT into school systems. These flexians want to do good while making a profit.

3

EDUCATIONAL POLICIES AND ICT
Superclass and Shadow Elites

"Today we live in a world where more people have access to ICT (usually mobile phone) than to toilets or clean water or the electric grid," was the appraisal of the World Economic Forum's *The Global Information Technology Report 2010–2011*.[1] Similar to my discussion in Chapter 1 of the general role of the World Economic Forum in promoting ICT, the Report presents a rosy future for ICT as the solution for most of the world's problems including expanding educational opportunities, poverty, and health care. An equally positive outlook for ICT in education is presented in the 2010 United States Department of Education's National Education Technology Plan *Transforming American Education: Learning Powered by Technology*: "Technology-based learning and assessment systems will be pivotal in improving student learning and generating data that can be used to continuously improve the education system at all levels."[2] Undergirding these optimistic predictions for the future role of ICT is a network of economic interests and shadow elites. It could be that this optimism is warranted. However, these two important reports contain many unanswered questions about the actual promise of ICT.

In this chapter, I will analyze these two reports because of the global significance of the World Economic Forum studies of ICT and the focus of the United States government on technology as the key to educational change. In the United States, the Bill and Melinda Gates Foundation acts like a shadow government by funding efforts to create online courses that are aligned with the recently created Common Core Standards. The Common Core Standards were released by National Governors Association and Chief State School Officers on June 2, 2010. As the world's richest foundation, the Gates Foundation is linked to a network of shadow elite supporting online instruction aligned with Common Core Standards.

The Gates Foundation plays an important advocacy role for education in the United States. The Foundation gave money to Achieve Inc. to coordinate the writing of tests to be aligned with the Common Core Standards. Achieve Inc. was created "by the nation's governors and corporate leaders ... [to] raise academic standards and graduation requirements, improve assessments and strengthen accountability."[3] In addition, the Gates Foundation funded Teach Plus which has been lobbying state legislatures to eliminate protection of senior teachers during layoffs; most teacher union contracts and many state policies favor layoffs based on seniority. The Gates Foundation has also funded groups such as the New Teacher Project to support changes in the way teachers are evaluated. As I will discuss later in this chapter, the Gates Foundation supports the Foundation for Excellence in Education, a major advocacy group for expanding online instruction by changing state laws, and it funds the Pearson Foundation to create online courses aligned with the Common Core Standards. *New York Times* investigative reporter Sam Dillon wrote about the attempt by Teach Plus to change state laws favoring senior teachers during layoffs: "In Indiana, some lawmakers accused the group [Teach Plus] of being 'part of a conspiracy by Gates and hedge fund managers' to undermine the [teacher] unions' influence."[4]

I will begin with an analysis of *The Global Information Technology Report 2010–2011*'s claims that it will be a panacea for world problems, including the expansion of educational opportunities. I will also outline the networks contributing to the optimism of the Report. This will be followed by a similar analysis of *Transforming American Education: Learning Powered by Technology* along with the impact of Common Core Standards on the work of other advocates of online instruction, foundations, and for-profit ICT companies.

World Economic Forum: *The Global Information Technology Report 2010–2011*

Analysis of *The Global Information Technology Report 2010–2011* provides an opportunity to judge the various claims that ICT will solve most of the world's problems. The Report is rich in arguments on how ICT ushers in a better world, including ending poverty, and improving health care and education. There is nothing in the Report that would dissuade the reader from thinking about ICT as anything but a global panacea. However, I will raise issues about these optimistic claims while trying to balance the positive and negative aspects of ICT. For instance, as I will discuss, there is little evidence that ICT will actually end global poverty.

Examining the production of the Report provides an opportunity to see the global networks influencing governments to subsidize improvements in ICT including expanding national broadband access. These networks, as I will show, again highlight the global shadow elite behind the expansion of ICT. These shadow elites are linked to both a global ICT community and the leaders of the World Economic Forum.

The Report also introduces several important new concepts. One is what the Report refers to as a "global internet culture."[5] The second is an important economic classification, namely the existence of a "global consumer class," which is defined as those who earn enough money to consume global products—there is no maximum income level for the global consumer class.[6] The Report itself promotes the concepts of "Transformations 2.0" and "Localization 2.0." The former refers to shifting from a focus on access to ICT to its use and the latter to adapting ICT to local cultures and languages.[7] I will first analyze the Report's assumptions about the promise of ICT and the development of a global internet culture and consumer class. I will then turn to claims that ICT is the panacea for global problems including education and poverty, and the problem of localizing Internet culture. Throughout these discussions, I will examine the network of shadow elites who produced the Report.

The Promise of ICT: Economic Growth

Reflecting what seems to be a generally accepted assumption among leaders in the World Economic Forum that ICT is the key to a better tomorrow, Robert Greenhill, Chief Business Officer of the World Economic Forum, opens his preface to the Report: "The last decade has seen information and communication technologies (ICT) dramatically transforming the world, enabling innovation and productivity increases, connecting people and communities, and improving standards of living and opportunities across the globe."[8] Sweeping statements like this are difficult to prove or disprove, particularly claims that ICT rather than other potential factors like national political and economic changes could be the source of possible increases in global standards of living. In the same opening paragraph, Greenhill stretches the argument even further by claiming, "ICT has also proven … an important instrument for bridging economic and social divides and reducing poverty."[9]

The Report's editors turned to global ICT leader César Alierta, Executive Chairman and Chief Executive Officer of Telefónica and member of the Boards of Directors of China Unicom and Telecom Italia, to summarize the general attitude about "The Promise of Technology." Globally educated with a law degree from the University of Zaragoza (Spain) and an MBA from Columbia University (USA), Alierta received in 2010 the Americas Society Gold Medal for his contribution to growth and development in South America. As leader of a global ICT firm, César Alierta is economically motivated to preach the future payoff for expanding ICT.

Posted on Telefónica's website is the following description of the company's global reach:

> Present in 25 countries and an average of 257,000 professionals. More than 60.7 billion euros and more than 287.6 million customers as of the end 2010: more than 220 million mobile phones accesses; more than 41 million fixed telephony accesses; more than 18.6 million Internet and data accesses and 2.8 million pay TV accesses.[10]

Its website also offers this description of its recent global activities:

- Strategic alliance with China Unicom; mutual investment agreement: Telefónica increases its stake in China Unicom up to 8.37% while China Unicom takes 0.88% of Telefónica capital (2009)
- Stake in Telefónica CTC Chile increased to 97.89% (2009)
- Acquisition of Hansenet in Germany (2010)
- Control of Vivo in Brazil obtained by buying PT out of Brasilcel (2010)
- Mobile license awarded in Costa Rica (2011)
- Strengthening of the strategic alliance with China Unicom (2009) and increase of the share exchange (2011): Telefónica reaches 9.7% in CU and CU gets a 1.37% in Telefónica[11]

Given this background it is hardly surprising that César Alierta declared in "The Promise of Technology" that the global transformations caused by ICT are "unequivocally positive" and that "this optimistic view rests on the broad platform of the liberation and democratization of information and of technology … Data have been liberated from the control of the few and are now accessible to the many."[12] Now there are serious questions about ICT being a source of liberation in contrast to domination. I will discuss this issue in more detail in the concluding sections to this chapter. But it should be mentioned in reference to Alierta's assertion that data collection and ICT can be used by governments for surveillance and control of their populations. The nonliberating aspects of ICT are highlighted by Evgeny Morozov in *The Net Delusion: The Dark Side of Internet Freedom*.[13]

Alierta's uncritical perspective on technological change becomes evident when he identifies ICT as the fifth technological revolution preceded by the industrial revolution, steam power, electricity, and oil.[14] He asserts each of these technological revolutions was disruptive and required that humans adapt, with the end result being a new technological paradigm that "unleashes widespread opportunities for generating wealth."[15]

However, there is little consideration of the negative along with positive aspects of each of these technological revolutions. Certainly the period he identifies as "oil" unleashed many economic opportunities for industries associated with the discovery and production of oil and gas, and the manufacturing of gas and diesel powered vehicles like cars and trucks along with building of new transportation infrastructures. But there was a downside to these technological revolution as air pollution increased, scientists warned of global warming and climate change, and health experts worried about obesity and lack of exercise as people drove to work and shopping, and drove in circles looking for a parking spot closest to their destination.

In other words, Alierta does not provide a balanced picture of the results of technological change. For instance, he does not provide a balanced view of one of the most significant results of the ICT revolution which is the growth and expansion of global corporations. I think he is correct that ICT has made possible the expansion of multinational businesses by providing the technological tools for an easy global flow of information and the ability to immediately communicate between different corporate divisions spread around the globe. But are these newly expanded global corporations having a positive effect on local businesses? Are these transnational corporations becoming more powerful than nation states? Are they creating a greater divide between rich and poor people and between rich and poor nations and geographical areas? These questions can only be answered after the dust has settled from the current ICT revolution. But the questions highlight the importance of considering the negative effects along with positive effects when considering the impact of new technology.

The Promise of ICT: Education and Data Management

It's not surprising that the uncritical perspective of Telefónica's CEO César Alierta would lead him to conclude: "The contribution of ICT to both social fields—education and health—is not only obvious, but is also one of the areas where the implementation of technology has enormous potential."[16] Among ICT's contributions to education, he states, are instant access to knowledge, opportunities to improve teaching methods, and distance and lifelong learning.

Besides these contributions of ICT to education, *The Global Information Technology Report 2010–2011* advocates the application of what it calls the "Transformation 2.0 agenda" to education and other social services. The two editors of the Report, Soumitra Dutta of INSEAD and Irene Mia of the World Economic Forum, along with Thierry Geiger of the World Economic Forum, state that the Report's focus is on the social impact of Transformation 2.0.[17]

What is Transformation 2.0? It is the application and analysis of data. As I discussed in Chapter 1, this approach contributes to the data mind that perceives educational improvement as a problem in data management; data management of school operations, student assessment scores, and instructional materials. Data collected on students, in this paradigm, could be used to match instructional materials with student abilities and predict the student's educational future. In other words, Transformation 2.0 reinforces the cultural perspective that sees students and schools as data.

The person chosen to write the Report's section on "Transformation 2.0 for an Effective Social Strategy" was Mikael Hagström,[18] the Executive Vice President of Europe, the Middle East, Africa, and Asia Pacific at SAS which, as described on its website, "is the leader in business analytics software and services, and the largest independent vendor in the business intelligence market."[19] Given this corporate background it is not surprising that Hagström believes that the use of analytic software, of the type produced by his firm, to interpret data is at the heart of Transformation 2.0.

Hagström argues that the use of data-driven decision-making has evolved through three stages; stages that can be used to frame its application to education. The first stage of data management occurred in business which used ICT to collect data and subject it to quantitative analysis. The second stage, and this encompasses public education, involved applying these methods developed in the private sector to government operations, including schools.

Today, he argues, the world is embarking on the third stage which involves "investing heavily in analytic capabilities and driving the development of new techniques and technologies, including high-performance computing, data integration, and complex event processing."[20] He compares the first two stages to looking in the rearview mirror while driving. Quantitative analysis involves looking at data collected on past events, such as the results of student test scores.

The third stage uses "analytics," which he defines as the software and processes that convert data into "actionable insights."[21] In this third stage, one is looking through the front windshield at potential future circumstances: "we can use analytics to spot patterns and predict future trends with far greater accuracy than ever before … Analytics gives you the ability to see forward, peek into the future and make meaningful judgments that result in better outcomes"[22] Analytics was exemplified in Chapter 1 by the Adaptive Learning Platform software produced by Knewton which promises to adapt educational content to meet the needs of each student. This involves applying analysis of students and content data to their future learning.

Hagström's article on Transformation 2.0 for the World Economic Forum Report reflects the business objectives of his own company SAS. The company uses the concept of "analytics" to sell its software products: "SAS Analytics provide an integrated environment for predictive and descriptive modeling, data mining, text analytics, forecasting, optimization, simulation, experimental design and more."[23]

SAS targets the education market along with many other markets including casinos. The company claims to have worked for over 30 years in the education field with its products now being used in 3,000 educational institutions worldwide. Under education on its website, SAS states that it offers a range of educational products "from online curriculum resources that enhance student achievement and teacher effectiveness to on-site or hosted administrative offerings that supply SAS customers with the accurate and reliable information and analysis they need to make the best data-driven decisions possible."[24] One SAS product, Education Value-Added Assessment System designed for current efforts to measure academic growth using data from standardized tests, is used in the United States by the Metropolitan Nashville Public Schools, Hershey Intermediate in Pennsylvania, and the High Point Central High School, North Carolina. The Education Value-Added Assessment System does not involve the sale of software but has states and school districts sending their "electronic data directly to SAS, where the data is cleaned and analyzed. SAS transmits the results via a secure Web application that is a powerful, but user-friendly, diagnostic tool for any user with security privileges to access."[25]

SAS's Education Value-Added Assessment System exemplifies the Transformation 2.0 championed by the World Economic Forum. Its website stresses the use of this product will provide a basis for future decision-making. As the most comprehensive reporting package of value-added metrics available in the educational market,

SAS EVAAS for K–12 provides valuable diagnostic information about past practices and reports on students' predicted success probabilities at numerous academic milestones. By identifying which students are at risk, SAS claims, educators can be proactive, making sound instructional choices and using their resources more strategically to ensure that every student has the chance to succeed.[26]

SAS promises that, "Effectively implemented, SAS EVAAS for K-12 allows educators to recognize progress and growth over time, and provides a clear path to achieve the US goal to lead the world in college completion by the year 2020."[27]

In conclusion, SAS's Mikael Hagström offers the World Economic Forum a crucial argument for supporting the organization's promotion of Transformation 2.0 through ICT and, at the same time, advances the economic interests of his company. In Transformation 2.0, the application of analytics to data promises to improve a whole host of the world's problems besides education, including health care, drug abuse, public safety, and government services. Probably the most tenuous claim is that ICT and Transformation 2.0 will solve the problem of global poverty.

Poverty, Consumer Class, and Internet Culture

Consumerism plays an important role in the supposed economic benefits of ICT, the global economy, and in driving technological development as buyers line up in the early morning hours to be the first to purchase the latest version of an iPad, smart phone, or game console. These relationships are identified in the *The Global Information Technology Report 2010–2011*'s section on "The Emerging Internet Economy: Looking a Decade Ahead."[28] This prediction of the global technological future identifies a "global consumer class" which is defined as having "annual income above US$6,000 (in real 2007 terms)—an arbitrary boundary but one that is roughly indicative of the income threshold above which consumption for non-basic items begins to grow rapidly in many economies."[29] The Report estimates the size of the global consumer class to be about 2.5 billion. The growth of the consumer class, according to the Report, will be primarily in developing economies.

It is the global growth of the consumer class that is supposed to spur the growth of purchases and use of ICT. In fact the authors choose the figure of U.S. $6,000 as the point at which people could afford to buy ICT products. They choose the term "consumer class" over "middle class" because: "For our purpose—related to consumption of ICT goods and services—we find it best to rely simply on an income 'floor' without considering the income 'ceiling' implicit in middle-class estimates."[30]

The authors of "The Emerging Internet Economy: Looking a Decade Ahead" are Cisco Systems, Inc.'s Enrique Rueda-Sabater and John Garrity. Founded in 1984, Cisco pioneered the development of Internet Protocol (IP)-based networking technologies. Cisco's 2010 Annual Report, which is titled "Together We Are the Human Network," boasts, "More than 85 percent of Fortune 500 companies use Cisco Unified Communications for robust and feature-rich communications services accessible from a wide range of clients and endpoints, including enterprise telephony, unified messaging, multimedia conferencing, and enterprise instant messaging."[31]

Both Enrique Rueda-Sabater and John Garrity are part of the global shadow elite promoting the use of ICT products. Before working for Cisco, Rueda-Sabater and Garrity worked for the intergovernmental World Bank. Enrique Rueda-Sabater spent two decades at the World Bank with his last position being Director of Corporate Strategy and Integrated Risk Management. At Cisco, Rueda-Sabater is Director, Strategy and Economics. He has also been an advisor to the United Nations on economic development. John Garrity is part of the strategy team in Cisco's Emerging Markets Business Development Group who previously worked at the World Bank and United States' Federal Trade Commission.[32]

The global consumer class is part of what the Report refers to as a "new global Internet culture," where users across countries generally share similar opinions and habits.[33] However, the Report advocates promoting consumerism through what it calls "Localization 2.0" where the Internet adapts to local laws, customs, and cultures.[34] The authors of this section of the Report, Jeff Kelly and Neil Blakesley, stress the role of "Localization 2.0" in promoting consumerism. The authors claim, "It has become common to talk about world citizens and the global village, but consumers are even more the 'children' of the cultures in which they grew up."[35] Businesses using the Internet, the authors warn, must in the future adapt to the consumer desires of local cultures. "The number of people who may want to buy products or use services that are linguistically and culturally localized," the authors assert, "to countries other than that in which they are based is increasing all the time."[36]

It is not surprising that Localization 2.0 focuses on consumerism. Both authors have backgrounds in marketing. Jeff Kelly is Chief Executive of BT Global Services where he is described as having "extensive experience working in the global IT services market."[37] Neil Blakesley is Vice President of Marketing at BT Global Services.[38] BT Global Services is described on its website: "BT Global Services … provides managed networked IT services for business and government organisations. We operate globally and deliver locally to most of the world's large multinational corporations."[39]

Poverty, in the context of the *The Global Information Technology Report 2010–2011*, involves having enough money to join the global consumer class when income exceeds the amount to purchase basic items for living. Torbjörn Fredriksson, Chief of ICT Analysis Section of the Division on Technology and Logistics at the United Nations Conference on Trade and Development, was selected to write the Report's section on "The Growing Possibilities of Information and Communication Technologies for Reducing Poverty."[40] Note that the article's title is about possibilities of ending poverty and it does not claim that ICT is actually ending poverty. Fredriksson provides anecdotal evidence of mobile phones helping farmers and fishers access information on prices, markets, and weather. Also, the selling of mobile phones and related equipment has created new occupations. He considers the mobile phone important for illiterate populations. The other source of possible relief from poverty is employment in ICT manufacturing units. Fredriksson states that ICT "can help reduce poverty in two main ways: through direct income generation, and through diversified and more secure employment opportunities."[41]

In summary, the participants in the World Economic Forum's Report express a belief that ICT is the panacea to most of the world's problems, including education. The backgrounds of the authors of the Report and its various sections indicate that they have an economic interest in promoting ICT. However, there are serious flaws in their arguments. One argument claims that ICT will result in liberation and democratization of information without considering how countries might use it for surveillance and control of populations, and restrict the access to information. Another argument asserts that the ICT revolution is moving into a new stage where analytics can be applied to data to guide future actions. Analytics, as I will discuss in the next section, is becoming an important part of education where student data is analyzed to adapt instructional material to individual students and to predict their possible educational attainments. However, the application of analytics in education might, as I will suggest later in this chapter, simply provide a cheaper and more ideologically controlling education rather than actually improving learning. There is also the on-going issue of the local versus the global where local cultures might be transformed as a result of the growth of a global Internet culture. Whether this will actually occur is debatable, but the concept of Localization 2.0 suggests that authors of the Report are primarily interested in using local cultures to market consumer items. This approach reinforces the concept of a global consumer class that is the target market for ICT products. While there is hope among the authors of the Report that ICT can reduce poverty there is little evidence that this is occurring. The next section will discuss these issues in the context of ICT being presented as a panacea for education in the United States.

National Education Technology Plan

This section focuses on the 2010 United States Department of Education's National Education Technology Plan *Transforming American Education: Learning Powered by Technology* along with a discussion of supporting documents and funding, including the Foundation for Excellence in Education's report *Digital Learning Now!*; the grant policies of the Bill and Melinda Gates Foundation; and the policies of the Pearson Foundation to create online courses aligned with Common Core Standards. This discussion will lead the reader into a tangled network of government officials, for-profit companies, academics, and foundation leaders. Central players in this drama are a shadow elite similar to those discussed in the previous two chapters.

U.S. Secretary of Education Arne Duncan declared in a speech at the time of the release of the National Education Technology Plan that, "We're at an important transition point. We're getting ready to move from a predominantly print-based classroom to a digital learning environment."[42] Similar to other plans for education and ICT the Plan contains only positive statements about what ICT can do for education and schooling. Duncan's speech used terms more familiar to the business world than education: "just as technology has increased productivity in the business world, it is an essential tool to help boost educational productivity."[43]

Woven through the discussions about the report and other ICT proposals is a belief that ICT can reduce educational costs and solve the problem of declining state and local budgets. There is a sense that not only would print disappear from the traditional classroom but also the teacher and the classroom itself. Even in Duncan's speech there is reference to "progress as virtual schools expand access to curriculum." Might the ICT revolution result in virtual schools and teachers with government money paying for-profit ICT companies for these virtual worlds?

The National Education Technology Plan is designed to help the United States Department of Education to implement national curriculum standards known as Common Core Standards and what are referred to as STEM (science, technology, engineering, and mathematics) subjects. The STEM subjects are considered important for ensuring the United States' ability to compete in global markets.

Common Core Standards are to be aligned with common national assessments that are benchmarked against global tests. The U.S. Secretary of Education stressed when the Common Core Standards were announced:

> The release of these Common Core State Standards is just the beginning of the effort. As states move forward to implement the standards, they will need to translate standards into classroom teaching that will help all students master these new standards. The Department plans to support state implementation efforts by providing federal funds for high quality assessments, professional development to help teachers enhance the knowledge and skills needed to help students master the standards, and research to support continual improvement of the standards and assessments over time.[44]

The National Education Technology Plan contains five major recommendations that are designed to use ICT to implement the Common Core Standards and assessments. The first recommendation is to use ICT to make learning more engaging and tailored to the student and curriculum standards. This goal involves the application of analytics to student data of the type previously discussed in reference to the World Economic Forum and SAS. It also involves what in the next chapter I will discuss as "edutainment" or making learning entertaining by the application of software designs used for digital games. Highlighted in the Plan is the role of technology in teaching STEM subjects. The report stresses, "In particular, technology can be used to support student interaction with STEM content in ways that promote deeper understanding of complex ideas, engage students in solving complex problems, and create new opportunities for STEM learning at all levels of our education system."[45] Implementation of the first goal involves pressuring local and state governments to "implement standards and learning objectives using technology for all content areas" and for state and local school districts to "develop and implement learning resources that exploit the flexibility and power of technology to reach all learners anytime and anywhere."[46]

The second recommendation links the use of technology to assessment—a big part of the U.S. government's educational plan. Technology holds the promise of continually assessing student learning and using analytics to analyze student assessments to determine future learning objectives. Many groups, as I will discuss, have an economic interest in the application of ICT to assessments aligned with Common Core Standards. In the words of the Plan, "Learning science and technology combined with assessment theory can provide a foundation for new and better ways to assess students in the course of learning, which is the ideal time to improve performance."[47] The Plan recommends the use of ICT based assessments in a variety of situations including virtual worlds and games. Specifically, the Plan calls for conducting "research and development that explores how embedded assessment technologies, such as simulations, collaboration environments, virtual worlds, games and cognitive tutors, can be used to engage and motivate learners while assessing complex skills."[48]

The third, fourth, and fifth goals are to link teachers to available resources, support access to online instruction in and out of school, and use ICT to spend less money to accelerate student achievement, or to use the language of the Plan, to increase "productivity." It is revealing that the Plan uses the language of business by referring to the use of technology to make education more "productive." In the words of the Plan: "What education can learn from the experience of business is that we need to make the fundamental structural changes that technology enables if we are to see dramatic improvements in productivity."[49]

The economic crisis at the time of the Plan's completion is used to justify the call for increased educational productivity, meaning spending less for better test results. As I will describe, the economic crisis is used in other situations to justify replacing teachers with online instruction. In the words of the Plan, ICT promises to relieve the budget plight of American schools:

> More money for education is important, but we must spend education dollars wisely, starting with being clear about the learning outcomes we expect from the investments we make. We also must leverage technology to plan, manage, monitor, and report spending so that we can provide decision-makers with a reliable, accurate, and complete view of the financial performance of our education system at all levels. Such visibility is essential to improving productivity and accountability.[50]

In comments introducing the Plan, Secretary of Education Arne Duncan stressed the use of technology to overcome the budget crisis: "the fifth goal is to harness the power of technology to help schools become more productive ... Despite difficult financial times, we must improve student outcomes in ways that historically may have seemed impossible."[51]

The Shadow Elite of the National Education Technology Plan

Contributors to the National Education Technology Plan included a 15 member technical working group and members of the U.S. Department of Education. Guiding the development of the Plan was Barbara Means of SRI International. In his speech introducing the Plan, U.S. Secretary of Education Arne Duncan specifically thanked Karen Cator, Director of the Office of Educational Technology in the U.S. Department of Education. Duncan stated, "Our team here, led by Karen Cator, who is doing a fantastic job, is absolutely committed to supporting the work necessary to bring this plan to life."[52] Another important player is James H. Shelton, Assistant Deputy Secretary for Innovation and Improvement in the Department of Education.

The network contributing to the National Education Technology Plan is linked to a larger network of advocates seeking increased use of ICT in education. Not surprisingly a pivotal network player is the Bill and Melinda Gates Foundation. The goal of using ICT to implement common core curriculum standards is also supported by the Foundation for Excellence in Education's *Digital Learning Now!* and the Pearson Foundation, a foundation sponsored by the global publishing and test producer Pearson. Both the Pearson Foundation and the Foundation for Excellence receive funding from the Bill and Melinda Gates Foundation. As I discuss later in this chapter, the linkage between the Gates and Pearson Foundations in aligning online courses with the Common Core Standards promises large profits for Pearson.

As demonstrated in the previous two chapters, these networks of shadow elites are extensive and could prove tedious for the reader to follow. Therefore, I will try to simplify my description in this and following chapters. However, the basic pattern of networks discussed in previous chapters persists, with interrelationships between ICT companies, government, universities, and foundations. Many members of the technical working group on the National Education Technology Plan are academics with backgrounds in using digital gaming in education and using ICT for student assessment, and authors of books on educational technology.

Some of those who developed the Plan exemplify the concept of flexian moving between business, government, and universities. For instance, consider the previously mentioned Karen Cator who Arne Duncan specifically recognized when introducing the National Education Technology Plan. Just prior to accepting the position of Director of the Office of Educational Technology, she directed Apple Inc.'s "leadership and advocacy efforts in education."[53] She moved to Apple in 1997 after working on ICT for the Alaskan state government. She is also on the board of a major ICT education lobbying group, Software & Information Industry Association—Education.[54]

Cator's colleague in the U.S. Department of Education, James H. Shelton, Assistant Deputy Secretary for Innovation and Improvement, deals with learning technology. Highlighting his flexian career was his prior work as Program Director for the Bill and Melinda Gates Foundation. His education business connections are extensive as reported in his official biography posted on the U.S. Department of Education's website:

> Shelton has also been a partner and the East Coast lead for NewSchools Venture Fund and co-founded LearnNow, a school management company that later was acquired by Edison Schools. He spent over four years as a senior management consultant with McKinsey & Company in Atlanta, Ga., where he advised CEOs and other executives on issues related to corporate strategy, business development, organizational design, and operational effectiveness. Upon leaving McKinsey, he joined Knowledge Universe, Inc., where he launched, acquired and operated education-related businesses.[55]

Barbara Means, who oversaw the development of the National Education Technology Plan, is Co-Director of the Center for Technology in Learning, SRI International. Also with an SRI International background and a member of the technical working group for the Plan is Professor Roy Pea of Stanford University and Co-Director of its Center for Innovations in Learning. Prior to joining the Stanford faculty in 2001 he served from 1996 to 2001 as SRI International Director of the Center for Technology in Learning. Currently, Pea is Director and Co-Founder of TeachScape.[56] SRI, originally called the Stanford Research Institute, describes itself as "an independent, nonprofit research institute conducting client-sponsored research and development for government agencies, commercial businesses, foundations, and other organizations. SRI also brings its innovations to the marketplace by licensing its intellectual property and creating new ventures."[57] SRI's staff pursues grants from both government and commercial businesses.

TeachScape, where Professor Pea is Director, is a for-profit company selling learning software and its board of directors indicates its profit-driven status: Phil Clough, ABS Capital Partners; Paul Mariani, ABS Capital Partners; Robert Finzi, Sprout Group; and Marguerite Kondracke, America's Promise.[58]

Pea is also Director of VIP Tone, another for-profit learning corporation, which is described on its website:

> VIP Tone helps educators create world-class school environments with one integrated solution for their learning, communication and collaboration needs. Founded by Robert Iskander in April 2000, VIP Tone, Inc. is a privately held Delaware Corporation headquartered in Alameda, California, with an Australian subsidiary, VIP Tone Australia, PTY, Ltd., based in Adelaide, South Australia.[59]

The company claims that it sells products that serve 3.6 million students and over 100,000 teachers around the globe.[60]

Another member of the technical working group with connections to ICT companies is John Seely Brown, who was Chief Scientist of Xerox Corporation and the director of its Palo Alto Research Center and is currently co-chairman of the

Deloitte Center for the Edge, which according to its website "helps senior executives make sense of and profit from emerging opportunities on the edge of business and *technology* [author's emphasis]."[61]

Not surprisingly I could not find one critic of the application of ICT to education in the group that prepared the National Education Technology Plan. The group was composed of those who advocate and/or profit from educational technology. Given the background in ICT and education businesses, the two government officials involved in the Plan might logically favor members of their network. Also, it would be logical that they would draw on academics noted for their contributions to educational technology to help develop the Plan. It could be that all participants were so myopic that they never thought of searching for a critic of educational technology; they seem to have unquestioningly assumed that ICT is the panacea for American education.

Foundation for Excellence in Education: *Digital Learning Now!*

The Foundation for Excellence in Education is campaigning for more extensive use of online education by advocating for changes in state laws that would make it possible for students to take online courses from public and private sources anywhere at any time. Jeb Bush, former governor of Florida and brother of ex-President George W. Bush, is Chairman of the Foundation for Excellence, which serves as an advisor on education policy to a number of mainly Republican governors. In 2011, Bush hit the road carrying the message of the Foundation's *Digital Learning Now!* to state governments. The message was simple—the economic crises provided an opportunity to reduce school budgets by replacing teachers with online courses.[62]

Who funds the Foundation's message? Not surprisingly major funding comes from the Bill and Melinda Gates Foundation along with the Walton Family Foundation and The Broad Foundation. The Walton Family Foundation was established by Sam Walton, the founder of the global retail chain Wal-Mart. One area of funding of the Walton Family Foundation is education with a primary concern of promoting school choice. The Walton Family Foundation website states, "The Walton Family Foundation invests in programs that empower parents to choose the best education for their children … We are interested in helping children to receive high-quality educations in public, charter and private school."[63] One choice option is of course online learning.

Exemplifying the web of networks between Foundations, the other major funder of the Foundation for Excellence is The Broad Foundation which also receives money from the Bill and Melinda Gates Foundation. The Broad Foundation was established by Eli and Edythe Broad who made their money in real estate and financial services through creation of two Fortune 500 companies—KB Home and SunAmerica.[64] *Forbes* lists Eli Broad as 132nd among the world's billionaires.[65] Part of the work of The Broad Foundation is devoted to education, including support for school choice options that are the same as Jeb Bush's Foundation: "We are interested in helping children to receive high-quality educations in public, charter and private schools."[66]

Training shadow elites in education is a conscious goal of The Broad Foundation. Funding from the Bill and Melinda Gates Foundation supports the Broad Residency Program in Urban Education. As a trainer of the shadow elite, the residency program trains executives from business and civic organizations to assume leadership roles in education at every level of government:

> The Broad Residency is a management development program that places talented executives with private and civic sector experience and advanced degrees from top business, public policy and law schools into two-year, full-time, paid positions at the top levels of urban school districts, state and federal departments of education and leading charter management organizations.[67]

Highlighting the goal of creating shadow elite is the title of a Broad Foundation news release, "Record Number of Broad Residents Take on Local, State, and Federal Roles Managing Education Reform."[68] This news release reports the extent of Gates Foundation involvement in training these shadow elite: "The Broad Center has received a $3.6 million grant from the Bill & Melinda Gates Foundation to recruit and train as many as 18 Broad Residents over the next four years to provide management support to school districts and charter management organizations addressing the issue of teacher effectiveness."[69]

A 2011 *Education Week* article raised issues regarding The Broad Foundation's general goal of training leaders to occupy the superintendencies of a third of the largest schools districts in the U.S. According to *Education Week* reporter Christina Samuels, by 2011 there were:

> Broad-trained executives in top leadership positions: Shael Polakow-Suransky, the chief academic officer in New York City; John E. Deasy, the super-intendent of Los Angeles Unified; and Jean-Claude Brizard, who became the chief executive officer of the Chicago schools last month. In all, 21 of the nation's 75 largest districts now have superintendents or other highly placed central-office executives who have undergone Broad training.[70]

Conspiracy theorists might see a well-planned agenda in The Broad Foundation's support of Bush's online education initiative and its training of school district leaders to carry this agenda into leadership roles in local schools. Critics claim that The Broad Academy trains administrators on how to consolidate their power, weaken teachers' unions and other means of protecting teachers, and reduce parental participation in decision-making. One critic suggests the goal is to align the functioning of school systems to the needs of the business community.[71]

Another supporter of Jeb Bush's agenda is IQity, a provider of online learning platforms, which is a sustaining contributor to the Foundation for Excellence in

Education (Gates, Walton, and Broad are founding contributors). IQity website describes the company's work:

> The IQity e-Learning Platform is the most complete solution available for the electronic search and delivery of curriculum, courses, and other learning objects. Delivering over one million courses each year, the IQity Platform is a proven success for students, teachers, school administrators, and district offices; as well as state, regional, and national education officials across the country.[72]

Other supporters are the publishing house giants Houghton Mifflin Harcourt and McGraw-Hill. Listed as Friends of the Foundation for Excellence in Education are ICT companies involved in education, namely Apex Learning, Cisco, Learning.com, Pearson Foundation, and SMART.[73] Pearson Foundation, as I will describe later, also receives funds from the Gates Foundation to write online courses based on Common Core Standards which in turn helps its parent company Pearson publishing to create and sell online courses based on the same standards.

Changing Laws to Expand Online Learning: *Digital Learning Now!*

With these wealthy and economically interested supporters, Jeb Bush's Foundation for Excellence in Education is urging legal changes that will expand opportunities for online education offered by both public and for-profit organizations. The Foundation's action report *Digital Learning Now!* lists in its "10 Elements of High Quality Digital Learning" actions that should be taken by lawmakers and policy-makers. These actions include states passing laws providing online courses to students in K–12 and providing access to online courses from public schools, charter schools, not-for-profit organizations, and for-profit companies. These laws will require that online courses be aligned with the common core curriculum and that all providers are treated equally, meaning that for-profit companies will be treated the same as public schools.[74] The Foundation's action plan calls for states to not place limits on the number of credits earned online, to allow students to take all or some of their courses online, and to make online instruction all year and at any time.

The above legal changes would open the floodgates to online K–12 instruction in the United States. An important part of this plan is the elimination of any laws that put a cap on the size of class enrollments. This opens the door to replacing teachers with online instruction since the elimination of class size requirements would allow schools to put all their students, if they make the choice, online for their education. *Digital Learning Now!* states, "Actions for lawmakers and policymakers: State does not restrict access to high quality digital content and online courses with policies such as *class size ratios and caps on enrollment or budget* [author's emphasis]."[75]

Proposals to expand online instruction and, as a result, reduce the cost of teachers' salaries are presented as answers to declining state education budgets. *Digital Learning Now!* states that budget crises open the door to educational changes like the expansion of online learning: "Growing budget deficits and shrinking tax revenue present a tremendous challenge for the nation's Governors and lawmakers, especially when education sometimes consumes up to half of a state's budget. However, what might appear to be an obstacle to reform can also present a great opportunity for innovation."[76] Another cost cutter in *Digital Learning Now!* is the proposal that textbooks be replaced with digital content.

The reader might think that publishers would not support replacing textbooks with digital content. However, publishers are rapidly creating and marketing of online courses. In the next section I will describe this development in the context of the Bill and Melinda Gates Foundation's financial support of the Pearson Foundation's creation of online courses aligned with the Common Core Standards. This is another example of the interconnections between foundations.

A Marriage of Common Interests: Gates and Pearson

The relationship between the Pearson and Gates Foundations highlights how these two organizations mutually reinforce each other's policy objectives and promote a common economic interest in online instruction. On April 27, 2011, the Pearson Foundation announced that it had received a grant from the Bill and Melinda Gates Foundation to aid in the creation of 24 online courses in math and reading/English arts that would be aligned with the Common Core Standards. The courses are to be implemented in 2013.

The economics of the relationship between the two foundations demonstrates how opportunities are created by nonprofits to help for-profits increase their earnings. The Pearson Foundation was established by the global publishing and ICT company Pearson. The Pearson Foundation explains this relationship as: "The Pearson Foundation is the philanthropic arm of Pearson plc one of the world's leading media and education companies. Pearson Foundation extends Pearson's commitment to education by partnering with leading nonprofit, civic, and business organizations to provide financial, organizational, and publishing assistance across the globe."[77]

The money given by the Gates Foundation to the Pearson Foundation will allow for the free distribution of four of the planned 24 online courses. Pearson, the company, will be able to sell the other 20 online courses. In their announcement of the award to the Pearson Foundation, the Bill and Melinda Gates Foundation stated, "Funding from the Bill & Melinda Gates Foundation will support the development of this robust system of courses, including four—two in math and two in English language arts—to be available at no cost on an open platform for schools."[78]

Pearson, the company, describes itself as the world's leading for-profit education company: "Pearson is the world's leading education company. From pre-school to high school, early learning to professional certification, our curriculum materials, *multimedia learning tools and testing programs help to educate more than 100 million people worldwide − more than any other private enterprise* [author's emphasis]."[79] Pearson reports that 60% of its sales are in North America though it sells books and tests in 60 countries. Its publishing subsidiaries are Scott Foresman, Prentice Hall, Addison-Wesley, Allyn and Bacon, Benjamin Cummings, and Longman.

Pearson, the company, does have an economic stake in the relationship between its Pearson Foundation and the Bill and Melinda Gates Foundation in the creation of online courses to meet Common Core Standards. A huge market for online courses aligned to the Common Core Standards is being created by the U.S. Department of Education's implementation of the National Technology Education Plan and Jeb Bush's lobbying of state governments to implement the recommendations in *Digital Learning Now!* Pearson wants to sell products in this burgeoning market. The company has a past history of marketing online courses with claims that they are one of the world's largest providers. The company boasts on its website that: "We are also a leading provider of electronic learning programs and of test development, processing and scoring services to educational institutions, corporations and professional bodies around the world."[80]

The Pearson Foundation is candid that Pearson, the company, will use the Foundation's work to market products to local school districts. The Foundation and company are not embarrassed at what on the surface appears illegal, with a tax-exempt foundation creating materials that will eventually be sold by a for-profit company. This intention is clearly stated in Pearson Foundation's announcement of the money it is receiving from the Gates Foundation:

> Pearson, the nation's leading education technology company, will offer these courses to school districts, complete with new services for in-person professional development for teacher transition to the Common Core and next-generation assessment. The Pearson Foundation will also work with other partners to explore opportunities for additional commercial development and distribution.[81]

Pearson will also earn money from assessments aligned with the Common Core Standards. These aligned assessments promise to be another major source of revenue. Pearson already claims:

> We are also the largest provider of educational assessment services and solutions in the US (Pearson Educational Measurement), developing, scoring and processing tens of millions of student tests every year. We mark school examinations for the US federal government, 20 American states, and score more than 100 million multiple-choice tests and 30 million essays every year. Pearson also scores the National Assessment of Educational Progress (the only federal nationwide test), and college entrance exams.[82]

Gates Foundation: Online Courses and the Common Core Standards

As I stated in the opening of this chapter, the Gates Foundation acts like a shadow government in promoting government policies related to online education and Common Core Standards. The money given to the Pearson Foundation is only part of what the Gates Foundation refers to as a "suite of investments." This suite of investments focuses on using ICT to implement the Common Core Standards. In the announcement of this suite of investments, including the money going to the Pearson Foundation, the Gates Foundation states it will support the following activities to be aligned with the Common Core Standards: "game-based learning applications; math, English language arts and science curricula built in to digital formats; learning through social networking platforms; and embedded assessments through a real-time and engaging environment of experiences and journeys."[83]

Besides funding the Pearson Foundation, the Gates Foundation's suite of investments also includes indirect support for state laws that are similar to those advocated by Jeb Bush's Foundation for Excellence in Education. Gates Foundation money goes to Florida's Virtual School which was founded in 1997 as the first state-wide system of K-12 online instruction. The courses are offered globally, with Florida residents taking the courses for free while non-Florida residents pay tuition.[84] The legal parallels between Florida's Virtual School laws and those advocated by the Foundation for Excellence in Education are highlighted in a memorandum issued by Florida's Commissioner of Education, Eric Smith, on January 8, 2009. The memorandum explains Florida's legal requirements, including "that school districts may not limit student access to FLVS courses" and that there are "no limits on the number of credits a student may earn at FLVS during a single school year or multiple school years."[85] While Jeb Bush's Foundation touts online courses as solutions to school budget problems, Florida law allows for the use of the Florida Virtual Schools by local school districts "to help ease overcrowding."[86]

A joint Russian and United States nonprofit effort in online math instruction, Reasoning Mind, also benefited from funding from the Gates Foundation's suite of investments. With offices in Moscow and Houston, Reasoning Mind cites the mantra that: "First-rate math and science skills are essential for success in the 21st century workforce. Unless we can come together to take our nation's math education to the next level, the United States will quickly lose its leading role in industry and innovation."[87] Reasoning Mind is supported by a host of foundations besides the Bill and Melinda Gates Foundation. While it is a nonprofit organization, Reasoning Mind receives sponsorship from global for-profit technology firms having an interest in online instruction including Cisco, Google, Oracle, FairIsaac, Sungard, and Atlassian.[88] Reasoning Mind has linkages to global firms including Russia's oil and gas industry. The founder and CEO of Reasoning Mind is Alexander Khachatryan who in 1992 founded and became President of Russian Petroleum Consultants Corporation and in 1999 became Vice President of Operations of the

ICT company Logexoft, Inc. Khachatryan's career stretches back to the Soviet period when he earned degrees from the Moscow Oil and Gas Institute. Consequently, it is not surprising that the American branch of Reasoning Mind is located in the oil and gas center of Houston, Texas.

The Gates Foundation suite of investments also funds 20 literacy based programs developed by the Digital Youth Network which is dedicated to literacy instruction online or place based.[89] Also funded is the Institute of Play to apply game design to instructional methods and curriculum. The Institute of Play is a nonprofit corporation founded in 2007 "by a group of game designers looking to apply game design principles to challenges outside the field of commercial game development. Within six months funding was secured to start up an innovative new public school in New York City, called Quest to Learn."[90] I will discuss game design and the Quest to Learn School in the next chapter. The application of game design to education was also the purpose of the Gates Foundation grant to Quest Atlantis to create video games for math, science, and literacy. Quest Atlantis serves 50,000 children in 22 states and 18 countries. As described on its website it "is an international learning and teaching project that uses a 3D multi-user environment to immerse children, ages 9–16, in educational tasks."[91] It was created by the Center for Research on Learning and Technology at the School of Education, Indiana University.

Regarding this suite of investments, the Bill and Melinda Gates Foundation emphatically states: "All these applications will support the Common Core Standards."[92] In addition, the Gates Foundation is funding Educurious Partners to develop high school courses based on Common Core Standards using a social network Internet application and Next Generation Learning Challenges to develop embedded assessments aligned with the Common Core Standards.

In summary, as a shadow education government the Bill and Melinda Gates Foundation is funding a wide variety of organizations to ensure that the Common Core Standards and aligned assessments are provided as online courses using a variety of methods including game design and social platforms. It is indirectly funding through some of these organizations efforts to have states enact laws similar to those in Florida and create schools similar to the Florida Virtual Academy. As exemplified by the Gates funding of the Pearson Foundation, this funding supports the involvement of ICT for-profit companies in public education.

Internet and Social Control: Analytics and China's State Internet Information Office

The World Economic Forum's "Transformations 2.0" promises a new era of online teaching with the application of analytic software to student data. However, there is a possible downside to this development. Using software to manage the future creates the possibility of introducing errors that could have lasting effects on the student. What happens if software designed to adapt curricular materials to student abilities based on collected data is wrong? Students might receive instructional material based on analysis of their data that is below their ability level and, consequently, dooms them to an inferior education, or the software might predict that the student is at risk of dropping out of school and therefore should receive remedial counseling which might result in them being identified as a poor student. This creates a level of expectation about dropping out that might lead to a self-fulfilling prophecy.

It is rare to read about the possible negative effects of ICT amidst a chorus of true believers in its beneficial effects. The best evidence of the potential downside of ICT can be found in government uses of ICT to control the ideas disseminated over the Internet. Investigation of this issue raises the specter of controlling the ideas of students through either the content of online instruction or the information students try to access on the Web. As an example of these possibilities consider the actions of the Chinese government in establishing the State Internet Information Office on May 4, 2011. *The New York Times* reported the announcement with the comment: "a move that appeared to complement a continuing crackdown on political dissidents and other social critics."[93] I discuss China's Internet censorship in more detail in Chapter 6.

In contrast to *The New York Times*, the Chinese *People's Daily*, the official publication of the Central Committee of the Communist Party of China, reported that the State Information Internet Office was for "healthy Web development" to counter "problems such as online porn, gambling and fraud, as well as illegal marketing tricks, [which] have hampered its sound development."[94] The *People's Daily* claimed that the regulation would be in "accordance with common international practice … [and that] governments of most countries monitor and regulate Internet content and deal with relevant violations of the law."[95] The *People's Daily* did not name the countries or governments whose practices on Internet regulations they were following. But officials did claim in the announcement that: "These facts indicated that the strategies and policies on Internet development by the Communist Party of China Central Committee and the Chinese government are proved to be right and effective."[96]

Methods used by Chinese authorities to manage the information disseminated over the Internet could be used to censor ideas reaching students in any country. Evgeny Morozov in previously cited *The Net Delusion* details the censorship methods used by Chinese authorities. One example is the software GreenDam which was originally to be installed on all computers sold in China. After installing millions of copies of GreenDam the government cancelled the program because of poor planning. GreenDam software reflects the sophisticated methods that can be used to control the flow of what authorities might classify as forbidden information.[97]

What GreenDam software does is to study users' Internet behavior including their browsing of websites, text files, and examination of online pictures. The software relays to authorities the behavior of the user, which can result in blocking the user's access to certain websites. The software is self-learning so that if a person tries to avoid detection by typing "demokracy" rather than "democracy" the software learns this attempt to avoid detection and adds "demokracy" to its list of words that it tries to find in users' browsing history or text files.[98] Morozov comments, "Think of this as the Global Brain of Censorship. Every second it can imbibe the insights that come from millions of users who are trying to subvert the system and put them to work almost immediately to make such subversion technically impossible."[99]

Hyperlinks add another dimension to the "Global Brain of Censorship." Imagine that people identified by government authorities as possible subversives send messages to others with hyperlinks to particular PDF files. Internet police can block access to these PDF files based on the profiles of the senders without ever actually reading the PDF files to see if they are in fact subversive. This can be done automatically by the software.

Imagine a government concerned about uprisings among youth. With online instruction, data collected on students, and access to students' browsing behavior, the government can easily create an Internet profile of each student. These profiles can be used to identify potential malcontents. Internet security could evaluate the Internet behavior of those labeled as potential rebels against the system. If these potential rebels show a pattern of visiting certain websites then access to those websites could be blocked. If rebels send Internet messages to others with hyperlinks to websites and/or PDF files then these could be blocked. If potential rebels try to avoid the long arm of Internet Security then they could be identified as potential leaders of rebellions and put on a watch list to be rounded up at the first glimmerings of public discontent with the government.

It is not beyond the realm of possibilities that governments might worry not only about potential dissenters to government policies but also about students that might be identified through analytic software as potential criminals or the most likely to be unemployed and a drain on the government's resources. Might governments act on this potential to seek to restrain these students?

What are the consequences of the combination of the use of this type of analytic software along with controls over the information disseminated through online instruction? Online instruction promises greater control over the ideas disseminated to students. Teachers in classrooms might go undetected in making references to material considered subversive by their government. In contrast, online instruction guarantees that the student will only be exposed to content approved by the government.

In other words, might online instruction result in greater control and censorship of ideas disseminated to students and in attempts to control students' potential rebellion against government authority?

Conclusion: Panacea or a New Form of Authoritarian Control?

ICT in the global and national plans discussed in this chapter promises to solve a range of problems including those facing education and global poverty. Education is targeted by ICT companies because of the size of the market—all the world's children. Undoubtedly ICT provides many educational advantages in its ability to access global knowledge and link students around the world. It also can enhance classroom lessons with the use of YouTube videos, online maps, virtual science demonstrations, and a whole host of other applications.

The downside of this utopian ICT vision is the use of online instruction to replace teachers, reduce educational expenses, and maintain control over what students learn. Ideological management could be a key factor in developing online instruction. Certainly it is easier for authorities to censor the content of online instruction than the speech of classroom teachers. Software can be applied to student data and Internet habits to identify potential rebels against authority. Similar software can be used to predict student success or failure. Online instruction could be the key for authoritarian governments' attempts to use education as a means of ideological control over their populations.

4

EDUCATORS EMBRACE GAMING AND ONLINE INSTRUCTION

"Are video games 'a waste of time'?" asked noted Professor of Literacy Studies and gamer James Gee.[1] Gee, more than any other academic, has added respectability to the game industry by arguing that the principles behind game design can be applied to helping students learn. In his now famous book, *What Video Games Have to Teach Us About Learning and Literacy*, Gee asserts "that one way (not the only way) to deliver good learning in schools and workplaces would, indeed, be via games or game-like technologies."[2] Professor Katie Salen, of Parsons New School for Design and editor of a volume in the MacArthur Foundation Series on Digital Media and Learning, argues that "a growing movement in K-12 education casts them [games] as a Holy Grail in the uphill battle to keep kids learning."[3]

Some claim that game design offers the key to organizing learning, workplaces, and institutions, including schools. Drawing on concepts of flow from positive psychologists, some game designers believe that the happiness resulting from playing video games can be adapted to other settings. Jane McGonigal offers this utopian vision of the application of game design to social organizations and personal problems: "I foresee games that fix our education systems … I foresee games that tackle global-scale problems like climate change and poverty … I foresee games that augment our most essential human capabilities … and change the world in meaningful ways."[4]

Even the United States government and First Lady Michelle Obama are promoting the educational value of games. Kumar Garg, policy analyst for the White House Office of Science and Technology Policy, gave a keynote entitled "Grand Challenges for Game Developers" at the 2010 Game Developers Conference in which he called on the gaming industry to be more involved in education. In his speech, he revealed "a new initiative spearheaded by First Lady Michelle Obama to encourage game creators to make games that encourage kids to eat right and exercise. The new Apps For Healthy Kids program offers cash rewards, in the style of the X-Prize, to encourage developers to participate."[5]

Games are being promoted for specific academic disciplines. Writing about "Games for Civic Learning," one group of game advocates claims "there is good evidence that youth who play games that incorporate civic experiences are more likely to be civically engaged."[6] There are also representatives of for-profit companies promoting games for learning. For instance, Cory Ondrejka of Linden Lab, which markets *Second Life*, argues, "Virtual worlds allow teaching to go beyond the classroom, extending learning beyond the limitations traditionally imposed by geography."[7] Ondrejka's article's title expresses his hope for the use of virtual worlds in education: "Education Unleashed: Participatory Culture, Education, and Innovation in Second Life."[8] The obvious economic motives of Linden Lab in promoting virtual worlds in education are highlighted by the investment orientation of its funders which the company proudly presents on its website: "Linden Lab is funded by a group of notable investors including Mitch Kapor, Catamount Ventures, Benchmark Capital, Ray Ozzie, Omidyar Network, Globespan Capital Partners, and Bezos Expeditions."[9]

Obviously, the belief in the ability of video games to improve education raises a whole host of questions about the relationship between government support of education and the games industry. First, there is the issue of consumerism as related to the playing of games and how these products are marketed; marketing of toys and games has changed over time. Second, there is the issue of the structure and economics of the game industry. And third, there are criticisms of the game industry about addiction problems.

From the standpoint of consumerism, it is important to note that Gee includes in his definition of video games a whole host of separately marketed products. He writes, "I mean games played on game platforms (such as the Sony PlayStation 2 or 3, the Nintendo GameCube or Wii, and Microsoft's Xbox and Xbox 360, or various handheld devices) and games played on computers."[10] Sony, Nintendo, and Microsoft dominate the game platform industry while other products include software sold in stores and over the Internet to be played on a computer or online as multiplayer games that create global communities such as *World of Warcraft*. Some of these games are criticized for their violence and for causing addiction that can lead players to neglect their schooling, family life, and jobs.

I will begin my discussion of the role of video games in education by tracing the history of learning software and the marketing of toys and games. A very important part of this history is the introduction of learning software designed to "curricularize the home," which means to turn the home into a space that conducts educational work usually associated with a school. The curricularization of the home parallels the attempt by the ICT industry to sell its educational and school management products. This history will allow me to discuss the organization and economics of the game industry and its potential role in schools.

Besides their potential to change the landscape of learning, some worry about the effect of video games on human brains. Do video games cause a form of addiction where some players forgo responsibilities to themselves and others as they spend endless hours in front of a monitor? Does possible gaming addiction cause students to be distracted and unable to concentrate in school? These questions lead to a series of other questions about the effect of the digital world on the brain, including multitasking and ability to concentrate, and lack of downtime for the brain as people constantly check e-mail, play games on their smart phones, and surf the Web.

Edutainment

Edutainment, the combination of entertainment with learning, looks like a panacea to teachers frustrated by their efforts to engage students. Create a game that children love to play and at the same time teaches something! This is the dream. However, the game involves a product most likely made to be sold at a profit. In the 1920s and 1930s, *Parents* magazine promoted the purchase of educational toys like wooden blocks and peg boards as early childhood learning tools. The promotion and marketing of educational toys turned play into a form of work as preparation for school. In the 1950s, television made it possible to market toys directly to children. Television advertising created a mass consumer culture among children. As consumerism advanced among children, many parents still demanded edutainment from both television and toymakers. By the late 1960s this was achieved through the broadcast of preschool programs such as *Sesame Street* and in the 1970s with the development of software learning games.[11]

Television programs like *Sesame Street* and the development of software learning games not only "curricularized the home," but also contributed to a shift from the concept of protected childhood to prepared childhood. In *Huck's Raft: A History of American Childhood*, Steven Mintz argues that there are two competing concepts of childhood.[12] One is "protected childhood" where the family focuses on ensuring that children have a carefree life with proper nutrition, shelter, health care, and schooling. Childhood is something to be enjoyed. The other conceptual framework is "prepared childhood" where the focus is preparing children for school and work. Parents emphasizing prepared childhood tend to seek games and other forms of entertainment that will be educational. These parents are a major market for edutainment, including software.

Pioneers of software learning games were often caught between a visionary goal of increasing children's opportunities to learn and making money. One of the early and largest creators of software learning games was The Learning Company founded in 1979 by Ann Piestrup (now McCormick). McCormick was a former nun and school teacher who used her knowledge of educational research to try to make learning not like school but like entertainment. Her visionary goal was, "I want every child in the world to be able to get the basic skills they need to function thoughtfully ... We want lifelong learning for the entire world."[13] In 1998, The Learning Company was sold to Mattel for $3.8 billion, highlighting the triumph of consumerism in learning software.[14]

The desire to teach as opposed to just earning profits was the goal of the 1973 funding by the State of Minnesota of the Minnesota Educational Computing Corporation (MECC) which became a public corporation in 1985. MECC created and sold popular edutainment software including *MathBlaster* and the 1971 adventure learning game *Oregon Trail*. *Oregon Trail* was a new type of game that added the element of role-playing to learning games. In this game, the user assumes the role of a wagon leader guiding his party of settlers along the Oregon Trail, with the player having to make decisions about rations and supplies.

Edutainment software is sold by large retail outlets, such as Wal-Mart, Costco, Best Buy, Toys R Us, Office Depot, and various computer stores. It is marketed as educational to parents and as entertainment to children. Cultural historian Mizuko Ito argues, regarding learning software, "In marketing materials, parents are told that these products will ensure that their children will internalize the dispositions and cultural capital necessary for competitive academic success."[15]

Edutainment remains an important industry. Eventually The Learning Company acquired *Oregon Trail* and the very popular learning game *Carmen Sandiego*. In 2001, The Learning Company was bought by Riverdeep, Inc. which was bought by the publishing giant Houghton Mifflin Harcourt in 2006. In 2011, Houghton Mifflin Harcourt listed Tony Bordon, president of The Learning Company, as part of its executive team. Bordon's career created networks through the world of education businesses. Bordon held presidential positions at the Princeton Review, Knowledge Adventure, and Riverdeep.[16]

Currently, The Learning Company promises, "The Ultimate Experience: The Learning Company engages families by combining classic characters and award winning educational materials with a commitment to making learning fun."[17] Therefore, the current marketing strategy adds the promotion of family activities ("engages families") with learning and entertainment. This promotion is truly to "curricularize the home" by suggesting family learning sessions. On its website The Learning Company also promotes its parent company Houghton Mifflin Harcourt with the claim: "Most students' backpacks contain books published by Houghton Mifflin Harcourt. Each day over 57 million students from 120 countries benefit from HMH's educational services."[18]

One of The Learning Company's software products *Carmen Sandiego* was designed to teach geography through an adventure scenario. Originally marketed by Broderbund Software in 1985, *Carmen Sandiego* exemplifies the ability of edutainment to link multiple markets.[19] Through the years, the *Carmen Sandiego* brand has been used for two television series, books, and movies. Its history of multimedia connections is provided by The Learning Company:

- 1991–96 *Where in the World is Carmen Sandiego?* airs on PBS
- 1991 Series of Carmen Sandiego *Choose Your Own Adventure* books are written and published
- 1993 PBS series *Where in the World is Carmen Sandiego?* wins the George Foster Peabody Award for Excellence

- 1994–98 *Where on Earth is Carmen Sandiego?* animated series airs on Fox and other stations
- 1996–98 *Where in Time is Carmen Sandiego?* airs on PBS
- 1997–2004 *Carmen Sandiego Mystery* books are written and published
- 2004 *Carmen Sandiego: The Secret of the Stolen Drums*—GameCube, Xbox, and PlayStation 2
- 2008 *Where in the World is Carmen Sandiego?* mobile adaptation is released by Gameloft
- Planetarium Movies: There were two Planetarium movies featuring Carmen produced[20]

One thing to note in the above list of *Carmen Sandiego* books, television shows, and movies is the 2004 release of *Carmen Sandiego: The Secret of the Stolen Drums* for game consoles made by Sony, Microsoft, and Nintendo. This meant that the product could be bought for direct use on a computer or as game to be played on a console. *Carmen Sandiego* also has its own Facebook site.

While *Carmen Sandiego* was originally marketed in retail stores its new parent company Houghton Mifflin Harcourt realized that money can be made by selling the product to schools. The company sells the product as supplementary learning material for social studies:

WHERE IN THE USA IS CARMEN SANDIEGO? FOR SCHOOLS
Designed just for schools! Students chase Carmen Sandiego and her gang through all 50 states as they try to recover the nation's stolen treasures by deciphering clues relating to U.S. and state history, geography, economy, and culture.[21]

The Learning Company's previously mentioned game *Oregon Trail* is also being marketed by Houghton Mifflin Harcourt for school use:

THE OREGON TRAIL 5TH EDITION EEV
Oregon Trail 5th Edition EEV features an improved interface, new characters, and even more engaging stories. Students build real-life decision-making, problem-solving, and writing skills as they immerse themselves in the history and geography of the Westward Movement.[22]

The marketing of these two learning games to schools links the home and parents with the school through consumption of similar software. Consider the following sequence of events. Learning software is developed and marketed to parents as educational and to children as entertainment. Purchased at a retail outlet, the learning software enters the home and provides a basis for organized study that has traditionally been associated with the school. Marketers then advertise the learning software as a family event with hints that it will bring the family closer as all work together in learning and fun. A global corporation identifies schools as another market for the learning software. Sold to schools, the learning software is now linked to retail stores, schools, homes, and family learning and enjoyment.

Knowledge Adventure, Inc.: Venture Capital, 3D Virtual Worlds, and Avatars

Created in the 1970s and 1980s, *MathBlaster* and *JumpStart* were transformed from learning games sold in retail stores to online 3D games using avatars. Another important transformation is from the early days of visionary educators creating new learning opportunities to an industry dominated by venture capitalists.

Currently, *MathBlaster* and *JumpStart* are successful edutainment products sold by Knowledge Adventure, Inc. The company began in the late 1980s with *JumpStart* which today is marketed as an online adventure game. *JumpStart* ads claim the company is motivated by a commitment to take the work out of learning: "But what really sets *JumpStart* apart is our commitment to education. We believe that learning *should be an adventure, not a chore* [author's emphasis]."[23] Besides teaching math and reading, the game is supposedly designed to make "critical thinking fun!"[24] In the late 1990s, Knowledge Adventure merged with another education software firm, Davidson and Associates, which had bought *MathBlaster* and was developing educational software for the toy giant Fisher–Price.

The important role of venture capitalism after 1996 in the financial history of Knowledge Adventure is provided on its website:

> Knowledge Adventure was purchased by Cendant in 1996 and acquired by Vivendi in 1998. In 2004, Knowledge Adventure spun out from Vivendi, led by Venture Investors. In September 2004, Knowledge Adventure completed a Series A financing led by venture capitalist firms Telesoft Partners and Azure Capital. In March of 2008, Knowledge Adventure completed a Series B financing, also led by venture capitalist firms Telesoft Partners and Azure Capital. These infusions of capital support Knowledge Adventure's continued innovation and expansion from educational software to the new frontier of children's learning – adventure-based 3D virtual worlds.[25]

Cendant's 1996 purchase of Davidson and Associates made Knowledge Adventure part of a global conglomerate of companies that included the hotel chains Ramada, Howard Johnson's, Avis Rent-a-Car, and Days Inn. A financial scandal in 1998 sent its vice chairman E. Kirk Shelton to prison for 10 years and resulted in the sale of the company's software holdings to Vivendi in 1998.[26] The purchase by Vivendi linked Knowledge Adventure to a network of ICT ventures. Vivendi is a global producer of video games and a world leader in music production (Universal Music Group) along with owning telecommunications companies in France, Morocco, and Brazil.[27]

Knowledge Adventure split from Vivendi with financial support from venture capitalist firms Venture Investors, Telesoft Partners, and Azure Capital. Venture Investors was founded in 1982 as a venture capitalist firm investing health care and technology.[28] Telesoft Partners was founded in 1996 with a focus on investing in software companies.[29] The founder and head of Telesoft, Arjun Gupta, who calls himself the company's "Chief Believer," has established corporate partnerships with global companies Alltel, Bechtel, Deutsche Telekom, Nexant, Salesforce.com, and Symphony. Arjun was ranked by *Forbes* magazine in the top 100 technology venture investors on the 2006, 2007, 2008, and 2009 Midas Lists.[30] Founded in 2000, Azure Capital is another venture capital firm invested in a variety of industries. Paul Ferris, a founding General Partner of the firm, has handled investment in a variety of ICT firms, including ADC Telecommunications, Broadcom, Calix, Cerent (acquired by Cisco Systems), Com21, Cyan Optics, Efficient Networks (acquired by Siemens), Lucent Technologies, Next Level Communications, New Focus, Nortel Networks, Packet Engines (acquired by Alcatel), Phone.com, Siara Systems (acquired by Redback Networks), Siemens, and Xros (acquired by Nortel Networks).[31]

This brief financial history illustrates the domination of venture capitalism and profit considerations in the current learning software industry. This is also reflected in the background of Knowledge Adventure's president and CEO David Lord who holds a Bachelor's degree in accounting from Northeastern University and has no background in learning theory or education. In fact, prior to leading Knowledge Adventure, Lord was president and CEO of RazorGator Interactive Group (RIG), "a leading full-service event experience company for *premiere sports and entertainment events worldwide* [author's emphasis]."[32] He also worked as CEO for Toysmart.com, a venture-backed catalog company for educational, ecommerce, and retail products.

On March 10, 2009, Knowledge Adventure took learning games to a new level with the marketing of *JumpStart* as the first educational game to be "delivered in a browser with high-quality 3D graphics and advanced game play."[33] Marketed as an online game, parents had to be assured that it is: "A completely safe and secure online environment where kids can interact, explore and learn, *JumpStart.com* is quickly becoming the epicenter of online gaming for the 3–10 year old demographic."[34] Thus, *JumpStart*'s targeted audience includes preschoolers with the assumption that children as early as three years old will be able to play online games. In January 2011, Knowledge Adventure issued *MathBlaster* as a 3D cyber space online game.

In marketing *JumpStart* and *MathBlaster* as online games, Knowledge Adventure felt that it needed to assure parents that their online games would be safe particularly with three year olds entering the world of online gaming. Advertising to parents declares for both games:

Is it Safe?
   Absolutely. Over the past 20 years, the JumpStart brand has earned the trust of over 30 million parents by providing safe, age-appropriate games

for kids. JumpStart.com is no exception. *Our parental controls, canned chat and pre-programmed names ensure that kids are completely safe and cannot share any personal information* [author's emphasis].[35]

Adventure Knowledge marketing also reinforces parental tendencies to emphasize prepared childhood over protected childhood. Its lineup of games promises preparation of children for academic success in school. The company claims that its "games help kids learn many of the skills needed throughout their early childhood education. Learning games are particularly useful for younger kids and can help build confidence while enhancing the skills *needed for success in school* [author's emphasis]."[36] The company particularly stresses the importance of its games for preschool education: "Educational games for toddlers prepare young ones for their first scholastic experience and educational games for preschool students teach kids important skills and concepts required by a preschooler."[37]

One could argue that marketers at Learning Adventure might be trying to capture both concepts of protected and prepared childhood. Protected childhood envisions children having time to play and use their imaginations while being protected from the world's dangers. Software and online learning games do promise a world of safe play. On the other hand, the games are seen as preparation for school. Learning Adventure ads promise: "The kids' games provided here allow children to have fun while they learn. Fun educational games encourage children to keep learning, even after school hours."[38]

In the past, protected childhood might have included a vision of children actively playing games and not just sitting in front of a monitor. Also, there is the problem of software and online game addiction. As I will discuss later in this chapter, software and online game addiction is considered a global problem. Does it result in children spending endless hours playing video games in lieu of physical activities? I will discuss the possibility of gaming addiction after reviewing in the next section the growth of learning apps for smart phones and discussing the general structure of the industry.

Learning Apps for Smart Phones: Carrying Your School in Your Pocket

Are iPhones the toy of choice for toddlers? According to *New York Times* reporter Hilary Stout, "just as adults have a hard time putting down their iPhones, so the device is now the Toy of Choice – akin to a treasured stuffed animal – for many 1-, 2- and 3-year-olds."[39] According to Stout, Apple has built its reputation on creating products that are simple and intuitive. Consequently, it is easy for children as young as two to operate the phone.

Software producers quickly learned that apps could be created for children that would turn smart phones and iPads into learning tools. For instance, an app for *JumpStart* is available through Apple's iTunes store with the description: "JumpStart

Preschool Magic of Learning 1, an application designed for little hands and big imaginations! Your preschooler is invited to join Frankie the Dog on a magical learning adventure that will show just how fun learning can be."[40] At the time of writing this book, BlackBerry offered 347 educational apps ranging from foreign language instruction to teaching math to toddlers. There are a whole host of apps for iPhones ranging from reference works for older students to teaching foreign languages to toddlers.

With smart phone apps, children carry the school in their hands. The home is curricularized the child's entire life. Educational apps are marketed as edutainment; learning for adults and fun for kids. For instance a BlackBerry app is advertised as:

> TVO's Polka Dot Shorts is a sequence matching game for kids aged 2–5 that supports the early learning and kindergarten math curriculum and has been teacher and classroom tested. It will keep them entertained, help them to learn, and keep your BlackBerry device safely locked – your little one can't send emails or make phone calls.[41]

There are several things to note in the above ad for the BlackBerry app Polka Dot Shorts. First is the claim to the parent who purchases the app that it will help the child prepare for a kindergarten math curriculum. This is an excessive form, I would argue, of prepared childhood. Holding their BlackBerrys in hand, toddlers are envisioned preparing for kindergarten math which, in the framework of prepared childhood, is preparation for work. Play or entertainment becomes instrumental to kindergarten preparation and working in the global economy.

Also, the app is legitimized with the claim that it is "teacher and classroom tested." The school is invoked to convince parents of the worth of buying the app. More importantly, the lines between school, home, and play disappear. As their favorite toy is carried in their pockets or held in their hands, the toddler lives in an integrated future of school, home, and work.

The Political Economy of Gaming

Gaming is big business, as illustrated in the previous discussions of Adventure Learning and apps for smart phones. Obviously, the edutainment part of the gaming industry is very interested in selling its products to schools and homes. A 2008 report in *Wired* announced that the U.S. video game industry had "record shattering sales" of $17.9 billion which was a 43 percent increase over 2006 sales.[42] That's only earnings for the United States. Now consider the number of gamers worldwide as reported in 2011:

China 200 million
United States 183 million
India 105 million

Europe 100 million
South Korea 17 million
Australia 15 million
Russia 10 million
Vietnam 10 million
Mexico 10 million
Central and South America 13 million
Middle East 4 million[43]

As these numbers indicate there is a large and profitable global market for gaming software.

Aphra Kerr's *The Business and Culture of Digital Games* provides a good introduction to the economic structure of the games industry.[44] A study of Japanese expenditures on leisure time activities found that more money was spent on video-game software than books, magazines, music CDs, DVDs, karaoke, and movies.[45] The majority of games are played on consoles made by Microsoft (Xbox), Sony (PlayStation), and Nintendo (GameCube and Wii). The rest of the market is divided between Massively Multiplayer Online Games (MMOG), the largest being *World of Warcraft*, and software games played on handheld devices and computers.[46]

The games industry is global in scope with the manufacturers of consoles and software being located in Japan and the United States. Some software companies produce games in South Korea and Europe. The market for games requiring special consoles include those that work on previously mentioned game consoles sold by Microsoft, Sony, and Nintendo. These three companies dominate the sales of game hardware. These companies sell the hardware at a loss expecting to earn more money from the sales of software.[47]

Some games are those played on handheld devices, not smart phones, which originally were dominated by Nintendo hardware but later competition appeared from companies like Nokia, Tapwave, and Sony. Similar to game consoles, manufacturers intend to make their profits from the sale of software. Games sold to use on computers are sold online and through retail shops. In Massively Multiplayer Online Games players purchase software and then pay a monthly subscription fee and online service charges.[48]

By 2007, gaming hardware was dominated by Sony's PlayStation and its handheld gaming device PSP followed by Microsoft's Xbox and Nintendo's Wii.[49] This gave these three companies a potential oligopoly over any gaming consoles sold to schools for edutainment. In 2009, the leader in software sales for game consoles was *Call of Duty: Modern Warfare 2* produced by Activision Blizzard for use on Microsoft's Xbox. The next seven in rank order were produced by Nintendo for use on its Wii. The eighth in the list was a version of *Call of Duty* for use on Sony's PlayStation followed by *Halo 3* for Microsoft's Xbox. Tenth was produced by Nintendo for its portable game player.[50]

Gaming software for computers is dominated by two companies: Electronic Arts and Blizzard Entertainment. In 2009, these two companies sold nine of the top

10 software games. The 10th was sold by Sega of America. Electronic Arts sold the top seller *The Sims 3* with its other top sellers being other versions of *The Sims* along with *Spore* and *Dragon Age: Origins*. Activision Blizzard held its rankings in the top 10 with the global popular online game *World of Warcraft* along with various add-ons to the game.[51]

How is the gaming industry organized? In the United States there is a trade group called Entertainment Software Association. Among its over 30 members are the big names in gaming platforms—Nintendo, Microsoft, and Sony. This organization reported in 2010 the following economic data illustrating the growing size of the industry:

- The U.S. computer and video game software publishing industry directly employs more than 32,000 people in 34 states.
- For the four-year period 2005 through 2009, direct employment in the U.S. computer and video game software publishing industry grew at an annual rate of 8.65%.
- The U.S. computer and video game software industry's value added to U.S. Gross Domestic Product (GDP) was $4.9 billion.
- The real annual growth rate of the U.S. computer and video game software industry was 10.6% for the period 2005–9 and 16.7% for the period 2005–8.[52]

More money can be earned with a popular game than a popular movie. Flashing across the Entertainment Software Association's website in early 2011 was the announcement that: "The best-selling video game of 2007, 'Halo 3,' took in more revenue ($170 million) on its first day of sales than the opening weekend receipts of 'Spider Man 3,' ($151 million), the highest-grossing movie opening ever."[53]

One reason for the growth of the entertainment software industry is the age of the users. The majority of purchasers are adults in contrast to children and teenagers who might have less money than their parents. In addition, a large percentage of gamers are women. The Entertainment Software Association provided the following demographic data regarding purchasers of game software:

- The average game player is 34 years old and has been playing games for 12 years.
- The average age of the most frequent game purchaser is 40 years old.
- Forty percent of all game players are women.
- In 2010, 26 percent of Americans over the age of 50 play video games, an increase from nine percent in 1999.
- Forty-two percent of heads of households play games on a wireless device, such as a cell phone or PDA, up from 20 percent in 2002.
- Sixty-four percent of parents believe games are a positive part of their children's lives.[54]

Similar to any other trade association, the Entertainment Software Association supplies its members with sales information, lobbies state and federal governments for laws favorable to the industry, and, particularly important for this industry, provides a global anti-piracy service. The Association is directly involved in legal cases such as the U.S. Supreme Court case *Schwarzenegger v. EMA/Entertainment Software Association* involving a California law regulating the sale and rental of video games. The case had not been decided at the time of writing this book, but the Entertainment Software Association claimed that software games should receive the same free speech protection as movies, books, and music.[55]

In summary, the gaming industry is dominated by Microsoft, Sony, Nintendo, Electronic Arts, and Activision Blizzard. There are many other software gaming companies belonging to the Entertainment Software Association but, in reality, this is an industry controlled by only a few companies.

Halo 3: Example of Game Industry and Game Design

A *Wired* article by Clive Thomson, "Halo 3: How Microsoft Labs Invented a New Science of Play," provides a good example of the political economy of gaming and how game designers entice players.[56] The first *Halo* was designed by the two person operated Bungie Studios in the early 1990s. The design included what was called "30 seconds of fun" which immersed players in a half minute of action before the player rested. The idea was balancing potential boredom (lack of action) with the storytelling animations in the game. This type of balance keeps players in the game as they seek another rush of adrenalin from the action. This type of balance between storytelling and action contributes, as I will discuss in the next section, to an addictive quality to digital games—players keep playing so they can have another rush of adrenalin.

The success of the first *Halo* game attracted the attention of Microsoft who bought Bungie Studios in 2000 for $50 million. Microsoft executives believed the popularity of *Halo* would increase sales of their Microsoft Xbox and its online service Xbox live. The purchase of *Halo* and Bungie Studios was considered key to making the Xbox successful in its competition with the more successful Sony PlayStation.

According to writer Clive Thomson Microsoft owner Bill Gates and CEO Steve Ballmer wanted a new version of *Halo* to enhance the sale of Xboxes. In 2005, Microsoft financed two Hollywood studios to make a movie adaptation of the game. While a good marketing idea for Xboxes and *Halo* software, the movie was never made.

Microsoft executives turned their attention to applying psychological research to game design by hiring an experimental psychologist, Randy Pagulayan, to help with the development of *Halo 2* at the Bungie Studios. *Halo 2* proved highly successful particularly because it could be played as an MMOG through Xbox live.

For the development of *Halo 3*, Bungie Studios employed 100 workers which made it one of the largest game design studios. Under Pagulayan's supervision, designers incorporated principles drawn from experimental studies. Combined with the original "30 seconds of fun," these principles included:

> Keeping the gamer playing by alternating short rushes of action with a storyline.
>
> It's just as fun to die. A group of Finnish scientists wired gamers with skin meters, cardiac monitors, and facial electromyographs [and] found that getting killed in a game produces the same positive emotions as beating an opponent or completing a level.
>
> Fellowship matters. Researcher Jonas Heide Smith ran a study with 19 gamers and discovered that even hyper competitive players tend to help others. Desire for fairness in play, it seems, is as strong as the desire to win.
>
> It's OK to cheat a little. In 24 interviews with gamers, researcher Mia Consalvo discovered that "a majority of game players cheat" though they also have strict social codes governing what's acceptable.[57]

The design principle "It's just as fun to die" requires further explanation. Studies find that players have their strongest rush of emotions when they make a mistake which results in them being eager to try again. The games are designed to make players optimistic about their eventual success. Failure gives gamers a sense of control over the game's outcome. Therefore, after an initial failure gamers continue with new eagerness knowing that they will eventually succeed.[58]

"Fellowship matters" is supported by brain research which shows that humans, because of evolution, have a predisposition to be social and want to be part of a group. Limited cheating is also supported by brain research which finds that human brains have a disposition to detect cheating. In evolutionary terms, social grouping and exchange were only possible if every person acted according to social rules.[59] While people playing games might cheat a little other players will be quick to detect when cheating goes too far and violates social rules.

The above are principles of game design associated with *Halo 3*. As I will discuss in the next two sections, these are all design features that prove very attractive to the brain and as a result they have created an ongoing discussion about addiction to video games.

Learning Games: The Brain, Addiction, and Adjusting to New Technology

Why do toddlers choose smart phones and iPads over other toys? Why do some students miss classes and/or drop out of school because they spend hours playing online games? Why does the brain seem to like the stimulus of the digital world? David Pogue, the *New York Times* technology columnist worries, "I think my 6-year-old is addicted to the iPad. He asks for it constantly. He wants to use it in the car. He wants to use it at every unscheduled moment at home. He brings it to the dinner table. When I tell him it's time to shut off the iPad and head up to bed, or put his shoes on, or head out to the bus, he doesn't hear me the first three times I ask."[60] Is Pogue's son addicted to the iPad?

But are worries about gaming and Internet addiction a matter of reaction to adjustments to new technologies? Each new technological development requires human adjustment to its workings. When the automobile began to replace horses and carriages, humans had to adapt and learn a new range of skills associated with driving, obeying the rules of the road, and changes in social relations as people were able to travel more quickly from one destination to another. In the 1950s, when television became a household item, the social life of families changed as they gathered around the new media. Also, articles began to appear about the deleterious effects of television to human health, reduction of human intelligence through the broadcast of inane programming, a rise in violence and the potential that children would replace active outside play for inert television viewing. Television was declared an "educational wasteland." Did television addict the population to a wasteland of game shows, soap operas, children's programs, and insipid network series? Or were critics of the time responding to a population adapting to a new technology that altered living styles and thus threatened the perspectives of those wedded to the values of a previous generation?[61]

Keeping in mind the possibility that current worries about gaming and Internet addiction may be the result of those holding older values confronting the ongoing adaption to new technology, I will consider current concerns about the effect of the digital world on the brain. Is there Internet and gaming addiction? Of course the answer depends on how you define addiction. My Merriam-Webster Medical Dictionary defines addiction as:

> compulsive physiological need for and use of a habit-forming substance (as heroin, nicotine, or alcohol) characterized by tolerance and by well-defined physiological symptoms upon withdrawal; *broadly*: persistent compulsive use of a substance known by the user to be physically, psychologically, or socially harmful.[62]

This definition links addiction to the use of a chemical substance which, of course, gaming is not. However, gaming can lead to compulsive use that can be harmful. Can the general use of the Internet become compulsive and harmful? Nicki Dowling, a clinical psychologist, studied college students and found that 10 percent of them were at risk of Internet dependence: Dowling prefers to use the term "Internet dependence" in contrast to addiction.[63] *New York Times* columnist David Pogue uses the term addiction in reference to his son's obsession with the iPad, "Sometimes, he gets bizarrely upset when I say I have to take it [iPad] away now – out-of-character upset. That's what makes me think he's addicted."[64] Throughout this section I will refer to addiction with the realization that it might be called simply dependence. I am using addiction because the results include compulsive behavior that can be damaging to a person's life.

In the book *iBrain: Surviving the Technological Alteration of the Modern Mind*, Gary Small and Gigi Vorgan write in reference to alcohol and drug addiction, "the same neural pathways in the brain that reinforce dependence on those substances can lead to compulsive technological behaviors that are just as addictive and potentially destructive."[65] Gary Small is a medical doctor who is the Director of the Memory and Aging Research Center at the Semel Institute for Neuroscience and Human Behavior and the Center on Aging at the University of California at Los Angles while Gigi Vorgan is his wife and a professional writer. What they refer to as "Internet addicts" can receive a rush of dopamine by booting up their computers, playing digital games, shopping and dating online, checking e-mail, or doing data base searches. They write about the feelings associated with the rush of dopamine, "These feelings of euphoria, even before the actual acting out of the addiction occurs, are linked to brain chemical changes that control behaviors ranging from a seductive psychological draw to a full-blown addiction."[66]

What percentage of Internet users become addicts? Small and Vorgan assert that Internet addicts spend 40 or more hours online per week in addition to online time spent at work. They report one study that found 14 percent of Internet users remain online while neglecting other aspects of their lives like "school, work, family, food, and sleep."[67] One estimate is that 18 percent of college students are "pathological Internet users."[68] In addition, 58 percent of college students report that excessive Internet usage has interfered with studying and class attendance, and has lowered their grades.[69]

There appears to be a global concern about addiction to online games. Recently, the South Korean government, a country considered the most wired in the world with 90 percent of homes having high-speed internet connections, provided counseling services to its estimated 938,000 teenage addicts with plans to open rehabilitation centers for an estimated 975,000 addicts in their 20s and 30s.[70] The stories from South Korea about Internet addiction picture a world where addicts neglect everything but their online games. One story is of a couple who left their one room apartment every night for the world of Internet fantasy at their local Internet café, often returning home in the early morning hours. What was the consequence of their addiction? They returned one morning to find their three-month-old daughter dead from malnutrition as a result of parental neglect. There are physical attacks on gamers who have killed opponents' online characters. In February 2010, a man killed his mother for nagging him about his incessant gaming.[71]

While the South Korean government worries about gaming addictions it promotes the development and exporting of online games worth $1.5 billion annually; online games are its number one cultural export. According to Dal Yong Jin and Florence Chee, "Although the largest market for Korean online games was Japan (42.6%) and China (20.8%), Korean online games also penetrated other regions, including the United States (15.7%) and Europe (5%) in 2005."[72] Professional gamers in South Korea are celebrities, with television broadcasts of organized leagues playing online games.

China, the country with the largest number of online gamers, wrestles with the issue of gamer addiction. The government has tried to control Internet content by creating what is called the "Great Firewall of China." In China, Internet cafés gained an unsavory reputation as a place to hang out. Consequently government has attempted to regulate Internet cafés. In general, the Internet has been problematic for China's Communist Party which worries about it being a source of rebellion and discontent.

In China tales of gamer addiction abound. In 2004, a child committed suicide and left behind a four page note explaining his despair over the emotional ties to his characters in *World of Warcraft*. In 2006, a boy murdered his uncle for money to play Internet games. Two children fell asleep on railroad tracks exhausted from a marathon gaming session. Their lives ended when they were hit by a train. A man was murdered over a sword in the online game *Mir II*. Nineteen gamers started fighting in an Internet café over an online game treasure leaving four gamers seriously injured from stab wounds. A seriously obese man died after a marathon gaming session. One man killed himself after meeting face-to-face with his online sweetheart who turned out to be ugly. And the addiction stories go on ... [73]

In 2005, a report of the Chinese Academy of Sciences stated that 50 out of 5,000 university students drop out, with 80 percent being Internet addicts.[74] An extreme critic of the Internet, Zhang Chunliang, compared Internet addiction to opium use:

> The allure of Internet games for children is like the poison of opium in China so many years ago; it doesn't discriminate between the poor and the rich, between those of high or low position. It doesn't matter if you're an unemployed worker, a wealthy businessman, or a Party cadre, the highest hopes of innumerable parents for their children's future may well be destroyed by Internet games.[75]

Ironically, the Internet offers a range of services for video game addiction. One popular site, at least according to a Google search, is "Video Game Addiction: When video games become more than just games ... "[76] The site states:

> Anyone who has experienced it knows all too well – video game addiction is real. Although gaming addiction is not yet officially recognized as a diagnosable disorder by the American Medical Association, there is increasing evidence that people of all ages, especially teens and pre-teens, are facing very real, sometimes severe consequences associated with compulsive use of video and computer games.[77]

This website identifies the following symptoms of video game addiction: unusual preoccupation with a game when they are away from it; unable to control the amount of time spent on gaming; person loses track of time while gaming; other parts of the gamer's life are neglected; spending a disproportionate amount of money on gaming and computer items; and a tension between the euphoria of gaming and guilt about the amount of time spent gaming.[78]

Netaddiction.com features "Dr. Kimberly Young [who] provides individual, couples, and family counseling for Internet addicts and their families. She also provides half-day and full-day intensive treatment."[79] Dr. Young provides "Treatment Services" for Cybersex/Cyberporn, Online Affairs, Online Gambling, Online Gaming, Compulsive Surfing, and eBay Addiction. Each of these so-called addictions is accompanied by a self-test. For determining online gaming addiction, Dr. Young asks a series of questions concerned with: spending increasing amounts of time gaming in order to achieve desired excitement; preoccupation with gaming when offline; irritability when forced to stop gaming; gaming jeopardizing social relations; and gaming interfering with work and personal life.[80]

An important issue raised by Young's list of potential addictions is the question Can the Internet itself be addictive or cause people to use it in a manner that it interferes with their lives? The questions asked in her self-test were found to be valid in a study published in *CyberPsychology and Behavior*, particularly those questions related to neglecting work and social life, excessive use, anticipation of being online, and lack of control.[81] The article reviewing Young's test states that addiction is difficult to define but uses the term dependency: "Dependence is characterized by overindulgence, tolerance, withdrawal, craving and loss of control."[82] The self-study test contains questions related to Internet usage: neglect of personal affairs; preference for Internet to intimacy with partner; neglect of school work; loss of sleep to late night logins; and feeling moody when offline.[83]

This discussion of possible gaming and Internet addiction raises questions about the effect of the Internet on the brain and what consequences it might have for learning in schools. As for-profit software companies market their products to schools with claims of edutainment, there is the question of what effect learning games and online instruction might have on students. While gaming and Internet addiction or dependency may appear in student behavior there remains the question whether this perception is just the reaction of an older generation to a new technology or whether it is an actual effect on the brain that results in an addiction or dependency.

The Panacea: Learning Through Gaming

Jane McGonigal, Director of Games for the Institute of the Future, offers an important alternative psychological argument to those worried about gamer addiction while championing the benefits of gaming. In *Reality is Broken: Why Games Make Us Better and How They Can Change the World*, McGonigal uses positive psychology to describe the psychological impact of gaming.[84] Rather than addiction, she draws on the psychological concept of "flow" to describe the desire of gamers to continue to play. Mihaly Csikszentmihalyi, the social psychologist who did the pioneering work on flow theory, provides the following description of its characteristics:

> Concentration is so intense that there is no attention left over to think about anything irrelevant, or to worry about problems. Self-consciousness disappears, and the sense of time becomes distorted. An activity that produces such experiences is so gratifying that people are willing to do it for its own sake, and [have] little concern for what they will get out of it, even when it is difficult, or dangerous.[85]

Csikszentmihalyi examined the nature of this intense experience by studying the play of children and adults. Traditional psychologists considered children's play a means for children to learn to be adults. However, Csikszentmihalyi suggested that among children and adults play was simply for an enjoyable experience. His team of researchers investigated the self-motivation of people to seek activities that would provide them with optimal experiences, such as dancing, rock climbing, basketball, and chess. Also, they examined workers who had similar optimal experiences.

Csikszentmihalyi referred to these activities as "autotelic experiences" which means a self-contained activity, one that is done not with the expectation of some future benefit, but simply because the doing itself is the reward. He argued that people seek the psychological state of intense concentration and the accompanying loss of self-consciousness and a sense of time. He called this experience "flow." The internal experience of flow is different from acting because of an external reward. For instance doing a job just to earn money does not necessarily provide an optimal experience. However, doing a job for the sheer joy of the experience is an optimal experience. Appropriately for our concern about education, Csikszentmihalyi uses the example of teaching: "Teaching children in order to turn them into good citizens is not autotelic, whereas teaching them because one enjoys interacting with children is."[86]

Flow is what McGonigal considers the greatest benefit from digital gaming and an important source of happiness. Consequently, digital games provide players with a source of happiness not found in their reality: "many gamers have already figured out how to use the immersive power of play to distract themselves from their hunger: a hunger for more satisfying work, for a stronger sense of community, and a more engaging and meaningful life."[87]

Since, McGonigal argues, digital games are a source of happiness then game design should be used to improve working conditions and create a sense of community. Of course, this would include schools and learning. In addition, she asserts, games are being created to teach people to understand how political, social, and economic structures work so that gamers learn how to engage in social reform. These types of games are labeled "games for personal and social change," "serious games," "positive impact games," and "leveraging the play of the planet."[88] These types of games could be used in school to help students understand how they can participate in improving human conditions.

What are the principles of game design that McGonigal believes could improve the quality of life for all people? First is the idea of hard work which complex games require of the gamer. The pleasure gained from the hard work of gaming can be distinguished from, for instance, boring work that might occur at the workplace or in school. Hard work, as she conceptualizes the term, is absorbing work that initiates the flow that brings about a sense of happiness. Another term she uses for hard work is "hard fun." Hard work or hard fun causes chemical changes in the brain: "By accomplishing something that is very hard for us ... our brains release a potent cocktail of norepinephrine, epinephrine, and dopamine."[89]

A potential source of addiction—McGonigal does use the word addiction—are the brain chemicals released when a player experiences "fiero." Fiero is a term used by game designers to describe the emotional experience of overcoming a challenging obstacle, winning a battle, or avoiding danger. The experience of fiero, according to Allan Reiss, professor of psychiatry and behavioral science at Stanford, can be measured in MRIs of gamers' brains. Reiss found an intense activation of the addiction circuitry of the brain "when gamers experienced moments of triumph. And as a result, the researchers identified fiero as the most likely underlying cause of why some gamers feel 'addicted' to their favorite game."[90]

According to McGonigal, the game industry is aware and concerned about gamer addiction. "Gamer regret" is a term used to describe those who play more than 20 hours a week of games and then are concerned about missing out on reality. This poses a problem for the gaming industry because some players who experience "gamer regret" might stop playing. As a result, the game industry is trying to curb potential addiction by building into games some form of extra rewards for taking a rest from playing. The industry wants to create lifelong gamers and not ones that drop out to overcome addiction.

In addition to the brain chemicals released through the flow of hard work or hard fun and fiero are the emotions evoked through the sociability resulting from online gaming. McGonigal believes that online gaming taps into our "feel good" emotions of love and compassion. Social contacts are an important ingredient, according to positive psychologists, in long term happiness. Game design deals directly with these social emotions when games are online.

Game designers attempt to achieve all of the above brain reactions in their potential players through game goals, rules, and feedback. Game goals force players to exercise hard work or hard fun in trying to achieve them. Game goals are eventually attainable and the quest to achieve them involves a feedback system of points, scores, progress bars, and so on. The feedback system is supposed to cause fiero and the associated emotions. Associated with the feedback system is "phasing" which allows players to see their impact on the virtual world of the game.

McGonigal eloquently defends the social connections aspect of online game playing against those claiming that online game playing results in players living isolated existences staring at a monitor. McGonigal not only defends online gaming communities as real communities but also claims that online games give meaning to our social lives. She writes, "Meaning is the feeling that we're part of something bigger than ourselves ... the single best way to give meaning to our lives is to connect our daily actions to something bigger than ourselves—the bigger, the better ... And that's exactly the point of working together in a game like *Halo 3*."[91]

She uses *Halo 3* as an example of a game that combines "awe" with meaningful online sociability. McGonigal claims that positive psychologists believe that feelings of awe are the most powerful and gratifying emotions felt by humans. Awe is felt in epic games like *Halo 3*. These games are epic because their contexts or game scenarios link the player to a world that surpasses the ordinary. They are also considered epic because online playing links gamers to collective actions and stories including cooperative efforts that can last for months.

The feeling of awe that is supposedly felt by players immersed in epic online games makes them feel part of a larger scheme of things. McGonigal claims that feelings of awe encompass heroic actions and a sense of service to others. Players feel heroic as they experience epic adventures in an epic world. In her words, "awe doesn't just feel good; it inspires us to do good."[92]

While McGonigal argues for the value of digital games, she introduces a factor that challenges their use in schools. McGonigal's list of game elements that contribute to flow includes the factor that they should be voluntary. Voluntary participation involves willing acceptance of the goals, rules, and feedback. She writes, "And the freedom to enter or leave a game at will ensures that intentionally stressful and challenging work is experienced as *safe* and *pleasurable* activity."[93]

Therefore, learning games that students are required to play in school might lose their potential for creating flow and igniting the brain chemicals that lead to happiness. A child who engages in edutainment using an app on a smart phone or choosing to play *MathBlaster* or *Oregon Train* at home is in a different situation than a child in school who is told to play a learning game. School attendance is not voluntary and can be considered a chore by some children. Does a learning game assigned in school lose its potential as a source of flow because it is not voluntary?

School as a Game

Quest to Learn may be the first school organized around the principles of game design. It is a public charter school in New York City that declares, "We believe that students today can and do learn in different ways, often through interaction with digital media and games."[94] As a school based on game design it advertises on its website:

> Quest supports a dynamic curriculum that uses the underlying design principles of games to create academically challenging, immersive, game-like learning experiences for students. Games and other forms of digital media also

model the complexity and promise of "systems." Understanding and accounting for this complexity is a fundamental literacy of the 21st century.[95]

In tune with the digital world, the school divides its academic curriculum into "domains" which in the world of the Internet refers to a subdivision of websites that have a common purpose and similar Internet addresses. The first domain in the school's curriculum from sixth to 12th grade is called "The Way Things Work" which encompasses math and science topics. The second domain is "Being, Space and Place" covering social studies and English language arts. The domain of "Codeworlds" includes math and English language arts. "Core Support" subjects in the curriculum include health and physical education and, of course, "Sports for the Mind (Game Design)."[96]

Quest to Learn presents itself not only as a school based on digital game design but also as one that integrates technology throughout its learning experiences. Its use of technology, the school explains in its official documents, is based on four core principles. An important factor in this plan is to support the centrality of the teacher and to provide some limits on technological use in the pedagogy. In the school's four core principles for the use of technology is the proviso that, "The technology should always support and be supported by good teaching. If at any time a teacher feels as if he/she would like to incorporate technology into a piece of curriculum they should always be asking themselves, 'how will this technology help the learning of my students increase?'"[97] The pedagogy involves some game principles with students being sent on secret missions searching for answers throughout the school and with students being "leveled up" in difficulty as in a digital game in contrast to receiving grades for assignments.

Who is funding this school based on game design? Not surprisingly the major sources of funding for Quest to Learn are the Bill and Melinda Gates Foundation and the MacArthur Foundation. In the next section I will look at the political economy of edutainment and organizations and people supporting its inclusion in education.

The Political Economy of Edutainment

What are the political and economic interests promoting the use of game design in organizing schools and selling digital games? I've already described the economic interests in promoting games, such as the oligarchy of Microsoft, Sony, and Nintendo which sell game platforms, and edutainment software companies like Knowledge Adventure and The Learning Company. One question that these companies might have asked in the past, when products sold at Wal-Mart and Costco seemed unsuitable for school use, is whether they should market their games through retail establishments or to schools. Resistance to digital gaming in schools is disappearing as proponents of the industry, such as previously discussed James Gee and Jane McGonigal, promote game design as an educational panacea.

Are there political forces along with economic interests promoting edutainment games and game design for schools? Government education leaders are trying to enlist video games in promoting two objectives, namely national curriculum standards and the placing of an emphasis on what is referred to as STEM subjects: science, technology, engineering, and math. Both of these topics were central to the educational objectives of President Barack Obama and his Secretary of Education Arne Duncan which are supposedly to contribute to economic growth and improve America's ability to compete in the global economy.[98]

The inclusion of digital games as helping to obtain national political objectives is present in the 2010 U.S. Department of Education's National Education Technology Plan *Transforming American Education: Learning Powered by Technology* which advocates the use of digital game design in schools.[99] The Plan asserts, "Interactive technologies, especially games, provide immediate performance feedback so that players always know how they are doing. As a result, they are highly engaging to students and have the potential to motivate students to learn."[100]

The Plan's "Model of Learning, Powered by Technology" recommends "engaging environments and tools for understanding ... [in which] game-based courses use features familiar to game players to teach core subject content, such as history."[101] The Plan also suggests the use of "educational computer games" to teach literacy to preschoolers.[102] Even research into using games for assessment of students is recommended in the Plan: "Conduct research and development that explores how embedded assessment technologies, such as simulations, collaboration environments, *virtual worlds, games*, and cognitive tutors, can be used to engage and motivate learners while assessing complex skills [author's emphasis]."[103]

One member, Roy Pea, of the 15 member Technical Working Group that produced the National Education Technology Plan, is directly linked to the Bill and Melinda Gates Foundation which has funded efforts to use digital games to achieve national education curriculum standards. Stanford University Professor Roy Pea—co-director of Stanford's Center for Innovations in Learning and director of two for-profit companies, TeachScape and VIP Tone, as discussed in Chapter 3— includes in his network of relationships the Bill and Melinda Gates Foundation. The Bill and Melinda Gates Foundation "partnered" with Pea's TeachScape. Of course, I cannot establish a causal relationship between the Gates Foundation and the National Education Technology Plan's promotion of digital gaming in schools. However, it is interesting to note that in 2010, the same year that the Plan was released, the Gates Foundation sponsored a conference whose purpose, as described by the Foundation, was to discuss the development of games that would be aligned with the common core standards of public schools. Attending were members of the commercial gaming industry. The Gates Foundation website states about the conference:

> **Purpose:** to convene the foremost thinkers in education and commercial gaming for a one-day summit at New York University with the purpose of

creating a framework for developing game standards and a toolkit for developers to increase effectiveness of games in terms of alignment with the common core standards, design principles, assessment, and other needed key elements.[104]

Another member of the Technical Working Group was University of Michigan's Professor Barry Fishman whose research focuses on digital games to teach national standards. Similar to the group that attended the New York University conference, Fishman is interested in how video games can be used to support standards-based schooling. His research focuses on video games as model learning environments, the use of technology to support teacher learning, standards-based systemic school reform, and the role of educational leaders in fostering classroom-level reform through the application of technology. He is a principal investigator at the Center for Highly Interactive Computing in Education which in its self-promotion states, "Most recently, we have focused on the *design and development of e-learning, gaming environments,* connections between formal and informal education, learning progressions, and assessment instruments, alongside our ongoing focus on student learning, teacher learning, professional development, and materials development [author's emphasis]."[105] The Center receives money for its research, which includes digital gaming, from a variety of sources including government, private foundations, and business: National Science Foundation, U.S. Department of Education, W.K. Kellogg Foundation, Centers for Disease Control, Joyce Foundation, Spencer Foundation, and Hewlett Packard Corporation.[106] With funding from the National Science Foundation, W.K. Kellogg Foundation, and the Hewlett Packard Corporation, Fishman constructed an online professional development tool called Knowledge Networks On the Web (KNOW).[107]

Another member of the Technical Working Group interested in applying game design to the government's objective of improving instruction in STEM subjects is University of Pennsylvania's Professor Yasmin Kafai who claims to have "been one of the first researchers to establish the field of game studies with her work on children's learning as designers and players of educational software and games."[108] She has gained notoriety in game design through her popular online game *Whyville* which is described as:

> Whyville.net provides free access to about 1,500,000 registered players ages 8–18. Our investigations focused on two aspects: How do children chose [sic] to spend their time and how they do they become engaged in science on Whyville? We were particularly interested in two events: the annual outbreak of a virtual epidemic, called Whypox, and related vaccine sales and trades. Our observations captured players' interactions online and offline in classrooms and afterschool clubs.[109]

An article in *Science* clearly identifies *Whyville* as part of the government's effort to improve learning in the STEM subjects. This article states that *Whyville* has

4 million subscribers with the majority being eight to 14 year old girls. The article's author Merrilea Mayo asks the question: "Is it possible to greatly expand the reach of STEM education with the use of video games as the medium?"[110] Her answer echoes the words of others promoting digital games as the panacea for schooling: "Although the field is still in its embryonic stages, game-based learning has the potential to deliver science and math education to millions of users ... Unlike other mass-media experiments in education (e.g., TV, Webinars), games are a highly interactive medium with many key attributes shared with sophisticated pedagogical approaches."[111]

The funding for *Whyville* identifies Kafai as a member of the shadow elite moving between business and government networks. Government and foundation funding for *Whyville* comes from the University of Texas, NASA, Woods Hole Oceanographic Institution, J. Paul Getty Trust, and AbilityFirst and the Grace Foundation.[112] For-profit sponsors include two companies with an interest in expanding Internet usage in schools, namely Adobe Systems and Sun Micro-systems along with Toyota, Scion, and Toyota Financial Services.[113] Why Toyota and its subsidiary Scion? One might guess that the company might have an economic interest in supporting STEM education as a source of future designers and engineers.

Assessment of students is another part of the political agenda for education that the National Education Technology Plan suggests could be turned over to gaming and virtual reality. Another member of the Technical Working Group is Harvard's Professor Chris Dede, whose research funding as described on his Harvard website include: "four grants from NSF and the US Department of Education Institute of Education Sciences to explore immersive simulations and transformed social interactions as means of student engagement, learning, and assessment."[114]

Indicative of his work in developing virtual reality games as an assessment instrument is his membership of the National Academy of Sciences Committee on Foundations of Educational and Psychological Assessment and the 2010 National Educational Technology Plan Technical Working Group. This combination of interests is embodied in the Harvard School of Education project, Virtual Performance Assessment: Using Immersive Technology to Assess Science Inquiry Learning.[115] Professor Dede's work on virtual assessment probably contributed to the National Technology Plan's call for research into games as a method of assessment.

The use of virtual assessment is tied to the political agenda of creating national standards and national assessments. The website for Virtual Performance Assessment provides this explanation of its goals and political agenda:

> Science inquiry process skills are difficult to assess with multiple choice or constructed-response paper-and-pencil tests. This project will develop three single-user immersive three-dimensional (3-D) environments to assess middle school students' science inquiry skills. The investigators will *align these assessments to National Science Education Standards (NSES) and will develop the*

assessments to serve as a standardized component of an accountability program [author's emphasis].[116]

A product of this research and development is a virtual reality game, *Save the Kelp*, which allows students to analyze the disappearance of kelp on a shoreline using virtual avatars.[117] As they play the game, students are continually assessed with regard to thinking skills and science knowledge. The project "will modify an existing commercial framework for immersive game development to provide the appropriate authoring platform for the assessments."[118] The goal of developing these virtual reality games is stated as: "The final product will include three immersive virtual performance assessments that test students' science inquiry skills. The assessments will run on computers currently in schools and will require little preparation for users and no additional paper-based materials."[119]

Conclusion

Digital learning games potentially link the home, school, and future career of students. Used in schools and played at home, digital learning games are one more element in prepared childhood. In protected childhood, children played games without parental concern about them preparing children for school and work. Now games are enlisted to prepare children for school and work. In this context, the lines blur between the home, school, and future work of children.

The future work of prepared children, as claimed in national policy documents, depends on national standards, national assessments, and an emphasis on instruction in the STEM subjects (science, technology, engineering, and math). Research in game design is now being supported to help achieve these policy plans. It is also argued that these policy plans will make a nation more competitive in the world economy.

The sale of learning games to schools provides another inroad into the commercialization of education. Toy manufacturers as early as the 1930s realized that there was a market for edutainment toys. This market was primarily focused on parents and resulted to a certain extent in the curricularization of the home. As the concept of prepared childhood dominated parental actions in the late 20th century software learning games were marketed to parents and children. Even toddlers are now being prepared by ICT for future work and to make their contributions to the world economy. Manufacturers of game platforms and digital learning games now consider both the school and home as marketing sites.

Another interpretation of this scenario is that the promotion of instruction in STEM subjects might provide the type of workers needed by ICT companies including those making digital games. It could be argued that flooding the market with graduates strong in knowledge of STEM subjects will keep salaries low in ICT companies. This will improve the profitability of these companies through lower salaries and the sale of products to schools. This type of thinking might occur among the owners and managers of these companies who primarily have business and not education backgrounds, and receive funds from venture capitalists.

The growing popularity and use of digital games in schools raises questions about their effect. There are two sides to this issue. One side worries about the effect of the Internet and learning games on the attention span of students. Is multitasking creating a generation that shows signs of an epidemic of symptoms associated with attention deficit disorder? Can an overload of data affect memory? Does game design promote addiction or dependency? On the other side of the argument are those who promote game design as the panacea for educational problems. It is argued that game design opens the door to learning by having fun and feeling a state of flow. Game design replaces the punitive nature of letter grades with levels of achievement. Students keep learning so that they can advance to the next stage of difficulty as they do in games. A major question about digital games in schools is whether the student will play them differently when they are required in contrast to being voluntary activities outside of school.

Whatever the final research findings are regarding the effect of digital games and the Internet on changing brain functions, game companies now consider the schools an important market for their products and they are contributing to the growing commercialization of education. There is a network of educators, government officials, foundations, and gaming companies pushing an agenda of using learning games in schools. Will edutainment be the new panacea for education?

5

THE DIGITAL MINDS AND BRAINS OF STUDENTS

Claims about the effect of the Internet on the recent generation range across the spectrum from *The Dumbest Generation: How the Digital Age Stupefies Young Americans and Jeopardizes Our Future* to a more positive portrayal in *Grown Up Digital: How the Net Generation is Changing Your World.*[1] The debate centers on changes in the brains and minds of those growing up in the digital world. I am using the terms "brain" and "mind" to distinguish between the brain as an organism and the mind as the product of the intersection of the brain with culture and environment. For example, I will discuss claims that multitasking on a computer changes the brain, making it more difficult to concentrate, and that the minds of ICT users see and know the world differently than nonusers. As I will discuss, most writers seem to agree that the brain changes with the use of ICT and ICT affects the mind or how people think. For some these changes are positive, for others they are negative.

All parties to this debate agree that the generation growing up—the date varies depending on the writer—since the late 1970s are major users and consumers of ICT. As noted previously in this book, the evolution of new technologies depends on a willing consumer market. Are youth a targeted market for new ICT products, games, social networking, and smart phones? Is there a digital divide between generations? What is the effect of these new consumer products on users' brains and minds?

Underlying this discussion is ageism. Youth are portrayed as speeding ahead of the previous generation in technological usage. In 2001, Marc Prensky sparked an ongoing debate with his claim of a major difference between what he called "digital natives" and "digital immigrants."[2] The debate continued into 2011 with a publication devoted to an analysis of his generational divide titled, *Deconstructing Digital Natives: Young People, Technology and the New Literacies.*[3] But does this divide actually exist? Are all members of the so-called digital generation the same in their usage of ICT? Is the older generation significantly different in their usage of ICT?

Economic interests are a driving force in claims that the brains and minds of digital natives have changed and we should adapt institutions, particularly schools, to these changes. ICT companies trying to sell educational software and online courses are interested in portraying the digital generation as needing their products because of changes in their brains and ways of thinking. What I call the "new" consumers of ICT, Marc Prensky presents as the "new" students: "Today's students—K through college—represent the first generations to grow up with this new technology. They have spent their entire lives surrounded by and using computers, videogames, digital music players, video cams, cell phones, and all the other toys and tools of the digital age."[4]

In the following sections I will sort out the various claims about the changing minds and brains of students. I will begin with those lauding the rise of the digital generation and calling for changes in education to meet its needs. I will then discuss those who claim the digital generation is actually getting dumber and suffering from an inability to concentrate. Both sides of this debate agree that there are changes in the brain and mind resulting from the use of ICT. Running through these debates are questions of ageism, economic interests, and consumerism.

Evangelists for the Digital Natives

A legacy of the previously mentioned 2001 article by Prensky is the common use of the term "digital natives." As he phrases it: "What should we call these 'new' students of today? Some refer to them as the N-[for net]-gen or D-[for digital]-gen. But the most useful designation I have found for them is *Digital Natives*. Our students today are all 'native speakers' of the digital language of computers, video games and the Internet."[5] Accompanying this declaration is a declaration that is echoing through education corridors in the early 21st century: "Our students have changed radically. Today's students are no longer the people our educational system was designed to teach."[6]

One question is Marc Prensky's location in the world of ICT and whether or not he has an economic interest in promoting the ideas that digital natives require new forms of education. His biography suggests that he is economically interested in selling educational products for students who he claims can no longer benefit from a traditional education. Prensky is founder of two companies selling e-learning products—Games2train and Spree Learning. Games2train's clients include IBM, Bank of America, Microsoft, Pfizer, the U.S. Department of Defense, and Florida and Los Angeles' virtual schools. Spree Learning markets online educational games.[7]

In other words, he defines the digital generation and then claims they need the type of digital games sold by his companies. This is all captured in his promotional biography in his 2010 book *Teaching Digital Natives: Partnering for Real Learning*: "Marc's professional focus has been on reinventing the learning process, combining the motivation of student passion, technology, games, and other highly engaging activities with the driest content of formal education."[8]

Prensky began producing educational games in the early 1990s as vice president of human resources at Bankers Trust. During the 1990s he produced a dozen training games for a range of activities from stock trading to sexual harassment. As a result he founded Corporate Gameware as a subsidiary of Bankers Trust. In a 1998 article, the *Wall Street Journal* extolled his work for Bankers Trust: "Mr. Prensky created some twitch-speed training games designed to keep younger workers from lapsing into narcolepsy in traditional training sessions. Now, Bankers trust has formed Corporate Gameware to sell them to other companies."[9] A 1998 *Newsweek* article described his goal as bringing "the excitement of Nintendo and computer gaming to what he calls the needlessly 'dry and boring' world of executive training."[10]

Today, Games2train continues to offer corporate training programs along with online certification programs such as for completion of corporate sexual harassment training. It is also offering a financial literacy game; middle school science games; a military game sponsored by the Defense Advanced Research Projects Agency; an Algebra game; and a corporate cell phone game.[11] Prensky's company Spree Learning offers a wide variety of digital learning games for math, science, and literacy.[12]

Obviously with this corporate background, Prensky has an interest in convincing others that digital natives require a different type of education, particularly one using edutainment with digital games. In his original 2001 article, he asserted, "Digital Natives are used to receiving information really fast. They like to parallel process and multi-task ... They thrive on instant gratification and frequent rewards. *They prefer games to 'serious' work* [author's emphasis]."[13] Digital immigrants is what Prensky calls the older generations: "Those of us who were not born into the digital world but have, at some later point in our lives, become fascinated by and adopted many or most aspects of the new technology are, and always will be compared to them, Digital Immigrants."[14]

In the second of Prensky's original articles, he emphasizes neuroplasticity or the ability of the brain to change. Neuroscience findings over the last several decades emphasize the ability of the brain to change in contrast to earlier notions that the brain was fixed in its structure after childhood. Based on the findings of neuroscience, he argues, "They [digital natives] have been adjusting or programming their brains to the speed, interactivity, and other factors in the games much as [baby] boomers' brains were programmed to accommodate television."[15] Also, regarding the mind, he declares that social psychologists find that different cultures think differently and therefore the thinking of digital natives is different from that of previous generations. Stressing the importance of learning games for digital natives, Prensky continues the same argument in his 2010 book in which he declares, "Today's students want to learn differently than in the past. They want ways of learning that are meaningful to them ... and ways that make good use of the *technology they know is their birthright* [author's emphasis]."[16]

Don Tapscott's popular 1999 publication *Growing Up Digital: The Rise of the Net Generation* presented arguments similar to Prensky's, namely that those growing up with ICT were different in their brains and minds than previous generations.[17] Currently, he is Chairman of Moxie Insight (originally nGenera Insight) which, according to its website, has since 1993 "provided clients with insightful, thought-provoking analysis of emerging technology trends and their business impact. We serve as a 'strategic early warning system' for our clients, helping them discern real imperatives from all the hype and noise."[18] Moxie Insight is a subsidary of Moxie Software which sells social enterprise software designed for customer and employee corporate engagement.[19]

Drawing on similar research as Prensky, Tapscott declares that "interactive technology—in this case video action games—can change the brain, and in particular, the way we perceive things."[20] Brain changes, according to Tapscott, include highly developed spatial skills, and the ability to multitask and process rapid-fire visual information. Tapscott recognizes a common complaint that multitasking using ICT is changing the brain, making it more difficult to concentrate. In this context, the digital generation shows signs of attention deficit disorder (ADD). Tapscott responds to this claim, "So why do some Net Geners seem to have attention disorder in class? Isn't it possible that the answer is because they're bored—both with the slow pace and the content of the lecture?"[21] He continues by quoting Prensky that the digital generation does not display symptoms of ADD when playing games.

What type of education is suited for digital natives according to those claiming major generational change? Besides advocating the use of learning games, the response is a form of education that sounds strangely like traditional progressive education with an emphasis on student's interests, learning by doing, and group work and projects. For instance, Prensky's 2010 book lists under a section titled "What Today's Students Want" that students do not want lectures but they want to follow their interests, create, work in groups, make decisions while sharing control, cooperate with others, and connect to students around the world.[22]

Tapscott prescribes the same progressive education for the "net generation." He makes a comparison between what he labels as "Broadcast Learning," which he considers the traditional form of school learning, versus "Interactive Learning" for the net generation. He characterizes Broadcast Learning as being teacher centered, with no individualized instruction, learning about things, and learning alone. In contrast, he asserts that the net generation wants instruction that is learner centered and individualized and involves learning by doing and cooperative learning.[23]

Technology is advocated as the means for implementing progressive education principles. In *Rewired: Understanding the iGeneration and the Way They Learn*, Larry Rosen presents "seven major arguments for changing our educational system to include more technologies."[24] Referring to the iGeneration as "iGen," he premises his arguments the assumptions that: iGens are wired 24/7; iGens are multitaskers; iGens socialize through ICT; iGens live in an Internet connected world at home; iGens have available high quality course material at low prices; for iGens technologically adapted curriculum material will develop higher order thinking; and iGens' "participation in the Web 2.0 via user-generated content, social networking, mobile learning, and virtual learning environments (just to name a few) is highly motivating for them and they are naturals at it."[25] Like others claiming changes in the brains and minds of the digital native, Rosen believes schools should change by combining elements of progressive education with interactive and social linking ICT.

Rightly or wrongly, Prensky and Tapscott introduced the assumption, often repeated by others, that digital natives or the iGeneration are different than previous generations in their brain wiring and how their minds perceive the world. Typical of this often repeated assumption of a generation gap is the 2010 book *Understanding the Digital Generation*: "The problem is the rapidly growing gap of understanding between the young people sitting in the classrooms and the adults who teach them."[26] Or Larry Rosen who asserts that not only is there a generational gap with the current generation immersed in "any form of electronic media" but also, as a result, "*They* [iGeneration] *hate school*. Why? Education has not caught up with this new generation of tech-savvy children."[27]

Is There a Digital Gap Between Generations?

Homogeneity of youth is an assumption of those claiming the existence of a digital generation. Are all youth today immersed in a digital world? Not according to Australian university professors Sue Bennett and Karl Maton who report research findings that some of the current generation has a high level of digital skills while many are only familiar with rudimentary computer usage. The majority of the so-called digital natives only use ICT for communication and not for creative purposes or online gaming. There are also major differences in how the current generation access information online. Many have the ability to find information online but only a few can make decisions about the quality of the information. Bennett and Maton conclude, "In summary it is clear that the claim that young people are digital natives has little or no basis in empirical evidence and that blanket statements about generational differences, however nuanced, provide little if any insight into current or future educational needs."[28]

ICT researcher Michael Thomas of the University of Central Lancashire, UK, also argues that today's college students are familiar with basic ICT functions but cannot create multimedia content. Students primarily use ICT, he found, for social purposes. In fact, he suggests that students sometimes see a conflict between their use of ICT for social purposes and educational purposes: "Where students do use them [digital technologies], it is most often in their social lives for communication purposes and rarely in educational contexts. Moreover, in certain cases, students see a conflict between the use of Web 2.0 technologies in their social and educational lives, and like them to remain separate."[29]

Chris Jones of the Institute of Educational Technology at the Open University, UK, also reports research that shows a great deal of diversity in ICT among college students. Regarding claims of differences between digital natives and digital immigrants, Jones writes that research suggests "that while age is a factor there is no single Net Generation or digital native group and that first-year university students show a diversity that is inconsistent with a generational hypothesis."[30]

One study found that youth did not express any difference between their use of ICT and that of their parents' generation.[31] Jones accuses Prensky and Tapscott of technological determinism by insisting that each generation is shaped by new technology, requiring adaptation by educational institutions. The idea that the current generation is fundamentally different because of ICT, Jones argues, has created a "moral panic" among educators who are rushing to meet the needs of the newly defined digital natives. But, Jones argues, rather than an entire generation leaving the previous generation in their dust as they rush to embrace ICT: "As new technologies arise we can expect adoption patterns to vary by age but they also vary in relation to the time that each technology was first introduced. Adoption patterns are also likely to be affected by other factors such as gender and ... national and regional contexts.[32]

There are also suggestions that the recent generation primarily uses ICT for frivolous purposes such as online shopping and social contacts. This was the conclusion of a three year study of the Internet usage by European Union youth. The purpose of the study was to determine whether or not the Internet increased civic participation. In analyzing this study to determine if online usage stimulates civic activity, Shakuntala Banaji of the London School of Economics reports: "Over half the respondents expressed most interest in entertainment (music, movies, news, and shopping) sites, and little interest in explicitly civic sites, with an interest in electoral politics lowest."[33] Actual participation in civic websites was more dependent on family background interest in politics than availability of the sites. This finding is congruent with University of Melbourne's Gregor Kennedy and Terry Judd's summary of research, "While few if any of these studies are directly comparable, they do appear to describe a student population that is far from uniform in its response to technology."[34]

Despite the impression given by Prensky and Tapscott of a generation enmeshed in the world of ICT, the above arguments indicate obvious differences in ICT usage among the so-called digital natives or iGeneration. In fact, the above findings suggest many so-called digital natives are lost in a frivolous world of online shopping and gaming and social networking. Are writers like Prensky and Tapscott really saying anything new when they assert that the current generation is bored in school because their brains and minds have changed with ICT? Haven't some students always complained about school being boring? Bennett and Maton wonder why the idea of a digital native generation spread with the lack of social analysis and over-generalization about the current generation. Why do Prensky and Tapscott call for a complete overhaul of schooling to meet the supposed needs of so-called digital natives rather than just view ICT as another classroom tool? Bennett and Maton offer this cynical explanation:

> There are, of course, vested interests at play in the dissemination of claims [that schools must adapt to digital natives]. Commentators and academics are eager to raise their academic and media profiles, consultants and technology vendors wish to promote their services and products, and educational administrators desire easy, quick, and simply understood policy ideas.[35]

The Internet and the Brain: The Effects of Multitasking and High Internet Usage on the Brain

Research suggests ICT usage causes changes in the brain. Depending on the commentator, these changes in brain functioning may or may not require changes in educational institutions or they may indicate a generation unable to concentrate and engage in what might be called deep and focused thought. This section will explore the debate about possible changes in the brain and what should be the resulting response.

A river trip by a group of neuroscientists attests to the disagreements about the effect of the digital world on the brain. The trip was planned to evaluate the effects of the digital world on the brain by isolating these scientists in an area of Southern Utah without their laptops, without e-mail access and without cellphone connections. The organizer of the trip, psychology professor David Strayer, stated the trip was for studying what happens when we stop using digital technology and whether or not attention, learning, and memory are affected. Strayer commented, "Attention is the holy grail. Everything that you're conscious of, everything you let in, everything you remember and you forget depends on it."[36]

The five scientists on the trip were divided between those with concerns about the effect of the digital world on the brain and those who used their digital devices without concern about their affect. Among the worriers were Professor Strayer and Professor Paul Atchley, who studies the compulsive use of cellphones by teenagers. Strayer and Atchley concluded from their studies that extended times on cellphones and other digital technology can cause anxiety and inhibit "deep thought."[37] The three non-worriers were Professor Todd Braver, a brain imaging expert, Professor Steven Yantis, who studies multitasking, and Professor Art Kramer, who studies the neurological effects of exercise.

The five scientists left the trip with a new appreciation of the possible effects of the digital world on the brain. The skeptics remained skeptics but in a new context. Professor Braver said that he would now use brain imaging to study the effect of rest and nature on the brain. Professor Yantis came away with new ideas about researching people who are distracted by irrelevant streams of information. Professor Kramer wants to examine if being in nature leads to "clear thoughts." And Professor Atchley said he could "see new ways to understand why teenagers decide to text even in dangerous situations, like driving. Perhaps the addictiveness of digital stimulation leads to poor decision-making."[38]

One of the things talked about on the trip was a Michigan study that concluded walking in the woods is more relaxing for the brain and people learned significantly better than if they walked through an urban area. This particular study is reported in a number of places in discussions of the effect of multitasking and information overload on the brain.[39] The issue is that smart phones, laptops, iPads, and desk computers are filling more and more of a person's time as their brains react to continuous streams of information. A short time ago I would ride my local commuter train during rush hour and passengers either would be glancing at some form of print matter or just lolled around staring out the window or into space resting their brains. Now most riders are hunched over some type of digital media, sometimes simultaneously using three forms, such as a smart phone, iPad, and laptop. "The technology makes the tiniest windows of time entertaining, and potentially productive," writes *New York Times* reporter Matt Richtel. "But scientists point to an unanticipated side effect: when people keep their brains busy with digital input, they are forfeiting downtime that could allow them to better learn and remember information, or come up with new ideas."[40]

Some researchers claim that multitasking and information overload make it difficult for students to concentrate and learn. In addition, long periods of time spent on digital devices do not allow the brain to rest. Professor Loren Frank at the University of California, San Francisco, argues, "Almost certainly, downtime lets the brain go over experiences it's had, solidify them and turn them into permanent long-term memories."[41] Frank claims that constant stimulation of the brain makes it difficult to learn. A similar argument is made regarding multitasking in the digital world when people sit in front of monitors checking their e-mail and Facebook accounts while surfing the Internet. Michael Rich, an associate professor at Harvard Medical School and executive director of the Center on Media and Child Health in Boston argues, "Their brains [children's] are rewarded not for staying on task but for jumping to the next thing. The worry is we're raising a generation of kids in front of screens whose brains are going to be wired differently."[42]

Researcher Eyal Ophir and his team at Stanford University divided test subjects into those who frequently used the Internet and were considered heavy multitaskers and those who weren't. The subjects played a computer game that tested how well they could filter out distractions. The heavy multitaskers were found to have more difficulty with this task. The researchers had similar results from another experiment and they concluded that heavy multitaskers were more sensitive to incoming information over the Internet and therefore were more easily distracted from the task they were performing. These researchers concluded that multitasking heightens the propensity of the brain to be attuned to possible dangers or in other words being distracted by an inflow of multiple cues from the environment. Another Stanford researcher, Clifford Nass, commented, "we've got a large and growing group of people who think the slightest hint that something interesting might be going on is like catnip. They can't ignore it. … [some] can't shut off their multitasking tendencies when they're not multitasking."[43] Other research studies found an increase in stress hormones when a person is interrupted by e-mail, thus adding a potential medical hazard to multitasking.[44]

The most extensive writing about the impact on the brain of immersion in the digital world is by Nicholas Carr in *The Shallows: What the Internet is Doing to Our Brains*.[45] He asks the question: "What can science tell us about the actual effects that the Internet use is having on the way our minds work?"[46] Carr finds the literature on this question disturbing and asserts: "Dozens of studies by psychologists, neurobiologists, educators, and Web designers point to the same conclusion: when we go online we enter an environment that promotes cursory reading, hurried and distracted thinking, and superficial learning."[47]

Carr argues, citing the findings of neuroscience, that the Internet is one of the most brain-altering technologies to appear in human history. Writing, books, and maps were major brain-altering technologies that reduced a reliance on memory since people did not have to depend as much on their memories because information is retained in writings and directions stored on maps rather than in the brain. With the Internet, Carr argues, the brain now faces the possibility of information overload. He writes, "With the Net, we face many information faucets, all going full blast ... We're able to transfer only a small portion of the information to long-term memory, and what we do transfer is a jumble of drops from different faucets, not a continuous, coherent stream from one source."[48] The result of this flood of information from the Internet, Carr claims, results in "cognitive overload" making it harder "to distinguish relevant information from irrelevant information, signal from noise. We become *mindless consumers of data* [author's emphasis]."[49]

Overloaded with the data, according to Carr, the brain has a difficult time concentrating and becomes easily distracted, resulting in behavior similar to ADD. In turn this affects our memories, Carr claims, citing research that people need to focus on information through either repetition or strong emotional engagement in order to store it in long term memory. Multitasking contributes to this difficulty of remembering by making it more difficult for people to focus their attention on a single piece of information. This situation, Carr argues, creates a self-reinforcing loop where our dependence on Web information makes "it harder for us to lock information into our biological memory, we're forced to rely more and more on the Net's capacious and easily searchable artificial memory, even if it makes us shallower thinkers."[50]

Gaming addiction, discussed in Chapter 4, is identified as part of the growing inattention among ICT users. Research reported by Gary Small and Gigi Vorgan substantiates the idea that Internet addicts suffer from ADD and attention deficit hyperactivity disorder (ADHD). A Taiwanese study found Internet addiction linked to ADD. South Korean researchers found 20 percent of Internet addicts suffering from ADD. Small and Vorgan state, "Other studies have shown that Internet addiction in elementary school children significantly increases the likelihood of ADHD and inattention symptoms."[51]

There is also an argument related to the Mihaly Csikszentmihalyi's concept of "flow" as discussed in Chapter 4 regarding Janet McGonigal's call for utilizing feelings of flow occurring during gaming in schools and workplaces. Sherry Turkle, Professor of the Social Studies of Science and Technology at Massachusetts Institute of Technology, relates the concept of flow to the potential of Internet addiction. She argues that there develops a desire within people for continual connectivity through the Web which produces a similar reaction to those experiencing flow during gaming. Regarding Internet connectivity to others as an addiction, she writes, "Connectivity becomes a craving: when we receive a text or an e-mail, our nervous system responds by giving us a shot of dopamine. We are stimulated by connectivity itself. We learn to require it, even as it depletes us."[52]

Turkle relates multitasking to the high associated with a "shot of dopamine" which, as others suggest, leads to problems in concentration and might promote ADD. She argues that psychologists find that multitasking does not lead to greater efficiency and that multitaskers do not do well on the tasks they are attempting. "But," she asserts, "multitasking feels good because the body rewards it with neurochemicals that induce a multitasking 'high'. The high deceives multitaskers into thinking they are being especially productive. In search of the high, they want to do even more."[53]

In summary, do digital gaming, data overload, and multitasking produce learners who might be addicted to the Internet or have problems with concentration and memory? Are digital natives shallow in their thinking? Will the digital generation show more signs of ADD and ADHD than past generations? What will be the effect on students who use online instructional software? Do they become shallow readers who have difficulty concentrating on a text for long periods of time?

Digital Natives: Sense of Community or Loneliness?

Some people assert that digital natives are more attuned to social interconnections, cooperation, and community. Larry Rosen claims that "iGen students are socializing constantly via technologies such as social networks and text messaging, and this communication has been shown to level the playing field so that all students feel comfortable participating in conversations."[54] This argument is often used to support the inclusion of the progressive education idea of group work and collaboration in school.

A counter argument is that digital natives are possibly experiencing a decline in social skills and increasing feelings of loneliness as a result of ICT's impact on the brain. Small and Vorgan assert: "As the lure of technology distracts people of all ages from their usual personal interactions, their neural circuitry changes and everyday social skills begin to decline."[55] This conclusion would seem to contradict arguments that the Internet maintains social relations through its interconnectivity. However, the brain is predisposed to use a variety of nonverbal communications to connect with others. Lost on the Internet are nonverbal communications such as general body language, facial expressions, eye contact, touch, and general appearance. Obviously, visual contact through Internet video streaming allows for the appearance of body language, facial expressions, and general appearance.

Neuroscience has found pathways in the brain that utilize these nonverbal forms of interactions in making social contacts, including spontaneous face-to-face reactions. These neural pathways are considered essential for a sense of social connectedness. Small and Vorgan claim: "In Digital Natives who have been raised on technology, these interpersonal neural pathways are often left unstimulated and underdeveloped."[56]

As a result, "Symptoms of loneliness, confusion, anxiety, depression, fatigue, and addiction can emerge and further erode their social skills."[57]

Social Networking: Feeling Alone and Without Compassion

Social networking through media such as Twitter, text messaging, Facebook, instant messaging, and e-mail has, in some cases, taken the place of spontaneous communications in face-to-face relationships. Social networking participants rely upon machine mediated interaction. Some writers consider social networking as adding another important dimension to educational technology. The MacArthur Digital Youth project hails the possibilities of this as a new educational frontier providing new learning opportunities.[58]

However, many questions are asked about the effect of social networking. Does social networking create authentic communities or is machine mediated interaction undermining communities and creating feelings of loneliness? These are important questions as children grow up in a world where face-to-face communications or even phone conversations are being replaced by regulated interactions. There are reports that Americans are becoming increasingly lonely and insecure. Are parents giving their full attention to their children as they too are distracted by their smart phones? Are people distracted by their smart phones from giving their full attention to conversations with others? What is the effect on the brain of social interactions shifting from spontaneous face-to-face interactions to ones mediated by technology?

The MacArthur Digital Youth project found social networking integrated into the lives of today's children and youth. Of course, adults also participate, sometimes to the detriment of their children. There is a wide variety of usages of social networking among all members of the population. Some people are constantly text messaging and checking their Facebook account while others only minimally participate in social networking or do not participate. The MacArthur Digital Youth project reports some children and youth begin text messaging after awaking and continue until bed time with Facebook and other social media being used simultaneously.[59] A 2010 Nielson report indicated that on average teenagers send about 3,000 messages a month.[60]

The MacArthur Digital Youth project divides teenage users into different modes of participation. One category is "friendship-driven practices." Many in this category use text messages and other social media to arrange actual face-to-face hanging out time and remain in contact to exchange gossip. Another category is "interest driven" which the report states is the domain of the "geeks, freaks, musicians, artists, and dorks." In the case of these so-called marginalized youth the interests come first: "It is not about the given social relations that structure youths' school lives but about both focusing and expanding an individual's social circle based on interests."[61] The friendship-driven practices are open to criticism by those who claim that ICT rather than expanding the knowledge of youth only provides another avenue for frivolous activities.[62]

How does friendship- and interest-driven use of social networking affect relationships? Does human use of new social media strengthen a sense of community and overcome feelings of loneliness? How does it affect the brain's predisposition to feel compassion and empathy for others? Certainly, the most provocative discussion of these particular issues can be found in the work of the previously mentioned Sherry Turkle who has specialized in the study of human interaction with technology, especially robots and social media. She teaches courses on computer culture at the Massachusetts Institute of Technology. Trained as an anthropologist and a psychoanalytic psychologist, Turkle studied computer culture in the 1970s and early 1980s when personal computers were first becoming popular. Initially, she decided early computer usage stimulated self-reflection. In her autobiography published as part of her 2011 book *Alone Together: Why We Expect More from Technology and Less from Each Other*, she reports a conversation with a 13 year old girl in the 1980s about working on a computer that captures her early findings: "there's a little piece of your mind and now it's a little piece of the computer's mind."[63] She called this initial study of computer culture *The Second Self: Computers and the Human Spirit*.[64] After the 1980s, she argues, there was a significant change in the human relationship to computers. Originally, the relationship involved a person alone with a computer. Computer culture changed dramatically in the 1990s with the ability of people to have parallel lives in virtual worlds. In 1995, her book *Life on Screen: Identity in the Age of the Internet* reflects a positive view on the possibilities of shaping identity. But, she claims, she was beginning to lose her positive feelings about the contribution of computer culture to human life. Some people were telling her that they preferred their online lives to their real lives. What did this mean for human relationships?

In her 2011 book, she reflects on both her study of human interaction with robots and social networking. Using her anthropological and psychological background to study computer culture, she has become more critical of the impact of computer culture on human life. The study of human interaction with robots provides a basis for Turkle's discussion of the impact of social media. In the 1990s robots began to be manufactured to serve as companions to children and to the elderly. For children, robots were marketed as toys.

The brain's functions regarding human interactions are the basis for Turkle's analysis of human interactions with robots and through social networking. Currently, neuroscience informs us that the brain, as result of evolution, is predisposed to seek social attachments. Most human brains are predisposed at birth to imitate the actions of others and develop an ability to read the emotions of others through facial expressions and bodily reactions. Tied to this ability is empathy or the ability to feel the emotions of others. I see someone reacting with fear and I feel fearful. These brain functions are key components of human interaction.[65]

Turkle defines "authentic" human relations as involving these brain functions and shared human experiences. This is something that a robot cannot provide. She writes, "Authenticity, for me, follows from the ability to put oneself in the place of another, to relate to the other because of a shared store of human experiences: we are born, have families, and know loss and the reality of death."[66]

Can machine mediated interactions be "authentic" according to Turkle's definition and the brain's predispositions? When we interact face-to-face all of the associated brain functions come into play including seeing the facial and bodily reactions of the other, empathy, smelling and possibly touching the other, and a shared human history. Body language includes how we stand, our gestures, and physical mannerisms. Facial expressions are crucial to nonverbal interactions. Eye contact can convey a range of emotions along with touch. Dress communicates emotions and personality. There is also an element of spontaneity in face-to-face interactions in contrast to the conscious planning that goes into writing an e-mail or posting on Facebook or other social platforms.[67]

Communication technology affects these factors in human relationships in a variety of ways. Previous generations used letters and telegrams to maintain contact over distances. Stripped of physical contact these forms of technology rely on a shared knowledge between the sender and receiver. Letters can convey emotion through words while the abbreviated language of telegraphs often conveyed little of the emotions of the sender. In both cases, the sender can't see the emotional reaction of the person receiving the message and the receiver cannot see the emotions of the message's composer. With the advent of the telephone, emotions are conveyed through the tone of the voice and there is a spontaneous interchange. Missing are the visual aspects of communication particularly being able to read facial expressions and body language.

In *iBrain*, Small and Vorgan worry that: "Spending hours in front of the computer can atrophy the brain's neural circuitry that controls recognition and interpretation of nonverbal communication ... Some studies suggest that these nonverbal signals constitute a higher proportion of what we communicate to other people than actual words we speak."[68] They are also concerned about developing the brain's predisposition to feel empathy—a key part of human evolution since empathy is necessary for forming social groups which is necessary for human survival. "Spending hours," Small and Vorgan write, "playing video games or working at a computer does little to bolster our empathic skills. Neuroimaging studies have identified the specific brain circuitry that controls empathy."[69] Spontaneous face-to-face interactions are essential for developing socially accepted behaviors.

One of Small and Vorgan's conclusions resonates throughout Turkle's study regarding human interactions with robots and through social media, namely that heavy use of social networking through computers and smart phones results in feelings of loneliness. As stated by Small and Vorgan, "Chronic Internet users risk other adverse psychological consequences. Symptoms of loneliness, confusion, anxiety, depression, fatigue, and addiction can emerge and further erode their social skills."[70]

Connection through ICT to millions of people without nonverbal forms of communication may result in a person feeling lonely. Sherry Turkle found feelings of loneliness among those whose social life is spent primarily through smart phones and computers. She cites findings in Hugh Gusterson and Catherine Besteman's *The Insecure American: How We Got Here and What We Should Do about It*[71] that

Americans are increasingly feeling lonely and insecure.[72] How could this be when everyone seems to be connected to a world of relationships through their smartphones, text messages, Tweets, social platforms, and cell phones?

For Turkle a central problem is that ICT promotes inattention along with the lack of nonverbal communications. Inattention now pervades relationships between children and their parents. Turkle reports children's complaints that their parents do not give them their full attention because they are busy on their smartphones or computer. Children complain that when their parents pick them up from school or other activity they are busy on their smartphones and only give them a nod or brief greeting. ICT has made it possible for companies to extend employee work time into family gatherings. In the evenings, Turkle reports, some children complain that their parents will set their smartphones next to their plates at dinner and they will be constantly distracted during family conversations receiving and answering messages. Also, many children, particularly teenagers, do not give their full attention to family dinner time conversation because they are constantly text messaging. After dinner, Turkle found, many family members disperse to their bedrooms or home work spaces to either work or connect with others through social messaging. In other words, there is a strong potential that ICT might be undermining authentic relationships within families.

Also, she states, inattention and/or distraction extend to social gatherings. She describes attending conferences where members of the audience, some of whom traveled many miles to hear a lecture, did not give their full attention because they were fiddling with their smartphones or working on their laptops. Conversations in the hallways of the meeting site were broken or disjointed by text messaging or other smartphone use. People were staring down at their phones while trying to converse. I experience this phenomenon in my classes when I look around and see students staring at their laps while text messaging or with their laptops open in front of them participating in Facebook. This type of inattention can be seen in restaurants when customers put their smartphones on the table as they sit down for a group dinner.

Turkle reports that teens prefer not to use a traditional telephone because it requires spontaneous give-and-take types of conversations. One teenager told her, "When you text, you have more time to think about what you're writing. When you talk on the phone, you don't really think about what you're saying as much as in a text. On the telephone, too much might show."[73] In other words, these teenagers prefer conversations mediated by technology. A similar issue arises with social networking sites like Facebook. Users can constantly change their image by posting new photos of themselves or by adding and changing their descriptions. The result is the possible presentation of an inauthentic self. In the case of Facebook, text messaging, and e-mail, technology mediates the relationship with others.

For Turkle a disturbing result is a decline in the brain's predisposition for compassion and empathy. This is similar to what Small and Vorgan report in *iBrain*. Machine mediated social relationships with their loss of spontaneous interactions, nonverbal communication, and presentation of an authentic self might be atrophying the brain's predisposition for empathy and compassion. Turkle reports a 2010 University of Michigan study of 14,000 college students that found a decline of interest in others and empathy or the ability to put oneself in the place of others. The study identified online games and social networking as the cause. Turkle writes about this study:

> An online connection can be deeply felt, but you only need to deal with the part of the person you see in your game world or social network. Young people don't seem to feel they need to deal with more, and over time lose the inclination ... psychiatrists, psychologists, and social workers ... talk to me about the increasing numbers of patients who present in the consulting room as detached from their bodies and seem close to unaware of the basic courtesies. Purpose-driven plugged into media, these patients pay little attention to those around them.[74]

The above arguments suggest that students who receive all their instruction online, spend hours playing online games, and rely on social media may be indirectly educated to not care about others. Their face-to-face social skills will decline along with their concern about others. Machine mediated social relationships may result in increasing feelings of loneliness, a decline in compassion, and possibly inauthentic relationships between parents and children and co-workers.

Of course, many who are casual users of social media might not face this prospect. But for those heavily involved in online gaming, creating online avatars, social networks, text messaging, and e-mail, they may face a future of loneliness and not caring for others. These findings suggest the following questions for the potential ICT addict: Do you bring your smartphone to dinner? Do you text message while talking to others? Do you text message or work on your laptop while in class, attending a business meeting, or listening to a lecture? The answers to these questions, the above authors suggest, might indicate whether or not a user will be feeling less compassionate and empathetic and be nagged by feelings of loneliness.

Online Communities

Don Tapscott's crusade for adapting schools to the so-called digital native contains the claim: "Social Networks: The Net Gen Version of a Global Community."[75] But what kind of community are students joining as they meet online? As online communities grow larger are they creating viable and lasting communities? Does an online community satisfy the human need for participating in social groups?

Nicholas Christakis and James Fowler characterize online communities as "superorganisms" that "can manifest a kind of intelligence that augments or complements individual intelligence, the way an ant colony is 'intelligent' even if individual ants are not, or the way flocks of birds determine where to fly by combining the desires of each bird."[76] Christakis is a Harvard Professor of Health Care Policy, Sociology, and Medicine and Fowler is an Associate Professor of Political Science at the Center for Wireless Population Health Systems and the University of California, San Diego. Using findings on communities from neuroscience and evolutionary biology, they argue that most humans have a predisposition to form social groups. These social groups were essential for the survival of humans. The brain, it has been found, is predisposed to deal with communities of about 150 members. Historically, this has been about the size of military units and wedding lists, and is currently the average number of friends on a social network site like Facebook.[77]

Participation in online communities taps into the brain's predisposition for social relations. What about virtual social relationships? Christakis and Fowler cite research that humans react in the same manner to emotional displays by avatars as they do with emotional displays by humans. In other words, humans can feel empathy towards avatars who express pain, anger, or other emotions.[78] If this is true then empathy can be felt within online communities. They write, "these experiments illustrate that life online can both emulate and extend real human interactions ... The sense of incredible realism that many people experience when interacting in virtual worlds with virtual people is known as *presence*."[79]

Christakis and Fowler use network theory to explore online communities. The brain, they argue, utilizes the same social skills with online social communities as it does with other human interactions. They claim this is true of even massive online communities like the 11 million plus playing *World of Warcraft*. In these online communities people create networks that allow for the exchange of information. From this perspective, online communities utilized in classrooms allow for the global sharing of knowledge.

However, Christakis and Fowler conclude, networks do not necessarily create economic, political, or social equality. One's location in the network determines one's status. They assert, "*Positional inequality* occurs not because of who we are but because of who we are connected to. These connections affect where we come to be located in social networks, and they often matter more than our race, class, gender or education."[80] From this perspective, one's exercise of power through online communities is determined by not only what type of online community one belongs to but also one's positionality within the community's network. For instance, President Barack Obama utilized a vast online network of supporters to ensure winning the 2008 election. However, people's political power in the network depended on their positionality; some members were just followers while others were central to the campaign.

As I discuss in more detail in Chapter 6, some educators argue that student participation in online communities will increase their civic knowledge and participation. There is also an argument, to be explored in more detail in Chapter 6, that online communities can be a source of democratic power by uniting disparate groups within a nation for political action. In these situations the actual goals and outcomes of political action may be determined by those in central positions in the network as compared to those on the network's periphery.

Sociologist Felicia Wu Song differentiates between different types of online communities. One type is what she calls "Lifestyle Service" which engages people in forums and chats about services and consumer goods. Another is "Visionary Communal" involving members in chats and planning on various social topics. It is this category of online community that is most involved in sharing interests and knowledge. There are also "Information Clearinghouses" for the general communication of information on a particular topic and "Technical Interface" communities that provide digital platforms for communication like Facebook.[81]

The title of Song's study, *Virtual Communities: Bowling Alone, Online Together*, reflects her interest in whether or not online communities are positive replacements for other forms of disappearing communities. The reference in her title to "*Bowling Alone*" is to Robert Putnam's *Bowling Alone: The Collapse and Revival of American Community*.[82] In his study, Putnam argues that there has been a decline in belonging to communities in the United States. He argues, as an example of this decline, that in the past people primarily bowled as part of an organized league. Today, as representative of the decline of community, people primarily bowl alone. Song interprets Putnam's findings as showing "patterns of not only weakened networks of civic engagement and informal sociability but also declining levels of social and governmental trust … Americans are no longer oriented as joiners."[83]

The question for Song is whether or not virtual communities can be an adequate replacement for what is perceived as the decline of community in American life. She identifies as problematic the ease with which one can join and withdraw from a virtual community. She writes, "With their high ease of exit, the majority of online communities foster relatively weak forms of membership that lack expectations for mutual obligation and reciprocity—two key dispositional goods traditionally associated with democratic life."[84] Most online communities, she argues, involve individuals seeking to fulfill their own personal needs. One problem with these communities is that they are often composed of likeminded people. Often members of these communities do not deal with diversity. In Song's words, "there are significant ways that the technological and institutional features of online groups work to keep people from encountering differences altogether and having to develop skills in negotiation or cooperation."[85]

This means, according to Song, that online communities should be considered from multiple perspectives. Considered as part of a democratic society, online communities can provide people with direct routes to political action and political information. They can serve as a call to action. On the other hand, online communities do not encourage deliberation and compromise between groups. Members often lack any real commitment since it is so easy to drop out. When one drops out of a bowling team, for example, it involves a withdrawal from emotional ties with other members and the commitment to play for the benefit of the team. In contrast, withdrawal from an online community can entail nothing more than a click of the mouse.

The above researchers provide a mixed message about the nature of these online communities. On the one hand, they seem to fulfill the brain's desire for social connectivity and contribute to maintaining social relationships. They can create global networks that provide both information and a potential access to power. On the other hand, online communities do not prepare participants to deal with difference or create a lasting commitment to group goals. While online community members might feel empathy towards other members as they seem to do towards avatars, there is still the question of whether or not they may develop feelings of loneliness as they are globally networked. What does this mean for the online student linked to the world but without face-to-face communication with others?

The Dumbest Generation: Are these the Digital Natives?

From 2003 to 2005 Mark Bauerlein served as Director, Office of Research and Analysis at the National Endowment for the Arts where he compiled studies of the reading habits and learning attitudes of American youth. He worked at the National Endowment for the Arts while on leave from Emory University where he is a Professor of English and author of a range of scholarly books from *Whitman and the American Idiom* to *Negrophobia: A Race Riot in Atlanta*.[86] Bauerlein's *The Dumbest Generation: How the Digital Age Stupefies Young Americans and Jeopardizes Our Future* quickly received national attention with reviews in the popular press, such as Don Campbell, *USA Today*, "If you're the parent of someone under 20 and read only one non-fiction book this fall, make it this one"; Lee Drutman, *Los Angeles Times*, "Throughout *The Dumbest Generation*, there are … keen insights into how the new digital world really is changing the way young people engage with information and the obstacles they face in integrating any of it meaningfully"; David Robinson, *The Wall Street Journal*, "Argues that cultural and technological forces, far from opening up an exciting new world of learning and thinking, have conspired to create a level of public ignorance so high as to threaten our democracy"; and Charles McGrath, *The New York Times*, "Delivers this bad news in surprisingly brisk and engaging fashion, blowing holes in a lot of conventional educational wisdom."[87]

Unlike those preaching that ICT is producing a generation using new forms of learning to advance their knowledge beyond that of previous generations, Bauerlein argues, "The Dumbest Generation cares little for history books, civic principles, foreign affairs, comparative religions, and serious media and art, and it knows less … Other things monopolize their attention—the allure of screens, peer absorption, career goals."[88]

Bauerlein compiles extensive research to buttress his argument. While one might disagree with his interpretations of these studies, one cannot accuse him of not providing a research base for his assertions. For instance, Chapter 1 reports on the state of knowledge and activities among American youth as found by tests and surveys, such as the National Assessment of Educational Progress; the National Geographic's *Geographic Literacy Survey*; the National Survey of Student Engagement; and the American Time Use Survey, Bureau of Labor Statistics.[89] These sources are only representative of the large number studies cited in each chapter.

What does he find in these reports about the present state of American youth? First, Bauerlein argues there has been a general decline in general knowledge despite the fact that youth spend more time in school. He blames this on ICT: "The Internet doesn't impart adult information; it crowds it out. Video games, cell phone, and blogs don't foster rightful citizenship. They hamper it."[90] Rather than accumulating general knowledge about arts, politics, history, geography, and science, youth spend most of their time outside of school using and consuming technologies. He reports the following findings of eight to 18 year olds' average daily personal use of media:

- Television: 3:04 hours
- Computer: 48 minutes online usage
- Magazine reading: 14 minutes
- Book reading: 23 minutes
- Play video games: 32 minutes console, 17 minutes hand held
- Prerecorded television: 14 minutes[91]

Youth primarily use ICT to contact friends, participate in social networks, and for gaming and shopping. Very little time is spent on using the computer to access different types of general information such as news. Youth demonstrate little skill in actually accessing and evaluating information on the Internet. One study found that only 1 percent of Google searches ever extend beyond the second page of search results. The Education Testing service, as reported by Bauerlein, found that youth in fact had little skill in searching and evaluating information found online. Most view online assignments as a matter of doing a simple Google search and then cutting and pasting from documents. A Pew Research report states that among college students seven of the top 20 websites they visited focused on clothes, four on entertainment events, and three on music, with other popular sites being video games and consumer electronics. Bauerlein concludes, "The Web is a consumer habitat, not an educational one. Digital-learning advocates might restrict one sphere of usage in a classroom or through homework, and parents might invest in educational games for their children, but whatever benefits the assignments and programs provide will dissipate in the many more hours students spend online alone."[92]

At the heart of the problem is reading and Bauerlein uses the terms "a-literacy" and "bibliophobia" to characterize the current generation's reading habits. Simply stated this generation reads less than previous generations as shown by a whole range of studies. A-literacy (knowing how to read, but choosing not to) Bauerlein claims sharply contrasts with previous generations. Even the 1960s generation, he points out, widely read favorite intellectuals such as Herbert Marcuse, Paul Goodman, and Beatnik writers. But this generation does not share common intellectual interests in any particular books or authors except for maybe the Harry Potter series. This generation, Bauerlein asserts, "wears anti-intellectualism on its sleeve, pronouncing book-reading an old-fashioned custom, and it snaps at people who rebuke them for it."[93] Bibliophobia refers to the present generation's supposed avoidance of lengthy books or ones that require concentration: "Bibliophobia is the syndrome. Technophiles cast the young media-savvy sensibility as open and flexible … But faced with 100 paper pages, the digital mind turns away. The bearers of e-literacy reject books the way eBay addicts reject bricks-and-mortar stores."[94]

Bauerlein is particularly critical of those promoting ICT as the panacea for schools. First, he cites one study that found that many students skilled in ICT had mixed feelings about using it in their classrooms. Second, when ICT is used in the classroom there is little proof that it actually improves educational achievement. Bauerlein lists a series of studies that reach this conclusion. Below is a summary list of these studies:

- Heritage Foundation analysis of National Assessment of Educational Progress found that students with weekly use of computer instruction did not do any better in reading.
- A 2004 analysis of the Programme for International Students Assessment (PISA) found that computer availability at home had a negative relationship to math and reading performance.
- The same analysis found computer availability in school was unrelated to performance in math and reading.
- A 2006 study of federal subsidies to public schools to provide Internet access found that investments in technology did not improve measured student outcome.
- A 2004 Texas program for providing schools with wireless technology had no effect on student achievement in reading and math.
- A 2004 study of ICT in Scotland's schools found no evidence of increased educational attainment.
- A 2007 evaluation of 132 schools using educational software where teachers were trained by the vendors found no difference in achievement as measured by tests as compared to students not using the software.[95]

Bauerlein accuses digital evangelists of youth worship. Since the 1960s, he argues, many commentators identified youth as the future hope for society. In the 1960s and 1970s, some people characterized youth as embodying new forms of social change linked to environmentalism and social justice. In the 21st century, writers like Prensky and Tapscott characterize youth as the generation leading the world into the use of ICT. But, as discussed before, Bauerlein considers this generation to be mainly technoconsumers without much wisdom but with plenty of ability to use ICT for social contacts, consumption, and entertainment. In this context, he argues, elders have abdicated their leadership based on wisdom to youth who act on consumer desires. "Few things are worse for adolescent minds," Bauerlein warns, "than overblown appraisals of their merits … The twenty-first-century teen, connected and multitasked, autonomous yet peer-mindful, marks no great leap forward in human intelligence, global thinking, or 'netizen'-ship."[96]

In summary, Bauerlein provides a counter argument to those claiming that the new generation harbors extraordinary abilities in using ICT and that ICT is increasing the generation's knowledge and skills. These contrasting arguments can be analyzed according to economic and social interests. Clearly, techno-evangelists like Prensky and Tapscott have an economic interest in lauding the value of ICT since their companies are selling these products. They also have a personal stake in justifying their arguments to the general public. Bauerlein has an economic interest as both a college professor of English and a receiver of royalties as a popular writer. Also, he is part of a network linked to the National Endowment for the Arts who are interested in promoting traditional liberal arts as necessary for passing on the wisdom of the ages.

Conclusion: The Brains and Minds of Digital Natives

In summary, many advocates of increased use of ICT in schools assert that the brains and minds of the present generation are altered through computer usage. Usually associated with a company reaping profits from ICT, these evangelists for the digital native push an educational agenda that includes progressive pedagogy, computer software, and games. Critics argue that there is little difference between the current and previous generations' use of ICT. Also, some members of the current generation are not well versed on computer usage. Others who frequently use ICT want to keep a separation between personal use and applications in the classroom.

There seems to be general agreement that brains change with computer usage particularly with constant multitasking. Critics claim that multitasking changes the brain to seek constantly shifting scenarios leading to symptoms of ADD and ADHD. Difficulty in concentrating is considered by some a result of computer multitasking. Advocates for more ICT in schools counter claims of ADD and lack of concentration by pointing out that these symptoms do not appear among game players who spend hours online. There are also concerns that parents are not giving their children their full attention as they constantly check their smart phones or hurry from their dinner tables to their work stations.

Social networking, according to those wanting schools to adapt to the digital native, results in desires for cooperative forms of learning. Others claim that social networking without nonverbal forms of communication may result in users feeling lonely even though they might be connecting to many people. Based on brain research, these claims include a concern about the lack of spontaneous interactions in machine mediated communications and a possible decline in empathy. There are also questions about online communities being real communities since it is easy to join and drop out and members may not establish emotional ties to other members because of the lack of face-to-face relations.

The most critical perspective on digital natives is that they are shallow and spend most of their online time shopping, playing games, and communicating with friends. Because heavy users of ICT show symptoms of ADD it is difficult for them to read long articles and books. These critics attribute a decline in reading books and long articles to ICT usage. They also provide data that the introduction of online instruction in schools has not raised achievement levels.

So what can we conclude from all these different claims? A common agreement is that ICT does affect the plasticity of the brain. However, more research and time, I would argue, is required to answer the following questions. Does this mean that heavy users show symptoms of ADD and ADHD? Is this the cause of the reported decline in reading among the current generation? Does online social networking result in feelings of loneliness?

In contrast, there are certain important conclusions that can be derived from current research. One is that digital natives do not have proficient skills at using the Internet to obtain and evaluate knowledge. If online instruction becomes the standard then instructional time would seem to be needed to increase their proficiency in using the Internet as a source of knowledge. Second, there is no proof that ICT actually increases educational achievement. Third, so-called digital natives primarily use ICT for shopping, games, and friends and not for increasing their store of general knowledge. And last, it would appear that those with an economic interest in selling ICT products are the ones claiming that the current generation needs and demands new forms of education utilizing social networking, games, and learning software along with progressive education methods of learning based on student interests, learning by doing, and cooperative learning. In the next chapter I will explore some of these themes by examining research on the relationship between ICT and social and civic education. Does online instruction increase student political and civic involvement?

6

POLITICAL EDUCATION AND LIBERATION TECHNOLOGY

How does ICT impact political and civic education? Will ICT provide opportunities for liberating political activities? At the heart of these questions is a world in which citizenship is made increasingly difficult to define with many people, called denizens, working or living in nations different from their birth places or where they hold legal citizenship. Among today's youth, according to sociologist Brain D. Loader, "citizenship identity appears to be more closely associated with development of individual preferences related to lifestyle and consumer politics."[1] There is also a concern, as explored in the previous chapter, about the decline of community or in this instance the decline of a civic community which serves to mobilize political activity. Does ICT contribute to a disaffection of youth from civic communities and political life? Can ICT provide a civic education that increases participation in the political life of a nation? Will ICT be a liberating technology for political activism by distributing information and connecting participants in political movements?

Discussions of ICT and civic education usually accept the existence of a sovereign state with defined geographical boundaries where citizenship is granted by birth within these boundaries or by some form of naturalization process. As a legal term, citizenship usually means that a person is subjected to the laws of a particular nation-state. Theoretically, the nation-state can have unlimited power over its citizens. However, as the nation-state evolved from the 18th century to the present, and its conceptual framework spread around the globe, citizens sought protection from the potential unlimited powers of the state by creating constitutions putting limits on government power.

The Internet creates a tension between the territorially bounded nation-state and the borderless world of social interaction in Cyberspace. Some people, as I will discuss, hope that ICT can counter the power of the nation-state and create an online system of global governance. Cyberlibertarians hope that the social connections of the Internet will create a new world of freedom and independence. But Cyberlibertarianism is countered by the growing efforts by nation-states to control access to and the content of the Internet. In *Networks and States: The Global Politics of Internet Governance*, Milton L. Mueller states, "The expectations and norms created by the early Internet were radically liberal in nature and gave new vitality to ideals of freedom of expression in politics and culture, and to concepts of freedom of exchange and open, competitive entry into information and communication markets in the economic sphere."[2]

Mueller declares himself an early Cyberlibertarian who worries about the lost potential for the Internet to be an "unfettered and borderless global communication" system.[3] He argues the four factors driving attempts to govern the Internet are protection of intellectual property rights, Cybersecurity, censorship of content, and Internet resources.[4] There is an increasing potential for the Internet to serve authoritarian governments and to create a new form of totalitarianism as citizen actions are monitored in Cyberspace. In *Access Controlled: The Shaping of Power, Rights, and Rule in Cyberspace*, Ronald Deibert, Director of the Munk Centre for International Studies, University of Toronto, and Rafal Rohozinski, co-principal investigator of the OpenNet Initiative and Information Warfare Monitor warn that Cyberspace is now an environment easily monitored by governments. "Today," they write, "with always-on devices that are fully connected to the Internet, and much of society's transactions mediated through information and communication technologies—including business, work, government, and play—cyberspace is not so much a distinct realm as it is the very environment we inhabit."[5] The Cyberspace environment is easier to monitor than the earthly environment.

Warning of the potential authoritarian uses of ICT, Evgeny Morozov, a Fellow at the Open Society Institute and former Yahoo! Fellow at the Institute for the Study of Diplomacy at Georgetown University, calls the Trinity of Authoritarianism to be propaganda, censorship, and surveillance.[6] In other words, authoritarian governments can use ICT to disseminate propaganda, censor Internet usage to control the spread of political ideas, and conduct close surveillance of its population's actions. Through control of ICT, governments can potentially restrict the political education of their populations and ensure conformity to government dictates.

ICT can be viewed as a tool for enhancing civic education and as an instrument for involving people in civic activities. Calls for citizenship education began in the 19th century as populations demanded more participation in controlling their governments. In reaction to these demands, nation-states introduced public education systems to attempt to control the future actions of their citizens by instilling patriotism and loyalty to the state. In addition, some nation-states wanted citizens to receive a public education that would ensure citizen participation in government and politics.

Thus citizenship education has two major functions. One is building nationalism and acceptance of state authority, with the most extreme forms exemplified by the educational systems of the former Soviet Union and North Korea.[7] The other civic education function focuses on political and civic engagement for social justice and protection from the potentially abusive authority of state officials. In the United States, the best example of this type of civic engagement is the civil rights movement of the 1950s and 1960s in which citizens demanded relief from state laws that discriminated against racial, cultural, and linguistic minorities.[8]

ICT can be used by nation-states to exercise authority over their populations and build loyalty to the state and its policies. ICT can also educate active citizens and enhance political activities to counter the potential authoritarian power of the nation-state. In this chapter I will begin with a discussion of the role of ICT in educating active citizens. Next I will discuss the potential role of ICT as a liberation technology designed to protect citizens against extreme state authority by spreading information and connecting dissidents. And last, I will consider the use of ICT to control its citizens through Internet propaganda, censorship, and surveillance.

ICT and Civic Education

Why is there a concern about the participation of youth in political activities? Can ICT increase student interest in civic activism? What are the most important factors motivating students to become politically active? Calling it a crisis in "modern democracy," a European Union sponsored study, "CIVICWEB: Young People, the Internet and Civic Participation," expresses concern about the decline in voting rates in local and national elections; the low level of citizens' interest in and knowledge about social and political affairs; and the lack of trust and confidence in politicians and in the political system.[9] The study reports a decline in civic cultures "and the processes on which they depend (the public sharing of information, the creation of community, the commitment to rational debate)."[10]

Is the decline in interest in politics and civil society a function of social class or other factors? The International Association for the Evaluation of Educational Achievement's 2010 "International Civic and Citizenship Education Study" of 38 countries (five in Asia, 26 in Europe, six in Latin America, and one in Australasia) concludes: "Student interest in politics and social issues appeared to be little affected by immigrant background or socioeconomic background (measured through parental occupational status), *but was associated with students' reports of parental interest in those issues* [author's emphasis].[11]

This is an important conclusion regarding the potential effects of ICT on students' political interests. Another group of academics also report that political use of the Internet is strongly dependent on students' prior political interests.[12] One study found that online civic interests replicate offline socioeconomic and gender differences in civic participation.[13] These are not surprising findings. If rich or poor families discuss politics at the family dinner table or other functions then their children's interest in the topic is likely to be stimulated. On the other hand, if there is little discussion in families about politics then their children may show little interest in the topic.

Similar results were reported for the United States in a 2011 study sponsored by the MacArthur Foundation and Center for Information and Research on Civic Learning and Education. This report, with the descriptive title "The Civic and Political Significance of Online Participatory Cultures among Youth Transitioning to Adulthood," concluded that the strongest predictors of online involvement in politics and civil society were parental political involvement, prior political interest, and the strength of the student's own political ideology. In other words, young people's use of the Internet for political and civil purposes involves a previous political interest related to parental influence.[14]

The relationship between family and youthful interest in politics suggests a limited effect of ICT on increasing youth's political participation. The European Union's CIVICWEB project concluded that "the internet can be a valuable tool for young people who are *already* engaged in civic and political activity."[15] The report warns policymakers that ICT *may not* be an effective means of engaging young people who are currently disengaged from politics and civic life. In other words, if young people's families are interested in politics and civic life then they will tend to be more interested than other youth and will be more likely to use the Internet for political and civic purposes.

The CIVICWEB study also found that the current generation of youth does not feel an obligation to inform themselves through news media about current political events. The minority of youth who are interested in political and civic activities "tend to favor protests of various kinds, political consumerism, 'lifestyle politics', and a focus on local or sectional issues—an approach which is sometimes called 'DIY' (do-it-yourself) politics."[16] This finding matches conclusions discussed in previous chapters about the use of the Internet by young people for purposes of consumerism and social relationships. For instance, "political consumerism" refers to purchasing products that are considered ethically produced such as not harmful to the environment or unnecessarily cruel to animals. "Lifestyle politics" refers to such things as gay and lesbian rights and gender equality. Missing from the interests of many of these youth is a concern about broader issues such as how the political structure and economic systems should be organized.

According to the CIVICWEB report there has been increasing hope that the Internet will stimulate political involvement by youth. The report describes how Internet usage might promote increased political and civic activities among youth through trying out new ideas, adopting different civic identities, and promoting political dialogue. Also, the Web is an egalitarian medium allowing all people access to political information and dialogue about political issues. It also allows equal access to political information from around the world.[17] However, the reality is that only youth who are already interested in political and civic issues use the Internet for these purposes.

The previously mentioned "The Civic and Political Significance of Online Participatory Cultures among Youth Transitioning to Adulthood" concluded that the Internet could be a gateway to political activities:

Drawing on two large panel studies, we find that youth engagement in nonpolitical online participatory cultures *may* serve as a gateway to participation in important aspects of civic and political life, including volunteering, community problem-solving, protest activities, and political voice [author's emphasis].[18]

The important qualification in this report is the word "may" regarding online participatory cultures leading to civic involvement. The large panel studies referred to in the above extract are the California Civic Survey of 5,505 junior- and senior-level high school students and the Mobilization, Change, and Political and Civic Engagement Project at the University of Chicago.

The report divides online participation into "politically driven," "interest-driven," and "friendship-driven." Obviously, politically driven online participation reflects political and civic involvement. Friendship-driven online activities, it was found, are not related to civic activity or political action. However, the study found that interest-driven online activities can be related to civic involvement. The authors compare interest-driven online activities to extracurricular activities in schools which some authors claim promote civic involvement. The report concludes:

We propose that online nonpolitical participatory activities can promote civic outcomes—just as offline extracurricular activities have been found to foster social capital by teaching skills, by developing a sense of agency and productive group norms, and by fostering an appreciation of the potential of collective action.[19]

The argument that participation in online communities promotes civic outcomes underlies the goals of using ICT in Northern Ireland schools to overcome the tensions between Catholics and Protestants. In 1921, 26 of Ireland's 32 counties were declared independent of Great Britain and formed the newly created Republic of Ireland. The other six counties remained part of Great Britain as Northern Ireland. Since that time there have been continuous tensions and violence in Northern Ireland between Catholics and Protestants. Reinforcing religious divisions is the segregation of Northern Ireland schools along denominational lines. Ninety-five percent of Northern Ireland's students attend either Protestant or Catholic schools, with the other 5 percent attending religiously integrated schools.[20]

A hope was that this religious divide and associated violence could be overcome through ICT linking Protestant and Catholic schools. In 1997, Northern Ireland launched a major program in education technology which became known as Classroom 2000 and later in 2001 as C2K. C2K ensures that ICT companies will profit from publicly supported schools. Called a "managed service," the government contracts and pays private companies to provide the infrastructure and hardware for e-learning to 1,224 schools. C2K service provided to schools 55,000 networked computers with broadband connections, 14,000 laptops for teacher use, and 200 centrally licensed educational software titles.[21]

Civic education is a key element in the ICT plan for Northern Ireland. The hope is that through the use of ICT the tensions and violence between Catholics and Protestants can be reduced and the population become more integrated despite a segregated school system. One element in this effort is a common curriculum exposing students to a shared knowledge. The common curriculum is a citizenship curriculum centered on Diversity and Inclusion, Human Rights and Responsibility, Equality and Social Justice, and Democracy and Active Participation. The overall goal of this curriculum is to ensure that despite religious differences Catholics and Protestants share a common culture and citizenship values.[22]

ICT is considered the key in the effort to reduce religious tensions and violence by linking schools in Northern Ireland, Great Britain, and the Republic of Ireland. The "Dissolving Boundaries" program initiated in 1999 started interschool work using video and computer conferencing. Small teams in each school worked with small teams in connected schools. Roger Austin writes that this work "has had a marked effect on the attitudes and skills of the pupils involved, in terms of an increased sense of self-esteem, improved communications skills and *in terms of their views about pupils on the other side of the border* [author's emphasis]."[23]

Can a common curriculum and cooperative school work using ICT overcome divisions in Northern Ireland? An important issue is whether connecting Catholic and Protestant students through ICT can create real social connections. This issue was discussed in previous chapters regarding social networking. Face-to-face and spontaneous interactions are *not* present in these interschool connections. Roger Austin considers this lack of spontaneity an advantage. He argues that asynchronous computer conferencing "is a particularly valuable medium for discussion of emotive issues ... [because] participants have time to reflect on what they want to say, can compose responses off-line, and discuss them with fellow pupils and with their teacher before posting them to make them 'live'."[24] But these virtual connections lacking spontaneity may not be enough to overcome centuries of religious antagonisms.

The 2011 founding of Facebook.com/yalaYL illustrates another attempt to use ICT to overcome violent religious and political differences. This Facebook site is designed for Palestinians and Israelis to learn about each other with the hopeful outcome of peace. Created by Uri Savir, the president of the Peres Center for Peace, the Facebook site brings together Palestinians, other Arabs, and Israelis in an effort to create understanding and peace between all groups. A friend of Savir, Salah al-Ayan, a Palestinian Authority official who is helping with the Facebook site, explained "Our goal is to start by talking about art and sports. Since Israelis and Palestinians don't meet face to face anymore, this is a virtual place to meet."[25]

In summary, there is little evidence that ICT fosters increased political and civil activity among students. If students come from a politically oriented family they are likely to use the Internet for political information and contacts. Otherwise, most students use the Internet for personal reasons some of which might lead, like extracurricular activities, to civic engagement. On the other hand, some scholars worry that participation in online communities might draw students away from civic involvement in their local communities which could ultimately undermine democracy.[26] A darker side of students' political use of the Internet, a theme that will be explored in more detail later in this chapter, is suggested by the European Union's CIVICWEB study: "Our research suggests that young people's civic and political participation and action, like that of adults, is not always viewed positively by figures of authority and those in positions of social power: in some cases it is even censored or punished."[27] Maybe ICT undermines attempts to educate engaged citizens.

Cyberlibertarianism and Liberation Technology

Cyberlibertarian dreams are challenged by the findings that the Internet is primarily a tool for those already interested in politics. Cyberlibertarians envision a world where ICT provides political freedom and maintains self-governing communities. In the 1990s, John Perry Barlow popularized the idea that the Internet would provide a new level of global freedom. During the 1990s, Barlow popularized his ideas in *Wired* magazine columns. Along with Lotus 1-2-3 founder Mitch Kapor and Sun Microsystems programmer John Gilmore, Barlow founded the Electronic Frontier Foundation to protect the freedom of Cyberspace from the intrusions of governments.[28] Currently, the Electronic Frontier Foundation pursues political and legal means to ensure freedom in Cyberspace. The Foundation's website states:

> From the Internet to the iPod, technologies are transforming our society and empowering us as speakers, citizens, creators, and consumers. When our *freedoms in the networked world come under attack, the Electronic Frontier Foundation (EFF) is the first line of defense* ... Blending the expertise of lawyers, policy analysts, activists, and technologists, EFF achieves significant victories on behalf of consumers and the general public. *EFF fights for freedom primarily in the courts, bringing and defending lawsuits* even when that means taking on the US government or large corporations. By mobilizing more than 61,000 concerned citizens through our Action Center, EFF beats back bad legislation. In addition to advising policymakers, EFF educates the press and public [author's emphasis].[29]

On February 8, 1996, Barlow released his now famous "A Declaration of the Independence of Cyberspace."[30] Modeled on the American Declaration of Independence, Barlow declared Cyberspace to be independent of the control of national governments. The manifesto opened: "Governments of the Industrial World, you weary giants of flesh and steel, I come from Cyberspace, the new home of Mind. On behalf of the future, I ask you of the past to leave us alone. You are not welcome among us. You have no sovereignty where we gather."[31]

Barlow declared Cyberspace to be an independent social space not existing within the territorial space of any government. Within Cyberspace, Barlow declared: "We are forming our own Social Contract. This governance will arise according to the conditions of our world, not yours [nation-states]."[32] This social contract would guarantee equality and freedom for those who enter Cyberspace:

> We are creating a world that all may enter without privilege or prejudice accorded by race, economic power, military force, or station of birth. We are creating a world where anyone, anywhere may express his or her beliefs, no matter how singular, without fear of being coerced into silence or conformity.[33]

A Declaration of the Independence of Cyberspace recognized that governments were attempting to limit and control Cyberspace. Calling it the "civilization of the Mind in Cyberspace," Barlow argued that virtual selves were immune to government sovereignty. In Cyberspace, he claimed, identities have no bodies and consequently are immune to physical punishment. He described Cyberspace as a world of transactions, relationships, and thought existing in a web of communication. "Ours is a world," the Declaration stated, "that is both everywhere and nowhere, but it is not where bodies live."[34]

Liberation technology, in contrast to Cyberlibertarianism, considers the impact on nation-states of the free flow of information and the existence of virtual communities. Within this framework, the free flow of information and the ability to establish virtual relationships will lead to the overthrow of autocratic governments and usher in a new era of global democracy. Consequently, liberation technology has two concerns. The first, similar to Cyberlibertarianism, is maintaining free and open access to information in Cyberspace. The second is using that freedom of information and social networking to spark liberation movements within nation-states.

In a 2004 article in the *Chronicle of Higher Education*, John Unsworth, Dean of the Graduate School of Library Information and Science at the University of Illinois at Urbana-Champaign and former president of the Association for Computers and the Humanities, declared liberation technology as the next wave in Cyberspace development.[35] With his background in library information and science, Unsworth stressed the importance of open source and open archives as creating a new era of ideological freedom. He quoted Thomas Jefferson that "ideas should freely spread from one to another over the globe."[36]

Exemplifying the liberation technology movement, according to Unsworth, was the 2000–2001 annual report of the Massachusetts Institute of Technology (MIT) in which the institution's president Charles Vest announced that MIT's Open-Courseware project would make materials used in its courses available for free online. Vest stated, "inherent to the Internet and the Web is a force for openness and opportunity that should be the bedrock of its use by universities."[37] In addition to MIT making course content available online there was a call for open software and information as part of what is called the Creative Commons.

The term "open source," according to the Open Source Initiative, was invented in 1998 to promote the free distribution of software and information. The Open Source Initiative's definition of the term includes the free distribution of software and making available a source code for downloading from the Internet without charge. Most importantly, open source material "must allow modifications and derived works, and must allow them to be distributed under the same terms as the license of the original software."[38] Open source material should be available to all people with no discrimination against individuals, groups of people, or fields of study. The development of Wikis, most notably Wikipedia, exemplifies open source material. The most widely used is TWiki which allows users to edit Wiki pages, add links, and track revisions.[39]

The major problem of providing free open source material on the Internet is existing copyright laws. In 2001, the Creative Commons was created to address this concern. In 2002, the organization began issuing free copyright licenses which allows free copying and redistribution of material along with the ability of users to modify the material.[40] The Creative Commons declares: "Our vision is nothing less than realizing the full potential of the Internet – universal access to research and education, full participation in culture – to drive a new era of development, growth, and productivity."[41] The vision of the Creative Commons is succinctly stated on its website and it reflects the general goal of the open source movement:

> The idea of universal access to research, education, and culture is made possible by the Internet, but our legal and social systems don't always allow that idea to be realized. Copyright was created long before the emergence of the Internet, and can make it hard to legally perform actions we take for granted on the network: copy, paste, edit source, and post to the Web. The default setting of copyright law requires all of these actions to have explicit permission, granted in advance, whether you're an artist, teacher, scientist, librarian, policymaker, or just a regular user. To achieve the vision of universal access, someone needed to provide a free, public, and standardized infrastructure that creates a balance between the reality of the Internet and the reality of copyright laws. That someone is Creative Commons.[42]

The political aspects of liberation technology assume that the free flow of information will promote more democratic societies. Larry Diamond, senior fellow at the Hoover Institution and the Freeman Sogli Institute for International Studies and director of Stanford University's Center on Democracy, Development and the Rule of Law, gives this political definition: "Liberation technology enables citizens to report news, expose wrongdoing, express opinions, mobilize protest, monitor elections, scrutinize government, deepen participation, and expand the horizons of freedom."[43] In addition, liberation technology allows for communication to spread word of impending demonstrations and other actions against authoritarian institutions. Cellphones, text messaging, YouTube, and Facebook played important roles in the 2004 Ukrainian Orange Revolution, the 2005 Cedar Revolution in Lebanon, the 2005 protests for women's voting rights in Kuwait, and Burma's Saffron Revolution.[44] In 2010 and 2011, liberation technology played an important role in the so-called Arab Spring in revolts in Egypt, Libya, Syria, and Tunisia. In 2011, Voice of America described the role of ICT during the Arab Spring:

> Six months ago, if someone told you that activists in the Middle East would use social media platforms to revolutionize – literally – the way information is used and disseminated, you probably would have been skeptical.
>
> Six months later, Twitter and Facebook have played a crucial role in providing disenfranchised Arab citizens with a space to pressure regimes to democratize power and increase transparency. The impact of social media in the Arab Spring is undeniable.
>
> But what about the use of crowdmaps? Similar to Twitter and Facebook, crowdmaps rely on user-generated videos, images, and reports; the difference is that information is verified and geo-plotted on online maps, usually by nonprofits or a trusted network of local citizens.[45]

In summary, political education is supposed to be aided by Cyberlibertarianism and liberation technology. The free flow of ideas and open source materials, it is believed, will stir revolt against authoritarian regimes by making government actions transparent and by exposing users to political ideas that might be in conflict with the dominant ideology of their governments. ICT can create virtual political communities that can be organized to revolt against oppressive regimes. Consequently, Cyberlibertarians and open source advocates want governments to not control Cyberspace. In this context, Cyberspace becomes a powerful political realm offering the promise of freedom and world peace.

Online Political Education and Censorship

Online political and civic education makes it possible to have greater control over the content and provides greater opportunities for political indoctrination. I argue that most governments do not provide a political and civic education that will lead to citizens revolting against their own governments. Any action against a government resulting from education in a government school would be unintended. In other words, governments are not in the habit of educating the population to overthrow them. As stated at the beginning of the chapter, most government schools are interested in educating populations who are loyal to the government and obedient to its laws.[46]

In face-to-face classrooms there is leeway for the teacher to interject some political comments and critiques that might balance the bias of government selected textbooks and curriculum. With online instruction there are few opportunities for spontaneous and critical comments by the teacher. If online instruction is based on national curriculum standards then political and civic education is standardized for all students. In fact, online instruction can ensure ideological management of students in the interest of the political power. As mentioned earlier in the chapter, political authorities are uneasy about civic education projects that might lead to youth protesting the actions of their governments.

Online instruction can be used to teach students nationalistic history and literature and how the government operates and its laws. However, it is difficult to achieve the level of emotional nationalism associated with group singing of national anthems and songs and the pledges of allegiance to national flags. Traditionally, group singing and pledges are used to create emotional attachment to symbols of the state such as a national flag.[47] Online instruction doesn't lend itself to building this type of emotional nationalism or patriotism. Maybe this could be achieved online with simulated patriotic exercises using avatars. But this seems unlikely to replace real group face-to-face contact while engaging in patriotic school activities.

China offers one example of online patriotic exercises. The Chinese government appoints "Internet Commentators" whose job is to secretly influence public opinion by participating in online chatrooms and other forums. In *Who Controls the Internet: Illusions of a Borderless World*, Jack Goldsmith and Tim Wu write that the use of the Internet by Chinese dissidents against the government has been replaced by "Internet support for a different ideology: Chinese nationalism, often laced with virulent anti-American or anti-Japanese sentiment."[48] For instance, in 2005 when the Japanese government approved a textbook that labeled Japanese troops that occupied China during World War II as "liberators," Chinese online chatrooms were used by Internet Commentators to generate crowd protests resulting in the storming of Japanese department stores and the chanting of anti-Japanese slogans.[49]

What about the ability of students to access Internet information to counter the nationalistic and politically controlling instruction of public schools? Certainly the dream of Cyberlibertarians and liberation technologists is for a global flow of free information to undermine the government propaganda both in and out of school.

However, the dream of a borderless Internet began to unravel in 2000 when Marc Knobel, a French Jew, was searching the web for Nazi memorabilia. Knobel was doing the search from Paris where French law banned trafficking in Nazi goods. A life-long fighter against Neo-Nazism, Knobel was shocked to find an American website at Yahoo.com selling a vast array of Nazi items ranging from SS daggers and arm bands to concentration camp photos which could be purchased from France. Knobel assumed that Yahoo would shut down the website after he complained. This had worked several years earlier when AOL shut down a website after he complained that it was a Nazi hate site.[50]

Yahoo's corporate head Jerry Yang was opposed to government restrictions on free speech on the Web. Ignored by Yahoo, Knobel brought suit in a French court claiming that Yahoo was violating French law against selling Nazi memorabilia. After becoming aware of suit, Jerry Yang warned that there would be terrible consequences if governments were allowed to control the content of the Internet.

What would happen to the borderless and uncensored Internet if every government were able to censor content based on their national laws?

Yang assumed that since Yahoo servers were in the United States French officials would have no jurisdiction. The director of MIT's Media Lab Nicholas Negroponte commented about the case, "It's not that laws aren't relevant, it's that the nation-state is not relevant. The Internet cannot be regulated."[51] The French courts took a different view of the matter and ruled that U.S. websites violated French law. Yahoo responded that the Internet was not organized around physical geography and it would be impossible to match content with legal requirements of a particular country. Then Cyril Houri announced the development of technology that would allow users to identify the geographical source of Internet content. Applied to this case it was discovered that the actual servers for France were located in Sweden and not the United States. The French court then appointed a panel to determine whether or not Houri's technology could be used to screen out French users from particular websites. The answer was yes!

The borderless Internet ended on November 20, 2000, when the French court ruled against Yahoo. The company announced that it would ignore the ruling. In turn, the court announced that it would seize Yahoo's assets in France. Yahoo agreed to remove the Nazi website. In addition, Yahoo announced that it would be using the geographical identification software to target advertising to a particular nationality. Adding to the growing acceptance by Yahoo and other Internet companies of the ability of governments to censor the Internet, Yahoo agreed to Chinese demands to filter Internet material considered by the government to be harmful to society. In 2002, Yahoo signed a Chinese government document titled *Public Pledge on Self-Discipline for the Chinese Internet Industry*.[52]

With the end of the borderless Internet and the development of Internet government censorship, the Internet could no longer be a driver of political change through the unfettered distribution of political ideas and information. As I will discuss, governments could now censor the Internet to ensure that their populations were not exposed to what they considered to be the wrong ideas. The inherent possibility of the Internet being a source of political education for freedom had ended.

Political Education and Censorship

Thus ICT makes it possible to provide more restricted and controlling forms of political and civic education through centralized control of the content of online instruction and through government censorship. Politically interested students, the ones most likely to use the Internet for political purposes, potentially confront a wall of censorship as they search for political websites and information. Internet censorship is monitored by the OpenNet Initiative in collaboration with the Citizen Lab at the Munk Center for international studies, University of Toronto; the Berkman Center for Internet and Society at Harvard University; and the SecDev

Group (Canada). This group has issued two major reports detailing how governments control the information available to their citizens through Web censorship: *Access Denied: The Practice and Policy of Global Internet Filtering* (2008) and *Access Controlled: The Shaping of Power, Rights and Rule in Cyberspace* (2010).[53]

As mentioned previously, Evgeny Morozov worries that ICT can be used to implement the Trinity of Authoritarianism: propaganda, censorship, and surveillance. He asserts that "policymakers are getting lost in the mists of cyber-utopianism, a quasi-religious belief in the power of the Internet to do supernatural things … Opening up closed societies and flushing them with democracy juice until they shed off their authoritarian skin."[54] The free flow of Internet information, he argues, threatens the exercise of state authority over the control of information. Consequently, governments are busily developing methods to counter Internet freedom.

Similar to the economic interests of ICT companies promoting online instruction, companies have found it very profitable to help governments and schools censor the Internet and to ensure the Trinity of Authoritarianism. In Chapter 3 I discussed China's attempted development of GreenDam software for censorship purposes. In another case, the American company Cisco was primarily responsible for creating China's so-called Great Firewall.[55] I recently watched a Cisco ad on television which showed a classroom in the United States connecting with Cisco technology to a classroom in China with students happily sharing greetings. While Cisco is selling the technology to schools to create intercultural understanding, it is also selling technology to maintain oppressive governments.

In China, Cisco's Gateway Router blocked Chinese citizens' access to websites that were on the Ministry of Public Security's "Access Control List."[56] Cisco's actions highlight both the rush by ICT companies to sell their wares no matter what the political implications might be and the potential impact on education. Similar to the Cisco TV ad its 2010 Annual Report is titled "Together We Are the Human Network."[57] Cisco designs, makes, and sells Internet Protocol (IP)-based networking products. Its networking products use digital video, social networking, and other forms of Internet collaboration. These networking products include the ability to censor network connections within countries as exemplified by China's Cisco Gateway Router and networks created within corporations. Cisco presents its work as a unified package designed to help both education and business:

> The network enhances every aspect of our lives. Our customers recognize this. Cisco is addressing this transition by unifying networking, computing, storage and software through a systems approach. This transforms the data center into a networked environment designed to deliver innovation in *business, IT, environment and education – all the ways we work, live, play and learn* [author's emphasis].[58]

Exemplifying corporate actions that ignore Internet censorship while selling educational products, Cisco CEO John Chambers at the January 2003 World Economic

Forum launched a Global Education Initiative. The initiative's goal is to use technology to reduce the gap between developed and developing countries. In June 2003, Cisco along with other partners to its Global Education Initiative launched the "Jordan Education Initiative" designed in part to create a global education model that could be replicated in other countries. According to Cisco, the Jordan Education Initiative serves as:

> a prototype for new partnerships in Egypt and the Indian state of Rajasthan. GEI [General Education Initiative] has a vision that extends beyond education to help accomplish the following objectives:

> - Eliminate poverty
> - Stimulate national economies
> - Improve health
> - Encourage environmental responsibility and social justice.[59]

Cisco's launch of its Jordan Initiative was done without any concern about Internet censorship. Jordan law requires that Internet Service Providers deny access to anyone who "violates public morals" and "endangers the public good." In addition, Jordan bans the publication of material against "national obligation ... and Arab-Islamic values" and material "bound to stir violence or inflame discord of any form among the citizens."[60] In 2010, it was reported that Jordan along with other countries of the Middle East "censored Websites containing content critical of governments and leaders, Websites that claim human rights violations and/or Websites of opposition groups."[61]

The language of Cisco's Global Education Initiative suggests that the company will work closely with local governments, including cooperating with efforts to repress free speech. The company's report *Equipping Every Learner for the 21st Century: An Action Plan for Educational Transformation* details its vision of cooperation between business and government in planning education:

> Accomplishing a successful educational transformation will require informed and impassioned leadership at every level, from government ministries through institutions of higher learning and school districts down to individual schools, teachers, and classrooms. It will also *require close partnerships among educators, government entities, and private sector participants*, all of whom have a compelling stake in educational improvement [author's emphasis].[62]

What will the partnership between Cisco and world governments mean for political education? Cisco appears to be willing to make money in education from any cooperative relationship with a government no matter how autocratic and willing to censor the Internet for political purposes. Cisco's educational money making extends around the globe including in the United States, Africa, and Asia.

Consequently, Cisco Global Education Initiative, besides selling and structuring online education, negates the Cyberlibertarian and liberation technology visions of the free flow of Internet information and connectivity undermining autocratic governments. Working with governments like Jordan and China, Cisco indirectly helps implement forms of political education designed to gain citizen acceptance of existing autocratic rule. Cisco's willingness to cooperate with authoritarian political systems in ideological management suggests that it would support any form of online instruction in countries like the United States even if the content of political education is centrally mandated and controlled and reflects particular political interests.

In Russia, state authorities have adopted a variety of methods for ensuring that all media including the Internet serve as the Trinity of Authoritarianism. Morozov argues that Russian officials have learned that the best method of censorship is to distract the population from political news to entertainment. Russia's experiment in Internet television, Russia.ru, provides apolitical entertainment while Russia's version of YouTube shows funny videos. This raises the question of whether or not the effect of the Web is the depoliticalization of society as users spend the majority of their time shopping and accessing entertainment sites. Morozov wonders, "Could it be that the vast online reservoirs of cheap entertainment are dampening the enthusiasm Russian youth might have for politics, thus preventing their radicalization?"[63]

Also, Russia controls and censors the Internet along with trying to distract youth from politics with entertainment. The previously mentioned monitoring of Internet filtering, *Access Controlled: The Shaping of Power, Rights, and Rule in Cyberspace*, contains a lengthy investigation of the Russian government's methods of information control which in recent years is guided by the Russian government's official *Doctrine of Information Security*. The doctrine declares that information, including media and Internet sources, is a national asset requiring government protection and policing: "the stability of the constitutional order, sovereignty, and the territorial integrity of Russian political, economic and social stability, the unconditional ensuring of legality, law and order, and the development of equal and mutually beneficial international cooperation."[64]

The OpenNet Initiative found the Russian government using three generations of controls over the Internet. The first generation blocks access to servers, domains, key words, and IP addresses. The second generation exercises "just in time" filters that deny access to immediate information such as ongoing demonstrations or election debates. This second generation of filters makes it possible for the government to deny their censoring actions. The second generation Internet controls require Internet sites to register with the government which then gives the government immediate power to shut down a site. The government uses a broad interpretation of defamation and slander laws to censor material critical of the government and allow the closing of websites during times of civil unrest. The third generation of controls focuses on "successfully competing with potential threats through effective counterinformation campaigns that overwhelm, discredit, or demoralize opponents ... [and actively] use ... surveillance and data mining as means to confuse and entrap opponents."[65] In this manner the Russian government is able to achieve Morozov's Trinity of Authoritarianism on the Internet through propaganda, censorship, and surveillance.

Online political education in Egypt provides a complicated example of government censorship and the use of ICT to foment anti-government demonstrations. Prior to 2011, the Egyptian government exercised legal power over media and the Internet for the purpose of maintaining social peace, public order, and national unity. In 2007, blogger Abdel Kareem Suleiman was sentenced to four years in prison for using his blog to insult the country's president and incite hatred towards Islam. The government required users of Internet cafés to register, including supplying their cellphone numbers, with the government for Internet identification numbers. The government used the cellphone numbers to track and monitor phone conversations of Internet users. In addition, the government had the power to tap all fixed lines and cellphones.[66]

In 2010 and 2011, anti-government protests erupted fueled by Facebook. In June 2010, a 28 year old businessman, Khaled Said, was arrested in an Alexandria Internet café and then beaten to death by police in the lobby of a residential building. Five days after the arrest an anonymous human rights activist—later identified as a Google executive—created a Facebook page called "We are all Khaled Said" on which cellphone photos of his battered face were posted.[67] By mid-June 130,000 people had joined the Facebook page. *New York Times* reporter Jennifer Preston wrote, "Mr. Said's death may be the starkest example yet of the special power of social networking tools like Facebook even—or especially—in a police state. The Facebook page set up around his death offered Egyptians a rare forum to bond over their outrage about government abuses."[68] A YouTube video was posted on June 11, 2010, called "We are all Khaled. Each one of us can be Khaled." From June 2010 to February 2011 an estimated 500,000 connections were made to the video which urged people to stand up against police brutality. Project coordinator for the OpenNet Initiative at Harvard's Berkman Center for the Internet and Society commented, "Prior to the murder of Khaled Said, there were blogs and YouTube videos that existed about police torture, but there wasn't a strong community around them. This case changed that."[69]

The Egyptian government responded by arresting Google executive Wael Ghonim on January 28, 2011, for being one of the people responsible for the Facebook and YouTube campaign against the government. Ghonim oversees marketing for Google in the Middle East and North Africa. Released on February 7, Ghonim quickly became a symbol of the new tech-savvy rebel. In a two hour television interview, Ghonim admitted creating the Facebook page "We are all Khaled."[70] How did Google respond to his arrest? Reflecting the doctrines of liberation technology, Eric Schmidt, the chief executive of Google, said the company was "very proud of Ghonim." Google sent a message from its Twitter account: "We're incredibly proud of you, @Ghonim, & of course will welcome you back when you're ready." Schmidt said that collaboration tools like Facebook "change the power dynamic between governments and citizens in some very interesting and unpredictable ways."[71]

For liberation technologists, the eventual overthrow of the Egyptian government confirmed their belief that ICT could be a source for undermining authoritarian governments. On the other hand, it would be considered a reason for governments, such as China, to increase their use of ICT for propaganda, censorship, and surveillance. In reaction to increasing government controls over ICT, the United States government announced on June 12, 2011, that it was deploying a "shadow" Internet and phone service that dissidents could use to overthrow repressive governments. The U.S. State Department is financing "stealth" wireless networks to enable dissidents to communicate outside of their governments. In what would prove to be an important new phase in Cyberwarfare, U.S. Secretary of State Hillary Rodham Clinton asserted, "We see more and more people around the globe using the Internet, mobile phones and other technologies to make their voices heard as they protest against injustice and seek to realize their aspirations."[72] In an e-mail response to a question on the "shadow" Internet, she wrote, "There is a historic opportunity to effect positive change, change America supports. So we're focused on helping them do that, on helping them talk to each other, to their communities, to their governments and to the world."[73]

In summary, political education is both hindered and aided by ICT. The new forms of media can politically educate a population, like Egypt, by spreading information and organizing government protests. In contrast, ICT can be used by governments to ensure a political education that serves the interests of the state through using ICT for propaganda, censorship, and surveillance. In addition, there is often self-selection by the population as to who participates in online political activities. As noted previously, the politically interested are the primary users of the Internet for political action and self-education. In the next section, I will discuss the Great Firewall of China which exemplifies the use of ICT for political control through the Trinity of Authoritarianism in ideological management.

The Great Firewall of China: Trinity of Authoritarianism

China exemplifies the use of the Internet for propaganda, censorship, and surveillance. Political education on China's Internet serves the world's largest number of users with 90 percent having access to broadband service. The OpenNet Initiative reports, "China has devoted extensive resources to building one of the largest and most sophisticated filtering systems in the world."[74] In addition, OpenNet asserts, the "Chinese government has undertaken to limit access to any content that might potentially undermine the state's control or social stability."[75]

China's government uses the Internet for propaganda purposes, the first of the Trinity of Authoritarianism. As mentioned previously, China uses "Internet Commentators" to broadcast pro-government opinion and information. Unofficially, these commentators are called the "Fifty Cent Party" referring to the supposed 50 cent per post received by over 280,000 Web commentators who guide online opinion. These commentators are recruited by the government. The original Web commentators were organized in 2005 at Nanjing University which provided work-study funds to students to post pro-Communist Party statements on an online forum. The government's Ministry of Culture has institutionalized the process by providing Internet Commentators with training, exams, and certificates. According to the OpenNet Initiative, "while the government continues to aggressively intervene in news media coverage, these Fifty Cent Party members are proliferating because the CCP [Chinese Communist Party] also has come to recognize the potential benefits of a public relations approach to online discourse."[76] Another source of propaganda is online news which Chinese Internet users now claim is their major source of news over television and newspapers. Online news is controlled and censored by China's Internet Network Information Center with supervision of all media under the control of the Propaganda Department of the CCP. Chinese news agencies can only cover specific events approved by the government.[77]

Censorship, the second of the Trinity of Authoritarianism, affects all media and online news and information. Content considered illegal on the Internet includes anything considered as endangering national security; any material that contradicts officially accepted political theory; information about illegal civil organizations; and notices and information about illegal gatherings that might threaten the social order.[78] Chinese officials also worry about Internet content that might undermine Chinese nationalism such as anything considered a distortion of Chinese culture and history, and negative statements about national heroes, the army, or the judiciary.[79]

Online surveillance, the third part of the Trinity of Authoritarianism, uses software designed to detect censored material and track online users. For example, TRS Information Technology provides content management to "90% of the ministries of the State Council, 80% of the provincial-level information centers of government departments or industry administration agencies, 50% of the newspaper press groups, 300 universities and colleges and many enterprises."[80] TRS proudly states on its website:

> TRS has become the NO.1 enterprise search technology provider in Chinese market and has been given the imagery as "Google in enterprise search field" by media. TRS has occupied the first position of Chinese content management software providers as well. TRS has experienced significant and consecutive revenue and profit growth for more than ten years since 1996 and has become one of the most successful core technology software developers with intellectual property rights.[81]

TRS provides a full text data base server that can store and retrieve structured and unstructured information. The system is capable of determining who is accessing information and the content of that information. According to TRS' website its software can monitor Internet text:

> TRS Text Taxonomy: Text taxonomy can classify the text without human interference to improve the efficiency of processing unstructured information resources. Text taxonomy classifies the text into categories based on contents and can be used to classify news, resume, email, office documents. It provides two ways to classify the text which are content based and rules based.[82]

Fang Binxing, the president of Beijing University of Posts and Telecommunications and "father of the Great Firewall," defends Internet censorship as necessary protection against Western governments and government protestors. During a 2011 commencement address, Fang warned about protestors: "They sit comfortably at home, thinking only of how, through their fingertips on a keyboard, they can bring chaos to China by taking advantage of the Internet's effectiveness as a multiplier."[83] Signs of reaction against the Great Firewall occurred when a student flung his shoes and eggs at Fang during a lecture on Internet security.[84]

Chinese surveillance and censorship methods are increasingly more sophisticated. Using lists of words that potentially indicate anti-government sentiment, software can be used to monitor cellphone conversations and Internet usage. For example in 2011, a Beijing business man reported that in a cellphone conversation with his fiancée he quoted in English from Hamlet, "The lady doth protest too much, methinks."[85] When he used the word "protest" again in a cellphone conversation with her, her phone was cut off. When he used Chinese to speak the same phrase on another phone it was cut off in midsentence.

The Chinese government insists that any foreign search engines or social media conform to Chinese censorship laws. In 2009, Li Changchun, a member of the Chinese Communist Party Politburo Standing Committee, did a Chinese language search for his name on Google's international website. The search produced critical comments about him. As a result, Li conducted a personal campaign against Google in China. Google moved its China office from Beijing to Hong Kong, which has more Internet freedom from censors.[86] The Chinese government has also blocked access to Facebook, Twitter, and YouTube.[87] In contrast to Google, Microsoft in 2011 reached agreement with the Chinese search engine Baidu to use its Bing search engine for English language searches. Microsoft agreed to conform to China's Internet censorship laws. A Microsoft spokeswoman explained the company's policies: "Microsoft respects and follows laws and regulations in every country where we run business. We operate in China in a manner that both respects local authority and culture and makes clear that we have differences of opinion with official content management policies."[88]

Responding to events in Egypt and other Middle Eastern countries, China consolidated its Internet regulation into a single new agency called the State Internet Information Office with officials drawn from the State Council Information Office,

Industry and Technology Office, and the Public Security Office. The official newspaper of the Communist Party of China, the *People's Daily*, in announcing the creation of the new office, criticized foreign complaints about Internet censorship. An unnamed official of the State Internet Office "refuted some foreign criticism of China's Internet regulations, saying the irresponsible remarks were deliberate and a groundless smear against China."[89] The same official claimed, "China's Internet regulations are in accordance with common international practice … governments of most countries monitor and regulate Internet content and deal with relevant violations of the law."[90] The official added regarding the economic value of the Internet, "These facts indicated that the strategies and policies on Internet development by the Communist Party of China Central Committee and the Chinese government are proved to be right and effective."[91]

In summary, China's Great Firewall fulfills the Trinity of Authoritarianism on the Internet through propaganda, censorship, and surveillance. The dreams of Cyberlibertarians and liberation technologists about spreading free information and undermining authoritarian governments are blocked by the Great Firewall. Rather than being an engine of freedom, the Internet has become a means for building nationalism, spreading propaganda, censoring ideas, and surveillance. What does this mean for the political education of Chinese youth? Within schools and on the Internet, Chinese youth will learn to defend the Chinese Communist Party and its political theories and the actions of the Chinese government.

Conclusion: Liberation or the Trinity of Authoritarianism

What is the effect of the Internet on political education? In schools online instruction in politics and civics provides the government with a clearly controlled form of ideological management. Free of any comments or criticisms by classroom teachers, the content of online political and civic education can be more tightly bound to government standards and curriculum goals. Most governments do not want their schools to teach political ideas that will lead to the government's overthrow or social unrest. The goal of most government political education is a loyal citizenry that is obedient to the law and emotionally attached to symbols of the state. One problem in achieving this goal through online instruction is the lost emotional and social feelings of group singing of national songs, group patriotic exercises such as marches, and group pledges of allegiance to symbols of the state.

Does the Internet by itself provide a political education? As I discussed, Cyberlibertarians and liberation technologists believe that the free flow of information will undermine authoritarian governments. However, studies of Internet usage by youth show that only those youth with a prior interest in politics actually use the Internet for political reasons. The Internet does not appear to be a solution for declining voter participation rates and the apparent alienation of youth from their political leaders. When youth do use the Internet for political purposes it is primarily related to issues of ethical consumption and lifestyle politics. Some researchers have suggested that "interest-driven" Internet usage may serve the same function as extracurricular school activities by being a gateway to civic involvement. There are efforts to use ICT to overcome religious and political divisions such as in Northern Ireland and in Israel and Palestine. Also, social media in situations like Egypt proved effective in organizing and spreading news of political activities and demonstrations and bringing down an authoritarian government.

The Internet can be a source of political education based on the Trinity of Authoritarianism as exemplified by the examples of Russia and China. Private companies are rushing to supply governments with tools to use the Internet for disseminating propaganda and maintaining surveillance of their populations. Ideological management is achieved through Internet censorship and control of online news. China's Fifty Cent Party demonstrates how governments can organize Internet participants to post nationalistic and pro-government messages. Combined with a nationalistic school curriculum, Internet propaganda and censorship are powerful tools for ensuring the continuation of authoritarian governments.

Supposedly Russia has discovered the importance of distracting youth from politics by emphasizing Internet usage for entertainment. But is Russia just an example of a worldwide phenomenon of youth being distracted from politics by entertainment and consumption? As noted in this and previous chapters, children and youth primarily use the Internet for shopping, social messaging, and entertainment including games. Maybe thoughts of shopping and text messaging are crowding out thoughts of social justice and how to improve political and economic systems.

7

SCHOOLS OF TOMORROW

The Effect of Technological Evolution

How will ICT affect the future structure and content of education? It is impossible to answer this question with any degree of certainty. Predicting the future is hard. But it is possible to explore the range of possibilities. For instance, the actual structure of schools may change as technology allows for new organizational forms. An influential factor in determining structural change is educational consumer patterns which may be determined by family wealth. One promise of ICT is equality of educational opportunity where everyone will have online access to the same quality education. However, it could be that wealthier families will buy their children an education that is quite different from that which is affordable to middle and low income groups. The current pattern suggests more online instruction for middle and low income families and more face-to-face education for higher income families. But, as I will discuss, this potential income divide is complicated by the fact that some parents utilize online home instruction as an alternative to attending a school. Also, some governments may utilize online instruction to reduce educational costs.

What will influence the evolution of educational technology? As I discuss in this chapter, technology seems to follow an evolutionary path, with new technology being dependent for its discovery and development on previous technology. The actual direction of technological evolution is difficult to predict since there are so many variables pushing technological development down different paths. As discussed in previous chapters, one variable is consumer patterns. What educational technology will educational authorities be willing to buy? What will be the consumer patterns of parents and students? There is also the factor of human resistance to technological advances. Some people may hate the idea of learning online in contrast to the social interaction of face-to-face classroom instruction. Others might love online instruction because it frees them from the classroom. Also as data mining is increasingly being used in schools, teachers and principals may demonstrate different forms of resistance. The most recent forms of resistance involve teachers and principals colluding in changing student answer sheets so that results in their classes and schools appear more favorable on data sheets processed by government agencies. "Garbage in, garbage out" is the central problem with educational systems that depend on data mining for strategic planning and evaluation.

Will the results of ICT be increased educational control or liberation? Another variable influencing the direction of educational technology, as discussed in the previous chapter, is whether governments or other educational authorities want to use online instruction for purposes of ideological control or as a means of increasing the freedom to learn a variety of ideologies. This chapter will explore these possibilities.

Schools of Tomorrow

Schools of Tomorrow is the title of John and Evelyn Dewey's 1915 review of progressive schools that promised to guide the future of education.[1] They considered the promise of progressive educational models to be equal educational opportunity. *Schools of Tomorrow* ends on the hopeful note:

> The democracy which proclaims equality of opportunity as its ideal requires an education in which learning and social application, ideas and practice, work and recognition of the meaning of what is done, are united from the beginning and for all. Schools such as we have discussed in this book ... are showing how the ideal of equal opportunity for all is transmuted into reality.[2]

Reflecting the same concern about equality of educational opportunity but with a different meaning, the Organization for Economic Development and Cooperation (OECD) launched its Schooling for Tomorrow project in 1997. Since that time, the project has issued a number of reports including ones emphasizing different possible scenarios for future schools. In the project's 2006 report *Schooling for Tomorrow: Think Scenarios, Rethink Education*, the researchers, like the Deweys, also stress the importance of equality of educational opportunity but from an entirely different perspective. For the Deweys, equality of educational opportunity meant a holistic education designed to prepare students to understand how society functions and how to use what they learn to participate in social change. Or, as the Deweys state, "learning and social application, ideas and practice, work and recognition of the meaning of what is done, are united from the beginning and for all."[3]

In contrast, OECD's Schooling for Tomorrow project emphasizes equality of educational opportunity to prepare students for the global workforce. Missing in OECD's definition is the Deweyian emphasis on preparing students to participate in democratic social change. The primary thrust of OECD's school scenarios is preparation for an information society. While the Deweys saw the socialization of students in progressive schools as preparation for active citizenship, the OECD project assigns media the socialization task: "In the information era, the job of socialization is largely accomplished by the media. The first signs of this functionality of the media came when families huddled around their radios ... ; today, the media beam American culture worldwide."[4] It could be argued that media in contrast to progressive schooling socializes for a world of shopping and entertainment.

There is another important difference in the meaning of equal education from the earlier perspective of the Deweys which stressed equal preparation by progressive educational methods. In the OECD definition of equality of education or as they call it "equity," equal education implies a different education for each student based on their talents and needs. OECD summarizes the principles that "will guide us going forward":

- First, there is equity as the equal right to life, liberty, and the pursuit of happiness which, in the information age, demands an end to ignorance.
- Second, in this information era, equity calls for *differences that make a difference*, not just a uniform spread of the same standardized inputs.
- Third, market mechanisms must supplement down-from-the-top bureaucracy when it comes to allocating different resources to different local needs.
- Fourth, while education is a local responsibility, central governments have a job to do to make sure that urban districts have the funds they need to level up.[5]

This conceptualization of equality allows for differentiated instruction based on the future place of the student in the global job market. OECD officials believe this can best be carried out through market competition rather than through an educational bureaucracy. This idea is in marked contrast to the era in which the Deweys were writing when government bureaucracy was considered key to clean government, and progressive education emphasized socialization in school for a cooperative society rather than one based on market competition. Whereas the models in the Deweys' *Schools of Tomorrow* emphasized the importance of schools operating as cooperative communities, OECD stresses the importance of the central government regulating the management of local schools.

While the progressive schools described by the Deweys were designed to empower graduates to participate in making a better world, OECD scenarios are based on the objective of preparing students for different work in a globalized information society. In this framework, it would be fair to say that OECD objectives may lend themselves to preparing students to be "servants of power" rather than "empowered citizens." Of course, the goals of schooling do not determine all of the future actions of students since, as claimed by OECD, today's socialization is primarily a function of media.

Schooling for Tomorrow: Bureaucratic School Systems and Teacher Exodus

What are the scenarios suggested by the OECD project Schooling for Tomorrow? One scenario, obviously not supported by the project, is the continuation of existing bureaucratic schools systems which they characterize as having centralized curriculum control and assessment. In this bureaucratic model, it is asserted, "The use of ICT continues without changing schools' main organizational structures."[6]

The second scenario involves attempting to maintain this bureaucratic model in the face of "a major crisis of teacher shortages ... triggered by a rapidly ageing profession, exacerbated by low teacher morale and buoyant opportunities in more attractive graduate jobs."[7] It is asserted that this situation could lead to meltdown of the educational system. However, the teacher shortage could lead to greater use of ICT to compensate for the added cost of trying to pay and attract new teachers. In this scenario, ICT supplants the work of teachers because of teacher shortages and costs without creating any innovation in school organization.

Schooling for Tomorrow: Re-schooling and Schools as Social Centers

The third scenario is called "Re-schooling: Schools as Core Social Centers" which reflects part of the Deweyian progressive tradition of making schools social centers. However, the emphasis is not on the progressive goal of empowered citizens but on being "the most effective bulwark against social, family and community fragmentation."[8] Originally, Dewey argued that schools should be social centers for community life so that they could "interpret to [the worker] the intellectual and social meaning of the work in which he is engaged: that is, must reveal its relations to the life and work of the world."[9] In other words, Dewey saw schools as social centers integrating work, community life, and education to give students a holistic understanding of the world in contrast to OECD simply wanting to end social fragmentation.

ICT is a key element of the re-schooling scenario: "ICTs are part of the structure and are used extensively for peer-to-peer and cross-border networking."[10] In this model, the school becomes a center for the entire local community, providing learning opportunities for students and facilities for community organizations. The social networking capabilities of ICT are used to link students with each other, the local community, and the world. This scenario could arise, according to OECD researchers, if families, work, communities, and religious institutions fail to provide the social capital needed to maintain social cohesion.

Below is my model of the integration of ICT into a school functioning as a social center.

In Figure 7.1, the school as a social center provides spaces for both student learning and community activities. The model completely changes traditional school organization with students being divided into separate classes by age. One section of school center contains computers where students of any age can learn through online instruction. There are no classrooms. Students would enter the social center and at their own volition or at a set time go to the computer center and access their assigned online instruction materials. The teacher functions as a consultant helping

School as Social Center

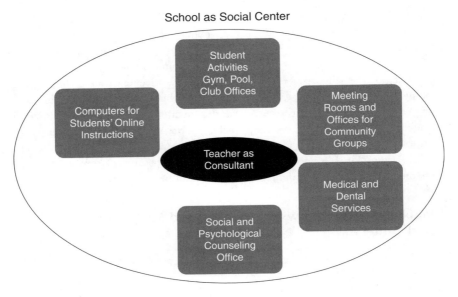

FIGURE 7.1

students with online instruction problems and other social and psychological issues. The school center provides meeting rooms and offices to community groups along with medical, dental, social, and psychological services. The teacher would also help with any organizational problems faced by community groups. There is also a section of the school center that provides a gym, pool, and club offices for students which could be used at any time by students or at specific times.

In this model students and community members cross paths with the possibility of face-to-face interchange. Medical, dental, social, and psychological services might be provided only for students or they could, in the spirit of building a sense of community, be provided to all community members. ICT would contribute to community building through social networking. A central responsibility of the teacher-consultant would be to ensure integration of students and community members and building a sense of community cooperation.

Schooling for Tomorrow: Re-schooling and Schools as Focused Learning Organizations

In contrast to schools as social centers, schools are operating as focused learning organizations with a flat hierarchy utilizing teams and diverse sources of expertise to achieve primarily knowledge goals. The schools work closely with parents and business. In carrying out the mission of education for global employment there is a "Focus on new knowledge in teaching and learning; strong links with knowledge-based industries; investments in educational R&D."[11] In this re-schooled organization,

ICT is used extensively alongside other learning media. In addition, these schools would use "ICT for communication and networking and as a tool for learning."[12]

Traditional age-graded classrooms would disappear in favor of teams of students of mixed ages and backgrounds. This organization could be done in large or small rooms equipped with ICT. The stated goal of this re-schooled institution is mixing "students variously by age, grade, and ability; links among schools, tertiary education, enterprises (local, national, international)."[13] This would be possible using ICT for communication and networking. Students would use national and international networks for sharing and acquiring knowledge.

So the OECD re-schooling scenarios change the traditional school organization of buildings divided into age-graded classrooms. In both scenarios ICT makes it possible to abandon age-graded classrooms for computer centers where students can access individualized learning programs. In both re-schooled institutions ICT links students to other students and the broader community and to knowledge resources. The major difference between the two re-schooled institutions is that one is focused on building social ties to the community and the other is focused on team-oriented learning.

Schooling for Tomorrow: Deschooling

The deschooling concept originated in the work of Ivan Illich and was popularized in his 1971 book *De-Schooling Society*.[14] Simply stated Illich's concept of deschooling abandons the traditional school with its age-graded classrooms, record keeping, and diploma system. In contrast, the OECD deschooling model also abandons the traditional school but with ICT carrying on traditional school record keeping. The reason for the difference is tied to the goal of ICT. Illich wanted to free learning from authoritarian institutions, while OECD's deschooling scenario would provide another means for educating global workers.

Illich advocated deschooling because he came to believe that schools were central institutions for justifying social class differences and creating dependence on technology and expertise. He argued that schools serve the function of translating economic differences into differences in schooling. One justification for universal schooling was the promise that it would serve as a ladder for upward mobility for the poor. But in reality what happens, Illich argued, is that family income determines the quality and amount of education received by students. Students from rich families attend better schools and receive more years of education than children from low income families. In addition, schools educate people to believe they are fair and just institutions. The poor, according to Illich, are told that school provides an equal opportunity for all people to improve themselves economically while at the same time schools convince students that they are fair and benign institutions. Consequently, when children of the poor do not advance economically and do not experience social mobility as a consequence of their education, they blame themselves for failing to achieve in school. If children believe in the goodness of schools, then they accept the social position the schools prepare them for as right and just. The myth of schooling, Illich argued, leads the poor to accept their poverty as their position in life. The traditional teacher–student relationship, Illich argues, teaches students to depend on expertise (the teacher) before acting. This relationship reinforces the patterns of dependency of modern society. People are taught not to act until they are told the correct way to act by some expert. Rather than believing in their own power to make choices, people are taught they should make choices only after consulting and paying experts.[15]

When I worked with Ivan Illich in 1969 and 1970 it was prior to the popularization of the Internet and development of the Web. I mention this because I think current ICT developments would have influenced his deschooling model. For instance, one of the things that we discussed was the creation of an information or learning center where people could go to either teach or learn. To avoid the social class consequences of the traditional school, Illich would not have this information center maintain records, grade students, or issue diplomas.

People who wanted to teach could offer courses through the information center. There would be no requirement of teacher certification to offer courses. Teachers would be paid directly by their students—one possibility that was discussed was that all children at birth would receive a government-funded educational credit card which could be used to purchase instruction throughout the person's life. People wanting to learn a particular subject or skill would register at the information center for courses.

The liberation aspect of Illich's deschooling model involved freeing learning from the curriculum requirements of governments. It would also undercut any attempts by government to use education for political indoctrination and nationalism. The political influence of business and other powerful interest groups on the content of instruction would be eliminated. Free of ideological management by government and business, learners would supposedly use knowledge to advance their own interests rather than the interests of the most powerful.

One wonders what path Illich's reasoning would have followed if the Internet and Web were widespread when he made his initial proposals. The OECD deschooling scenario envisions the end of traditional schooling and its replacement with learning networks. Similar to Illich, this OECD scenario envisions a reduction of existing governance and accountability systems. In the words of the OECD project researchers:

> This radical, perhaps anarchic, scenario would see the replacement of school systems with universal networking instead. The abandonment of the schools might be driven by public dissatisfaction with available schools and the widespread access to powerful new learning media. As government involvement decreases, parents and students assume more responsibility for education.[16]

With education occurring through interlocking learning networks, authority becomes widely diffused. Regarding teachers in this deschooling scenario: "There is no longer reliance on particular professionals called 'teachers': the demarcations between teacher and student, parent and teacher, education and community, break down. New learning professionals emerge, whether employed locally to teach or act as consultants."[17] Like Illich, the OECD scenario envisions the disappearance of classrooms to be replaced by different types of settings. There would be a blurring "of the boundaries between teacher and student, parent and teacher, education and community."[18]

OECD emphasizes the following in its deschooling scenario:

- Traditional curriculum structures decline as school systems are dismantled; new values and attitudes are key.
- The schools' demise also brings new arrangements for child and youth care, through e.g., sports, cultural activities, and community groups.
- Emphasis on the use of ICT for information, guidance, and marketing, and on new ways to certify competence.
- Possibility for inequalities between those operating within the network society and those left outside.[19]

With ICT anyone can learn at any time and any place. Informal educational settings can be utilized including homes, voluntarily organized groups, and individual settings wherever access to the Internet is available. Deschooling would stimulate the production of educational software including edutainment.

The educational experiences of my grandson Max illustrate this form of deschooling. When a student in a public school pulled a knife on him his mother began home schooling him. A local home schooling cooperative hired university students to provide courses that were quite different than those offered in the local public schools. Max then won an all-expense paid fellowship to travel to Japan and live with a Japanese family and attend a local school. His primary interest was learning Japanese language and culture. He maintained contact with home and friends through social networking. Through his contact with other foreign students in Japan he became part of an international network of learners. After returning to the United States, he decided that he would complete high school solely through online instruction utilizing courses offered by public and for-profit websites. Shortly after returning from Japan, he traveled to France to stay with a friend he met in Japan. While in France he studied for the SAT college entrance exam by taking an online course. On returning to the United States he enrolled in a variety of online courses to fulfill college entrance exams. Now his schooling can take place anywhere—at home, in coffee shops, in public spaces with Wi-Fi, and wherever he travels and with whomever he visits. He is now part of a global learning network.

Deschooling: Extending the Market Model

Deschooling lends itself to an educational system based on consumer choice. The idea of an education system based on consumer choice in a free market appeared in the 1950s in the work of economist Friedrich Hayek who in his 1944 book *The Road to Serfdom* argued that governments make decisions based on the interests of their bureaucracies rather than in the public interest.[20] Hayek, an Austrian economist and Nobel Prize winner, moved to the United States to teach at the University of Chicago from 1950 to 1962. Hayek influenced a number of American economists, including Milton Friedman, who first proposed school vouchers.[21] Hayek's ideas suggest that public schools operate in the interest of educational bureaucrats and teachers and not in the interest of students or parents. To return power to the public, Hayek argued for turning over government services to the competition of the marketplace where the public could wield power through their consumer choices. In this framework, for schools to serve parents and students they must have a choice as to which school to attend.

Essentially Hayek's argument makes the consumer supreme. "In this scenario," OECD researchers write, "education takes on market characteristics and choice becomes prominent. This is triggered by dissatisfied 'strategic consumers' and by government authorities who encourage diversification and a reduction of their own involvement in schooling."[22]

In the OECD market scenario public schools continue to exist alongside private and for-profit educational systems. Market diversity supposedly creates comparable diversity in teaching careers, including a growing international market for teachers. ICT becomes "powerful and indispensable" in all educational institutions and particularly for those students who work on their own or are home schooled.[23] This scenario includes new accreditation arrangements including a major role for international agencies. It also sees government agencies playing a role in providing information to help consumers make wise educational choices.

Unlike Hayek's desire to restrict government influence in the consumer market, OECD's scenario sees government as contributing to market choices:

> Reduced public-sector involvement in education does not necessarily mean small government – the market model could expand because of different not less government activity. It could decide to radically change funding structures, incentives and regulation, while setting the rules for the "learning market", overseeing quality assurance, and managing a potentially painful transition.[24]

Funding methods are important in this consumer model of schooling. Illich retained a financial role for government including the possible issuance of educational credit cards. In the OECD scenario is the startling statement: "Inequality tolerated; perhaps greater homogeneity of learner groups."[25] This statement suggests that access to learning opportunities would reflect differences in family income.

In summary, ICT plays a variety of roles in these different OECD scenarios. A continuation of bureaucratic school systems might result in greater reliance on online instruction in schools to ease the cost of teachers. The traditional school disappears or becomes part of an alternative educational system in other OECD scenarios with ICT playing a strategic role. In the re-schooling social center scenario, ICT provides the main instruction and serves to network students with each other, the community, and the world. The traditional role of the classroom teacher is replaced with social center counselors who help students with their online instruction and coordinate access to other functions of the social center such as medical, dental, and psychological services, and community meeting spaces. In the re-schooling focused learning organizations scenario, ICT plays a crucial role in networking students and providing access to online instruction. In this scenario, the traditional age-graded classroom disappears to be replaced by teams of learners and teachers who use ICT for international social networking and access to knowledge. Teachers in this model work in teams coordinating student learning and helping with access to online learning.

The rebirth of Illich's deschooling scenario provides the most radical alternative to the traditional school by allowing students to learn online any place and at any time. Professional teachers are replaced by online instructional packages or function as independent professionals hired by students or parents. Deschooling promises, but may not deliver, freedom from political decisions about what knowledge is most worth learning and the importance of nationalistic and patriotic instruction. ICT could serve a similar function in the extended market scenario. Consumers in the extended market scenario would be able to choose online instruction from public and for-profit providers along with attendance at public or for-profit schools.

Global Education Scenario: Avenues: The World School and the Florida Virtual Global School

In this section I explore two scenarios for global education. One scenario is a school designed for the global elite called Avenues: The World School, while the other is the Florida Virtual Global School. The Florida Virtual Global School is an offering of the Florida Virtual School discussed in Chapter 3. The reader may remember from Chapter 3 about how courses from Florida's Virtual School were substituted for classes without teachers in Florida's public schools. Avenues: The World School serves a global elite while the Florida Virtual Global School serves a more general population. The school being designed for the global elite uses ICT as an educational tool while the Florida Virtual Global School is completely online. It is not my intention to make judgments about the quality of these two schools but to simply offer them as alternative visions of a global education.

Are upper income families rushing to provide their children with primarily online instruction rather than just using ICT to enhance their children's learning in traditional classrooms? One answer might be found in parental response to plans for the for-profit Avenues: The World School opening in September 2012 which *New York Times* reporter Jenny Anderson calls "The Best School $75 Million Can Buy."[26] The school has a projected tuition cost of $40,000. Its organization and curriculum are planned to meet the needs of upper income global denizens whose work requires them to move their families around the globe. The school plans envision covering all grade levels from early learning through secondary school. The school was initiated by Chris Whittle, an educational entrepreneur who was founder of EdisonLearning, Inc. and a person with a great deal of experience in what makes for-profit education work.

Avenues: The World School does appeal to some upper income families, as testified by the 1,200 families who applied for early admission a year before the school was actually opened. Adding to the school's credentials is the reputation of its co-leader, Robert Matoon, who has run two other schools serving the elite—Phillips Exeter Academy and Hotchkiss School. Co-founder Benno Schmidt, former president of Yale University and partner at Edison, adds another prestigious name to the list of those involved in Avenues.[27]

Given the school's globetrotting parents you would expect online instruction to be high on their list of priorities. But this turns out not to be true. What appeals to upper income families wanting to send their children to Avenues? Students will learn bilingually with half the instruction in Spanish or Mandarin from nursery school through fourth grade. A goal, as stated by the school, "is to have every graduate achieve real fluency in a second language by graduation. For many people around the globe, this degree of language fluency is taken for granted. For students in the United States, it is much less common."[28]

Central to the curriculum is a World Course of global studies offered at every level of instruction with actual face-to-face world contacts. The World Course of global studies will utilize global teams of experts directed by Fernando M. Reimers, Ford Foundation Professor of International Education and Director of the International Education Policy Program at the Harvard Graduate School of Education. The course will infuse global topics in the study of "demography, environmental sustainability, world geography, economic trade, world religions and more."[29] Face-to-face global networking will be achieved through a planned 20 schools in cities around the globe. It is envisioned that:

> Once realized, this system will allow fluid exchanges between campuses of students and teachers, as well as a full range of interactive collaborations. Experiences ranging from multi-week exposure trips to semester exchanges will be offered, and in the course of their time at Avenues, students here and abroad will have the opportunity to study on five continents. No other system of schools currently offers such opportunities.[30]

New York Times reporter Jenny Anderson offers this vision of the global networking of the school's students through its other campuses: "If Mom and Dad move to London, little Mateo doesn't have to find a new school, or maybe even miss any class. When Sophia is in middle school, she can spend her summers in Shanghai, and when she's in high school, she can globe-trot by semester."[31] Face-to-face contact is the key to global networking at Avenues: "In the Upper School, students will begin to take full control of their learning environment, which extends well beyond the school building itself. In addition to taking advantage of Avenues' partnerships in the surrounding community, students will have the opportunity to travel extensively to multiple countries during the summer."[32]

Compare this globetrotting curriculum and face-to-face contacts to the Florida Virtual Global School operated by the publicly funded Florida Virtual School. The school is open to non-residents of Florida and promises students that they will be joining a global network. The school advertises: "Enroll your students today in a school that is also a global community. Our complete middle and high school online curriculum is accessed by students around the world."[33] The promise of global contact is through the online Socratic Café where the "Global School allows students to have many opportunities to collaborate with each other all over the world."[34]

A for-profit company 360Ed, Inc. provides the school's global services. On January 14, 2009, 360Ed, Inc. issued this descriptive announcement of its relationship to the Florida Virtual School. The announcement indicates the size and extent of the school's operations:

> 360Ed, Inc. announces that it has agreed to be a Global Service Channel Partner for the Florida Virtual School. The Florida Virtual School is the nation's largest state-led virtual K–12 education provider with over 100,000 enrollments annually. 360Ed will partner on the sales and service of over 90 courses in 30 states, including the District of Columbia and international clients.[35]

The involvement of 360Ed highlights the public-private relations confronting government schools as compared to the more independent and for-profit Avenues: The World School. 360Ed is a software company focused on edutainment through the production of learning games, most notably *Conspiracy Code*, and the Learning Management Environment Spark. *Conspiracy Code* is described by the company: "In this, the first game in the series, students will learn a full course of American History as they control two young spies on a fast-paced adventure to unravel a vast conspiracy."[36] Spark is described as "cross-platform compatibility software that uses the power of social networking, educational games, and mobility to engage students in learning content and developing critical thinking skills."[37] McGraw-Hill publishers partnered with 360Ed in the development of Spark and in 2011 360Ed proudly announced the launching of Spark: "Spark is a suite of online courses that provides access to McGraw-Hill content in a compelling and connected framework. It may be the best example of what online 21st century education is supposed to be about."[38]

Unlike Avenues, the Florida Virtual Global School lacks a theme like the Avenues' World Course running through its online curriculum. The Florida Virtual Global School relies on social networking media and an instructional staff located across the country to achieve a sense of being part of a global community: "Our staff goes above and beyond to involve students in engaging learning experiences with others around the globe."[39] Even the school's extracurricular activities are conducted online. On the school's website is posted under "Extra-curricular Activities" this description: "Global School students may participate in any of eleven online clubs, including Spanish and English honor societies, International Club, Future Business Leaders of America, Science Club, and Newspaper Club."[40]

These two scenarios provide contrasting approaches to global schooling. In Avenues: The World School the plan is to use ICT as a tool and not as a central method of instruction. Planned for upper income families, students are expected to globally network through travel and education at global branches of the school. Face-to-face contacts along with the World Course are important for preparing students for a global society. As discussed in Chapter 5, face-to-face contact allows for nonverbal forms of communication. Neuroscience asserts that nonverbal forms of interactions are important in making social contacts, including spontaneous face-to-face reactions. These neural pathways are considered essential for a sense of social connectedness. In contrast, the Florida Virtual Global School relies on social media networking which lacks nonverbal forms of interactions. This is true in both student participation in virtual extracurricular activities and global meetings in the online Socratic Café. While the Florida Virtual Global School is government operated its contractual relationship with 360Ed networks it with for-profit education similar to the network between Chris Whittle's EdisonLearning, Inc. and the for-profit Avenues: The World School.

Who Wants Online Schooling?

The choice between Avenues: The World School and the Florida Virtual Global School might reflect differing attitudes about online instruction. Certainly elite parents signing their children up for Avenues are expressing an interest in their children relying on face-to-face contact between students and teachers, students and other students, and a world community. But are those signing up for the Florida Virtual Global School embracing online instruction as an alternative to face-to-face instruction or are they enrolling because it is convenient? Given the variety of factors that might lead a student to online instruction it is difficult to make any sweeping statements about student preferences between the two forms of instruction.

Obviously, my grandson loves online instruction because it allows him to travel and study on his own time. The flexibility of online instruction helped to make the University of Phoenix the largest private university in the United States. It was founded in 1976 by Cambridge-educated economist and professor-turned-entrepreneur John Sperling, who it is claimed "saw an opportunity—and seized it—to cater to working adults seeking higher education by offering convenient class times at local sites."[41] The stated mission of the University of Phoenix is, "To use technology to create effective modes and means of instruction that expand access to learning resources and that enhance collaboration and communication for improved student learning."[42]

In general, many students enjoy certain features of online instruction. Besides appreciating the flexibility, some students like asynchronous online instruction because it gives them time to formulate thoughtful responses to discussions and questions in contrast to the face-to-face communication of the classroom. In addition, some students find that online discussions allow for better and more comprehensive class participation.[43]

One of the problems with online instruction is the lack of face-to-face contact. A literature review for a research project on blended learning found that online instruction that supplements traditional instruction increases students' perceptions that learning is occurring in the course and increases student camaraderie through online discussions. The literature review also found students, despite online discussions, disliked the loss in blended courses of "some face-to-face" contact.[44] The research project itself found that online discussions were the most highly rated by students as part of blended courses. The next most important aspects of online communication as rated by students in descending order were daily announcements, the posting of an online syllabus, the availability of an online gradebook, and the posting of course information and external links.[45] The authors of this research study concluded that students "perceived web-based instruction as enhancing the quality and quantity of class discussion, promoting a sense of connectedness among classmates and instructor, and contributing to their enjoyment and effectiveness of the course."[46]

This book explored other reasons for supporting online education. One is reducing school district costs for teachers by substituting online instruction for regular and makeup courses. Online instruction can fill the gap when a school district is unable to find a qualified teacher in such areas as foreign language and math instruction. Also, ICT companies are campaigning for incorporation of more online instruction in the school curriculum and to provide edutainment for learning and assessment. Companies like Cisco are advertising global networking as a method for cross cultural learning. Some educators hope that social media can be used to create greater cooperation between conflicting groups such as in Northern Ireland. Online instruction and assessment makes it easier to collect student data and maintain data banks. Software can be used to adapt instructional materials to student abilities. And, of course, ICT can enhance the regular classroom by providing access to learning materials, instructional examples, and virtual learning opportunities.

In the next section I will offer a more pessimistic view of the consequences of online instruction. It is questionable whether or not governments would be willing to limit their ideological management abilities by allowing the deschooling scenario. On the other hand, governments can maintain their traditional exercise of ideological management by regulating the content of ICT in schools and in the marketplace. Even in the extended market or consumer scenario, governments can mandate the curriculum for all choices available in the marketplace including for-profit and public online instruction, public and for-profit schools, and home schooling.

ICT and Authoritarian Schooling

ICT has the potential for creating a completely authoritarian education system through online instruction using a standardized curriculum provided by online instruction and standardized computer assessments that are computer scored and stored in a data bank. Online instruction eliminates any critical comments about the content of instruction which might have been made in the past by classroom teachers. Government controlled and regulated online instruction could ensure a more tightly controlled form of ideological management where the student is only presented in online instruction with material approved by government authorities. As discussed in Chapter 6, governments are developing better Internet filters to censor material and monitor social networking. In addition, computer storage and data mining methods will ensure that students can never escape their educational records, which could include warnings about students being potential troublemakers and dissidents.

The above scenario seems quite possible when considering the role of shadow elites who are dependent on continued government financing of ICT companies. For-profit ICT companies will continue promoting their products to schools for instruction, assessment, and data mining. As discussed in Chapter 6, most of these companies do not care if governments censor the Internet and, in fact, many actually supply governments with the technology for censoring and surveillance. ICT companies might find it easier to collect revenues by having government fund ICT in schools in contrast to the market model of consumers purchasing online instruction and related products in a competitive market.

In other words, ICT makes it possible for a person to never be able to escape the results of a highly controlled and censored education. Imagine that some negative test score or incident is entered into the student's records which is then placed in a national data bank. Interested parties, including potential employers, can hire companies like Social Intelligence to do background checks by mining personal data available on the Internet and in data banks. *New York Times* reporter Jennifer Preston provides this description of the services offered by Social Intelligence:

> It assembles a dossier with examples of professional honors and charitable work, along with negative information that meets specific criteria: online evidence of racist remarks; references to drugs; sexually explicit photos, text messages or videos; flagrant displays of weapons or bombs and clearly identifiable violent activity.[47]

With Internet surveillance tools used by countries like China, software can be used to identify key words in student essays or in text messages and other forums that might indicate any form of anti-government sentiment. Data mining using the services of Social Intelligence would be able to detect unpatriotic and anti-government ideas in the student's record. In other words, ICT in education has the potential of fulfilling the Trinity of Authoritarianism by including propaganda in instructional materials, by censoring instructional materials and student work, and by providing surveillance of student ideas.

The potential reality of the Trinity of Authoritarianism is enhanced by the utopian promise that the Internet will make available all the world's information to all people; certainly the dream of liberation technologists discussed in Chapter 6. By the 1980s, computer researchers were questioning the usability of the vast quantity of information available on the Internet. In his brilliant book *The Information*, John Gleick notes that in the 1980s researchers began to worry about the information overload paradigm, which "was a paradigm based on a truism: that people can only 'absorb' or 'process' a limited amount of information."[48] In Gleick's words Internet information represents the "Library of Babel," requiring search and filtering tools. It is these search and filtering tools that enhance the government's ability to disseminate propaganda, censor instruction, and maintain surveillance over student work. Reflecting both the promise and reality of ICT, Gleick writes:

> This is the curse of omniscience: the answer to any question may arrive at our fingertips ... We are all patrons of the Library of Babel now, and we are the librarians, too. We veer from elation to dismay and back ... What good are the precious books that cannot be found? What good is complex knowledge, in its immobile perfection?[49]

However, this very sense of omniscience might lead ICT users and online students to forget that their government might be censoring and surveilling their online work.

Authoritarian Education: Consumerism and Technological Evolution

The Trinity of Authoritarianism in schools might be achieved through a combination of consumerism and technological advances. The expanded use and potential ubiquitousness of ICT education is tied to consumerism and technological evolution. Schools are consuming institutions which in the past meant primarily buying books and other classroom materials. Today, as discussed throughout this book, schools are major consumers of ICT including hardware, software, and broadband infrastructure. A good example of the movement from a popular consumer item to a consumer item for schools is Apple's iPad introduced in January 2010. The iPad created a new consumer market. *InformationWeek* announced on October 7, 2010, that "iPad Is Top Selling Tech Gadget Ever: Tablet-style computers are flying off store shelves almost as fast as Apple can manufacture them."[50] The estimate was 8.5 million units sold to date. When the iPad2 was put on sale on March 11, 2011, Internet orders swamped the company and crowds lined up overnight at Apple stores. Adding to the hype was Apple's publicly announced sales schedule as reported by *The New York Times*:

Apple will commence online ordering of the iPad 2 at 4 a.m. Eastern time on Friday, March 11, according to the company. In-store sales will begin at 5 p.m. on March 11, a date and time set by Apple stores and honored by brick-and-mortar partners like Best Buy, Target and Wal-Mart. Online sales times from partners will be more scattered, but expect Friday to be a well-orchestrated onslaught of times and products from various iPad retail partners.[51]

Shortly after the sale of the first iPad, Apple began working with textbook publishers and holding workshops for teachers and administrators. Within the first year of its appearance on the market there were 5,400 educational applications available for the iPad with 1,000 being available for free. Houghton Mifflin Harcourt developed an iPad algebra program that includes a video on solving problems, individualized assessments, and practice problems.[52]

Exemplifying the network between government funding and Apple sales of iPad, public schools using federal funds from the Race to the Top's competitive grant program began buying iPads. Educators acted like any other consumer gripped by the excitement of purchasing a new product. Millburn, New Jersey, principal Scott Wolfe declared, "I think this could very well be the biggest thing to hit school technology since the overhead projector."[53] A Scottsdale, Arizona, principal asserted, "Of all the devices out there, the iPad has the most star power for kids."[54]

Technology advocates did not agree with the educational consumer rush for iPads. According to *New York Times* reporter Winnie Hu, "Elliot Soloway, an engineering professor at the University of Michigan, and Cathie Norris, a technology professor at the University of North Texas, question whether school officials have become so enamored with iPads that they have overlooked less costly options, like smartphones that offer similar benefits at a fraction of the iPad's base cost of about $500."[55]

Driven by consumer passion, ignoring cheaper alternatives, and using federal money, educators within the first year of production began buying iPads for their classrooms. These purchases were made despite the shortfall in funding that was causing many school districts to lay off teachers. *The New York Times* a year after the release of the first iPad reported the following educational purchases:

- New York's Roslyn High School hopes to provide iPads to all 1,100 of its students.
- New York City public schools have ordered more than 2,000 iPads.
- Two hundred Chicago public schools applied for 23 district-financed iPad grants totaling $450,000.
- Virginia Department of Education is overseeing a $150,000 iPad initiative to replace history and Advanced Placement biology textbooks at 11 schools.
- Six middle schools in four California cities (San Francisco, Long Beach, Fresno, and Riverside) are teaching the first iPad-only algebra course, developed by Houghton Mifflin Harcourt.
- Kindergartners are getting their hands on iPads in Scottsdale, Arizona, in a lab containing 36 iPads.[56]

The iPad illustrates how the combination of technological evolution and consumerism opens the door to ICT usage in education. Technological progress is dependent on the continued consumption of its innovations. Like biology, technology follows an evolutionary path determined by a number of factors including previous technological advances, military needs, government dictates, environmental factors, and, most importantly, what consumers are willing to purchase.

In *What Technology Wants*, Kevin Kelly describes the evolution of technology, with each developmental stage being dependent on previous technological advances.[57] In his framework, technology is a tool that extends the operation of the human mind and body. Kelly argues that that there is a self-propelling quality to technological advances which he calls the "technium." Technium refers to the globally interconnected system of technology. Kelly writes, "The technium extends beyond shiny hardware to include culture, art, social institutions, and intellectual creations of all types. It includes intangibles like software, law, and philosophical concepts."[58] Kelly argues that the technium as the outgrowth of the mind wants to perpetuate itself by continually expanding and becoming more complex. What technology wants is contained in the desire of the brain to continuously create new tools to master the environment. Kelly compares technological evolution to biological evolution: "The evolution of both systems moves from the simple to the complex, from the general to the specific, from uniformity to diversity, from individualism to mutualism, from energy waster to efficiency, and from slow change to greater evolvability."[59]

Consumption of new technology feeds its evolutionary development. Humans, he argues, tend to define progress as an enlargement of knowledge, comfort, and greater choices. New technology offers this progress. As an example, Kelly describes that wherever he travels "people who walk will buy a bicycle, people who ride a bike will get a scooter, people riding a scooter will upgrade to a car, and those with a car dream of a plane."[60]

The development, production, and personal and educational consumption of the iPad exemplifies Kelly's concept of the technium. Apple's development of the iPad was dependent on the existence of previous technological developments. It was also a reflection of a culture wanting more and more devices to enlarge knowledge, increase choice, and add comfort, particularly in the form of entertainment. As a human tool, the iPad extends the operation of the brain and mind.

However, Kelly's paradigm does not explain why the public and educators were enveloped in a consumer frenzy when others were saying that smartphones could do the same thing as iPads at lower costs. Consumerism as an economic doctrine developed in the early 20th century in the United States in part out of a fear that technological advances would reduce work time. Fear of workers having too much leisure time was rooted in a Protestant Christian belief that "Idle hands are the devil's tools." The argument for an economic system driven by consumption was made in a 1907 book by economist Simon Patten, *The New Basis of Civilization*.[61] He argued that the desire to buy the new technological and commodified leisure products would spur people to work harder. In Patten's words, "The new morality does not consist in saving, but in expanding consumption."[62] Patten explained, "In the course of consumption ... the new wants become complex ... [as a result the] worker steadily and cheerfully chooses the deprivations of this week ... they advance onto a period of restraint and morality, puritan in essence ... Their investment in to-morrow's goods enables society to increase its output and to broaden its productive areas."[63]

An important premise of consumerism is that economic growth is good and that it is based on the continual development and sale of new products. In this paradigm, consumer demand is a measure of the health of an economy. Products are made obsolete either by new designs or by the creation of an alternative product. Consumers often replace clothing and cars because of new styles. A consumerist economy relies on a throw-away culture in which people work to buy more stuff.

Modern advertising, also born at the same time as consumerism, provides the motivation for continuous consumption. Shops and establishments have always used some form of signage to indicate their wares. What's different about modern advertising is that it is designed to specifically tap into consumers' emotions, such as sexuality, status, fear, anxiety, and loneliness. After World War II high school students were defined as a particular consumer market that could be influenced by advertising. This is illustrated by the publication in 1944 of *Seventeen* magazine with its slogan "Teena means business."[64] The word "teenager," according to Kelly Schrum, was invented by marketers. At first marketers experimented with "teenster" and "petiteen," then "teenager" was popularized during the 1940s to mean a group defined by high school attendance. In a crass commercial effort, *Seventeen* magazine advertised the potential teenage market with provocative questions, such as "When is a girl worth $11,690,499?"[65] The question referred to the amount of money spent on teenage ads in *Seventeen* magazine.

In *Educating the Consumer-Citizen: A History of the Marriage of Schools, Advertising, and Media*, I formulated the following principles of consumerism:

Basic Ideas of Consumerist Ideology

1. Work is a virtue and it keeps people from an indolent life that could result in vice and crime.
2. The major financial goal of society should be economic growth and the continual production of new goods.
3. Accumulation of material goods is evidence of personal merit.
4. Differences in ability to consume (or income) are a social virtue because it motivates people to work harder.
5. A belief that the consumption of products will transform one's life.
6. People will want to work hard so that they can consume an endless stream of new products and new forms of commodified leisure.

7. Advertising is good because it motivates people to work harder to consume products.
8. The consumer is irrational and can be manipulated in his/her purchases.[66]

Technium and consumerism help to explain the frenzied purchasing and rapid educational adoption of the iPad. Technology evolves as humans try to develop new tools that extend their abilities. However, for the technium to exist requires a consumer economy that is supportive of a continuous stream of new tools. Advertising grips basic human emotions and directs them to new consumer products. Wanting to be the first to own and use a new technology, customers line up in the early hours to buy it. Using government money, educators try to be the first to adopt an unproven technology for teaching. Ironically, interaction between technology and consumerism might ensure government's ability to practice the Trinity of Authority. Are people buying their own enslavement?

Conclusion: Is Online Schooling Part of a Steady March to an Authoritarian Society?

ICT is making it possible to create authoritarian school systems that can serve governments by ensuring that schools become a conduit for their propaganda, enhance their ability to censor learning materials, and maintain surveillance over student work. ICT allows educational systems to collect data that potentially could follow students for their entire lives. Through life-long data collection by schools, public records, bank and credit documents, and other sources, people can now be tracked, measured, and reported on throughout their entire lives. Online learning programs that conform to government curriculum standards can be a vehicle for propaganda particularly in the social sciences. Current software can identify any potential student dissenter to government policies by analyzing the student's online written material and their social media messages.

As I discussed in Chapters 1 and 2, global superclass networks combined with a shadow elite are instrumental in the spread of ICT to educational institutions. Moving between government and private business, shadow elites tied to ICT companies promote government spending on educational technology by claiming it will be a panacea for global schooling by providing inexpensive schooling that will be made fun by advances in edutainment. For-profit educational software and hardware companies along with the gaming industry see government supported schools as an ideal place to market their products because they can be purchased with government money. A shadow elite operating between private foundations, for-profit educational technology firms, and government agencies work to convince government officials to invest in educational technology rather than other school needs. As discussed in Chapter 1, ICT moguls, global superclass members like Rupert Murdoch and Michael Bloomberg, support limiting the power of teachers' unions and reducing school expenses by laying off experienced teachers and replacing many with online instruction.

The global superclass and shadow elite are promoting ICT as a means of managing school data, including student test scores and principal and teacher ratings. In Chapter 1 I argued that some school and ICT leaders have a data mindset which results in them relying on data crunched by software programs to guide educational policy. Government policymakers and the shadow elite support policies that rely on data to evaluate the educational quality. The rotating staff at the Bill and Melinda Gates Foundation, a foundation that I call the shadow education government, exemplifies the movement of personnel between government, foundations, and business as represented in part by the Gates Foundation's support of the publisher Pearson to produce online courses for public schools that conform to national curriculum standards.

As I noted in Chapter 4, the gaming industry sees edutainment as the panacea for education by making learning fun for all students. Again this involves a for-profit industry that can earn government money by having their learning games used in schools. Schools using learning games must buy or subscribe to gaming software and buy appropriate hardware. Swept up in consumerism, educators believing in the power of learning games must choose between a variety of hardware options which today include smartphones, iPads, notebooks, and standard computers.

The use of analytic software, as described in Chapter 1, may result in a new form of tracking as educational text is adapted to the abilities and interests of students. Of course, these abilities and interests are determined by data crunching of test scores and interest inventories. In the past, students were tracked by being placed in classes with other students with similar abilities. This resulted in complaints that the composition of these class divisions reflected family wealth and racial or ethnic background. Promoted by for-profit ICT companies as meeting the needs of individual learners, the end result may be a new form of tracking which is more powerful than the past because it becomes part of a data set that follows students throughout their lives and determines their employment and economic status.

Some critics of the promotion of ICT forms of learning, as discussed in Chapter 5, worry that online instruction and the use of learning games could result in students being unable to concentrate for long periods of time and leave them feeling lonely in a world of social media. Multitasking is often cited as one possible reason for recent complaints that many current students suffer from ADD as their brains are trained to move quickly from one task to another. There are also suggestions that social media and text messaging create virtual communities in which a person can be networked to thousands but still feel lonely because of the lack of nonverbal communication that occurs in face-to-face communications. The possibility of Internet addiction may add to the sense of loneliness; there is the image of addicted gamers sitting for hours before a monitor with only brief bathroom breaks and kitchen forays for snack food.

The Trinity of Authoritarianism may be accompanied by a depoliticalization of the population through Internet shopping, social media, and entertainment, and a data system that locks students into their social and economic place at a young age and accompanies them throughout their lives. ICT may also, as discussed in Chapter 6, be replacing political and civic involvement with social media, text messaging, and online shopping and entertainment. The majority of youth primarily use the Internet for shopping, social contacts, and entertainment. Only those already interested in politics and civic causes use the Internet for these purposes. The more cynical may agree with the analysis of the Russian government's ICT policies as being designed to distract the population from politics by providing primarily Internet entertainment.

Some readers might object that this is not possible in so-called free countries like the United States and that it will only be a problem in countries like China. However, consider the following. In the United States, as discussed in Chapter 3, there are government and foundation plans to increase the use of ICT in schools. These plans include ICT usage for instruction, assessment, and data management. Instructional materials include edutainment, virtual reality, and other forms of online instruction. These instructional materials are to conform to a national standardized curriculum. Online assessments are to conform to the same national standards.

In the United States, the problem is not just the standardization of the curriculum but also the long history of struggle over the content of courses, particularly those in the social studies. Since the beginnings of the public schools in the 19th century there have been protests about instructional content, particularly by those worried about "un-American" and "radical" ideas. Particularly since the 1920s, groups have censored teachers and books for anything that smacked of socialism or communism. Even the content of tests is scrutinized for political bias. I have catalogued these ideological conflicts in a number of places. Examples of censorship struggles include the nature of the economic system, environmentalism, evolution, birth control, Aids education, racism, multiculturalism, religion, and history.[67] As mentioned previously, traditional classroom instruction does allow for critical comments by both teachers and students. Online criticism might appear on discussion boards. There is the potential that a standardized curriculum put online could result in a uniformity of ideas being taught along with government censorship of content and propaganda. Analytic software might be used to identify potential "troublemakers" or "criminals" and that information placed in a data file that will accompany the student throughout her/his life.

There may also develop clear income divisions between different types of education. Will the global elite be sending their children to globally franchised schools like the for-profit Avenues: The World School where ICT is used as an instructional tool with most learning involving face-to-face contact with teachers and other students around the world? Will middle and low income students be primarily learning through online instruction as school systems cut teachers and costs? Is there a difference between using Rosetta Stone software to learn a foreign language and learning a language from face-to-face contact with a teacher in a classroom and with other students around the world?

In summary, ICT may usher in an educational era where governments are better able to use schools to propagandize, censor, and maintain surveillance of students throughout their lives. It may also create a depoliticized population more interested in shopping and social media than economic and social problems. People may never be able to escape their pasts as data sets follow them from school to employers. For-profit ICT companies are primary promoters of this new form of authoritarianism as they market and sell software that allows governments to analyze, control, and record the education of students and make it possible to propagandize, censor, and maintain surveillance of school graduates. The Trinity of Authoritarianism through ICT can be used to maintain the power of the global superclass by strengthening their protection by governments and ensuring a population that doesn't care about their power because it has been depoliticized, suffers from an inability to concentrate, and tries to fill its feeling of loneliness through more social media, gaming, entertainment, and shopping.

NOTES

Chapter 1

1 Sarah Sparks, "Data Mining Gets Traction in Education: Researchers Sift 'Data Exhaust' for Clues to Improve Learning," *Education Week* (January 12, 2011), p. 1.
2 Ibid.
3 For a history of the advancement of corporatism in education see Joel Spring, *Education and the Rise of the Corporate State* (Boston: Beacon Press, 1972) and *The Sorting Machine: National Educational Policy Since 1945* (New York: David McKay, 1976).
4 Laura Herrera, "In Florida, Virtual Classrooms with No Teachers," *The New York Times* (January 17, 2011). Retrieved from http://www.nytimes.com/2011/01/18/education/18classrooms.html?ref=education on January 25, 2011.
5 Ibid.
6 Claire Cain Miller, "Google Unveils Tool to Speed Up Searches," *The New York Times* (September 8, 2010). Retrieved from http://www.nytimes.com/2010/09/09/technology/techspecial/09google.html?scp=1&sq=google%20unveils%20tool%20to%20speed%20up%20searches&st=cse on September 16, 2010.
7 Patricia Cohen, "In 500 Billion Words, New Window on Culture," *The New York Times* (December 16, 2010). Retrieved from http://www.nytimes.com/2010/12/17/books/17words.html?ref=todayspaper on December 16, 2010.
8 Ibid.
9 Keith Bradsher and Claire Cain Miller, "Google Sees Rules Violations in Limits on Internet Access," *The New York Times* (November 16, 2010). Retrieved from http://www.nytimes.com/2010/11/17/technology/17google.html?scp=3&sq=google%20china&st=cse on November 20, 2010.
10 Nicholas Carr, *The Shallows: What the Internet is Doing to Our Brains* (New York: W.W. Norton & Company, 2010).
11 David Rothkopf, *Superclass: The Global Power Elite and the World They Are Making* (New York: Farrar, Straus and Giroux, 2008).
12 *Forbes* 400, "Michael Bloomberg." Retrieved from http://www.forbes.com/profile/michael-bloomberg on December 15, 2010.
13 *Forbes*, "The World's Most Powerful People." Retrieved from http://www.forbes.com/wealth/powerful-people#p_3_s_arank on December 16, 2010.

14 Nicole Perlroth and Michael Noe, "One In A Billion: The Most Powerful People On Earth," *Forbes* (November 3, 2010). Retrieved from http://www.forbes.com/2010/11/01/obama-china-power-opinions-powerful-people-10-intro_print.html on December 15, 2010.

15 Bloomberg, "About." Retrieved from http://www.bloomberg.com/about/ on December 15, 2010.

16 Bertelsmann: Media Worldwide, "One Company—Six Divisions." Retrieved from http://www.bertelsmann.com/bertelsnann_corp/wms41/brn/index.php?ci=99&language=2.

17 Bloomberg, "About."

18 Wireless Generation, "About Wireless Generation." Retrieved from http://www.wgen.net/about-us/about.html on December 15, 2010.

19 Ian Quillen, "Rupert Murdoch Moves Into k-12 Tech. Market," *Education Week* (December 8, 2010), p. 16.

20 *Forbes*, "Rupert Murdoch Profile." Retrieved from http://www.forbes.com/profile/rupert-murdoch on December 15, 2010.

21 See News Corporation's "2010 Annual Report" for a listing of companies at http://www.newscorp.com/Report2010/index.html, retrieved on October 17, 2011.

22 Press Release, "News Corporation Appoints Former New York City Department of Education Chancellor Joel Klein as Executive Vice President, Office of the Chairman" News Corporation (November 9, 2010). Retrieved from http://www.newscorp.com/news/news_462.html on March 22, 2011.

23 See News Corporation's "2010 Annual Report."

24 Sarah Sparks, "When Joel Klein Resigned as Chancellor in 2010 He Accepted a Position as Executive Vice President at Wireless Generation," *Education Week* (November 12, 2010). Retrieved from http://blogs.edweek.org/edweek/DigitalEducation/2010/11/securing_private_capital_for_n.html on March 22, 2011.

25 Jeremy W. Peters, Michael Barbaro, and Javier C. Hernandez, "Ex-Schools Chief Emerges as Unlikely Murdoch Ally," *The New York Times* (July 23, 2011). Retrieved from http://www.nytimes.com/2011/07/24/business/media/joel-klein-ex-schools-chief-leads-internal-news-corp-inquiry.html?_r=1&hp=&pagewanted=print on July 25, 2011.

26 Ibid.

27 Sharon Otterman, "Amid Layoffs, City to Spend More on School Technology," *The New York Times* (March 29, 2011). Retrieved from http://www.nytimes.com/2011/03/30/nyregion/30schools.html?_r=1&ref=todayspaper&pagewanted=print on March 29, 2011.

28 Ibid.

29 Ibid.

30 Sarah Sparks, "When Joel Klein Resigned as Chancellor … "

31 Wireless Generation advertisement appearing in *Education Week: Technology Counts* (March 17, 2011), p. 9.

32 New York City Government, "Mayor Bloomberg Appoints Cathie Black – History-Making Business Leader With Proven Expertise Making Great Organizations Even Better – Chancellor Of New York City Public Schools." Retrieved from http://schools.nyc.gov/Offices/mediarelations/NewsandSpeeches/2010-2011/cathie-black110910.htm on December 5, 2010.

33 Ibid.

34 Ibid.

35 Fernanda Santos, "Shael Polakow-Suransky Is Believer in (More) Testing / New No. 2 at City Schools Believes in More and Better Testing," *The New York Times* (December 13, 2010). Retrieved from http://www.nytimes.com/2010/12/14/nyregion/14deputy.html?scp=1&sq=new%20york%20schools&st=cse on December 10, 2010.

36 Ibid.

37 For a brief analysis of this tradition see E. Doyle McCarthy, *Knowledge as Culture: The New Sociology of Knowledge* (New York: Routledge, 1996).

38 Richard Nisbett, *The Geography of Thought: How Asians and Westerners Think Differently … and Why* (New York: Free Press, 2003).

39 Ibid., p. 100.

40 Ibid., p. 114.

41 Ibid., pp. 111–35.

42 Thom Shanker and Matt Richtel, "In New Military, Data Overload Can Be Deadly," *The New York Times* (January 16, 2011). Retrieved from http://www.nytimes.com/2011/01/17/technology/17brain.html?ref=todayspaper&pagewanted=print on January 17, 2010.

43 Ibid.

44 Ibid.

45 Ibid.

46 See the research reported by Carr in *The Shallows*.

47 Nicholas Christakis and James Fowler, *Connected: The Surprising Power of Our Social Networks and How They Shape Our Lives* (New York: Little, Brown and Company, 2009), p. 300.

48 Ibid.

49 David Knoke and Song Yang, *Social Network Analysis Second Edition* (Los Angeles: Sage Publications, 2008), pp. 1–3.

50 Associated Press, "Facebook's CEO Visits China's Top Search Engine," *The New York Times* (December 20, 2010). Retrieved from http://nl.newsbank.com/nl-search/we/Archives?p_product=APAB&p_theme=apab&p_action=search&p_maxdocs=200&s_dispstring=Facebook's%20CEO%20Visits%20China's%20Top%20Search%20Engine&p_field_advanced-0=&p_text_advanced-0=("Facebook's%20CEO%20Visits%20China's%20Top%20Search%20Engine")&xcal_numdocs=20&p_perpage=10&p_sort=YMD_date:D&xcal_useweights=no on October 28, 2011.

51 Ibid.

52 Ibid.

53 *Forbes*, "The World's 100 Most Powerful Women," (2010). Retrieved from http://www.forbes.com/profile/cathleen-black on December 21, 2010.

54 James Brady, "The Boss Entertains," *Forbes Magazine* (December 7, 2006). Retrieved from http://www.forbes.com/2006/12/06/cathie-black-holiday-party-oped-cx_jb_1207brady_print.html on December 2, 2010.

55 Winnie Hu, "Christie Picks Klein Ally for New Jersey Schools" (December 17, 2010). Retrieved from http://www.nytimes.com/2010/12/18/nyregion/18cerf.html?ref=education on December 17, 2010.

56 Ibid.

57 EdisonLearning, "EdisonLearning Leaders, Jeff Wahl." Retrieved from http://edisonlearning.com/index.php?q=search/node/jeff%20wahl on October 28, 2011.

58 Ibid.

59 Ibid.

60 Sangari Active Science, "About Us" and "What We Do." Retrieved from http://www.sangariglobaled.com/whoweare/ and http://www.sangariglobaled.com/whatwedo/ on December 20, 2010.

61 Sangari Active Science, "Distinguished Leadership." Retrieved from http://www.sangariglobaled.com/whoweare/leadership/ on December 20, 2010.

62 Rothkopf, *Superclass*, pp. 290–92.

63 Andrew Ross Sorkin, "A Hefty Price for Entry to Davos," *The New York Times* (January 24, 2011). Retrieved from http://dealbook.nytimes.com/2011/01/24/a-hefty-price-for-entry-to-davos/?hp on January 24, 2011.

64 Rothkopf, *Superclass*, p. 266.

65 World Economic Forum, "Annual Meeting of the New Champions 2010." Retrieved from http://www.weforum.org/events/annual-meeting-new-champions-2010 on January 3, 2011.

66 Ibid.

67 World Economic Forum, MENA (Middle East and North Africa) Roundtable on Entrepreneurship Education, Global Education Initiative (October 2010), "Manifesto." Retrieved from http://www.weforum.org/s?s=global+education on January 3, 2010.

68 Ibid.

69 *Empowering People and Transforming Society: The World Economic Forum's Technology Pioneers 2011* (Geneva: World Economic Forum, 2011).

70 Ibid., p. 3.

71 Ibid., p. 4.

72 Ibid.

73 Ibid., p. 20.

74 Knewton, "About Knewton." Retrieved from http://www.knewton.com/about on January 4, 2011.

75 Robert Greenhill, "Preface," *The Global Information Technology Report 2009–2010: ICT for Sustainability*, edited by Soumitra Dutta and Irene Mia (Geneva: World Economic Forum, 2010), p. v.

76 Boao Forum for Asia, "Profile." Retrieved from http://www.boaoforum.org/Html/adoutjs-en.asp on January 4, 2011.

77 Boao Forum for Asia, "Board of Directors." Retrieved from http://www.boaoforum.org/html/adout-lsh-en.asp on January 4, 2011.

78 Boao Forum for Asia Annual Conference 2011. Retrieved from http://www.boaoforum.org/html/ac2011/rcen.asp on October 17, 2011.

79 *The Boao Forum for Asia: The Development of Emerging Economies Annual Report 2009* (Beijing: University of International Business and Economics Press, 2010), pp. 3–6.

80 Ibid., p. 12.

81 Ibid.

82 Shadow elite is a term used by Janine R. Wedel in *Shadow Elite: How the World's New Power Brokers Undermine Democracy, Government, and the Free Market* (New York: Basic Books, 2009).

Chapter 2

1 Wedel, *Shadow Elite*, p. 86.

2 Public Law 107–10-Jan. 8, 2002, "No Child Left Behind Act of 2001," p. 58. Retrieved from the U.S. Department of Education, http://www.ed.gov/policy/elsec/leg/esea02/107-110.pdf on October 28, 2011.

3 Ibid., p. 70.

4 Sylvan Learning, "No Child Left Behind." Retrieved from http://yessylvan.com/nclb.html on January 14, 2011.

5 Schools Matter, "Kaplan Gets Fat on School Money for Kids." Retrieved from http://www.schoolsmatter.info/2008/08/kaplan-gets-fat-on-school-money-for.html on January 14, 2011.

6 Wedel, *Shadow Elite*, p. 40.

7 American Dialect Society, "Truthiness Voted 2005 Word of the Year" (January 6, 2006). Retrieved from http://www.americandialect.org/index.php/amerdial/truthiness_voted_2005_word_of_the_year/ on January 30, 2011.

8 Park Si-soo, "Jeju Seeks to Become Mecca for English Education," *The Korea Times* (December 12, 2008). Retrieved from http://www.koreatimes.co.kr/www/news/nation/2008/12/117_35830.html on January 14, 2011.

9 Ibid.
10 Kang Shin-who, "[Exclusive] Dulwich College Accused of Bribing District Officials," *The Korea Times* (November 18, 2010). Retrieved from http://www.koreatimes.co. kr/www/news/nation/2010/12/117_76604.html on January 14, 2011.
11 Ibid.
12 Chadwick International, "About Chadwick International." Retrieved from http:// www.chadwickinternational.org/page.cfm?p=356 on January 14, 2011.
13 Do Je-hae, "Incheon to House World's Largest Ubiquitous City," *The Korea Times* (December 9, 2009). Retrieved from http://www.koreatimes.co.kr/www/news/ nation/2010/07/281_56996.html on January 16, 2011.
14 Ibid.
15 Choe Sang-Hun, "Western Schools Sprout in South Korea," *The New York Times* (August 22, 2010). Retrieved from http://www.nytimes.com/2010/08/23/world/ asia/23schools.html?scp=1&sq=western%20schools%20sprout%20in%20South% 20korea&st=cse on September 1, 2010.
16 North London Collegiate School, "History." Retrieved from http://www.nlcs.org. uk/history_of_school/History_of_the_School.php on January 14, 2011.
17 North London Collegiate School, "Assistance." Retrieved from http://www.nlcs.org. uk/fees/Assistance-with-fees.php on January 14, 2011.
18 North London Collegiate School, "NLCS in Korea Agreed" (March 16, 2010). Retrieved from http://www.nlcs.org.uk/Latest_News/NLCS-in-South-Korea-agreed. php on January 15, 2011.
19 Ibid.
20 Education Industry Association & ESEA Organizing Principles (December 28, 2009). Retrieved from http://www.educationindustry.org/ on March 12, 2010.
21 Ibid.
22 Steven Pines, Executive Director Education Industry Association, PowerPoint: "Weather Report for SES: Storm Warnings are Posted!!!" (June 8, 2010). Retrieved from http:// www.google.com/search?sitesearch=www.educationindustry.org&q=Weather+Report+ for+SES%3A+Storm+Warnings+are+Posted on October 28, 2011.
23 Ibid., Slide 14.
24 Emil Protalinski, "Microsoft's Principal: Ars Interviews Michael Golden," Arstechnica (July 6, 2009). Retrieved from http://arstechnica.com/microsoft/news/2009/07/ microsofts-principal-an-interview-with-michael-golden.ars on January 27, 2011.
25 Ibid.
26 See biography Milken Institute Global Conference 2009, April 27–29, 2009, L. Michael Golden Corporate Vice President, Education Products Group, Microsoft Corp. Retrieved from http://www.milkeninstitute.org/events/gcprogram.taf?EventID=GC 09&SPID=3691&function=bio on January 27, 2011.
27 "About Pearson," Pearson School. Retrieved from http://www.pearsonschool.com/ index.cfm?locator=PSZ19 on January 28, 2011.
28 See biography Milken Institute Global Conference 2009.
29 The William & Ida Friday Institute for Educational Innovation, "What We Do." Retrieved from http://www.fi.ncsu.edu/what-we-do/teaching-learning on January 28, 2011.
30 Consortium on School Networking, "Core Beliefs." Retrieved from http://www. cosn.org/AboutUs/CoreBeliefs/tabid/4330/Default.aspx on January 28, 2011.
31 Maine International Center for Digital Learning, "About Us." Retrieved from http:// www.micdl.org/about_us on January 31, 2011.
32 SOFTPEDIA, "Microsoft Partners with UNESCO for Higher Education ICT Task Force" (July 6, 2009). Retrieved from http://news.softpedia.com/news/Microsoft-Partners- with-UNESCO-for-Higher-Education-ICT-Task-Force-115880.shtml on January 17, 2011.

33 Randall Stross, "Online Courses, Still Lacking That Third Dimension," *The New York Times* (February 5, 2011). Retrieved from http://www.nytimes.com/2011/02/06/business/06digi.html?ref=business&pagewanted=print on February 5, 2011.

34 UNESCO, "Microsoft Commits $50 Million in Higher Education Resources, Training and Certifications to Drive Economic Recovery" (July 9, 2009). Retrieved from http://www.unesco.org/en/higher-education/dynamic-content-single-view/news/unesco_and_microsoft_announce_higher_education_ict_task_force/back/11995/cHash/dc357a2085/ on January 30, 2011.

35 Microsoft, "UNESCO and Microsoft Announce Higher Education ICT Task Force" (July 7, 2007). Retrieved from http://www.microsoft.com/presspass/press/2009/jul09/07-09UMTFEdResourcesPR.mspx on October 28, 2011.

36 Ibid.

37 Microsoft, "MSDN Academic Alliance." Retrieved from http://msdn.microsoft.com/en-us/academic/default on January 27, 2011.

38 Microsoft, "Microsoft Partners in Learning Alliance Agreement." Retrieved from http://www.microsoft.com/education/leadership/partnersinlearning/alliance.aspx on January 27, 2011.

39 UNESCO, "Microsoft Commits … "

40 Ibid.

41 Ibid.

42 Ibid.

43 Ibid.

44 Ben Wildavsky, *The Great Brain Race: How Global Universities Are Reshaping the World* (Princeton: Princeton University Press, 2010), p. 42.

45 Ibid., pp. 56–57.

46 Ibid., pp. 42–43.

47 Tamar Lewin, "In Oil-Rich Mideast, Shades of the Ivy League," *The New York Times* (February 11, 2008). Retrieved from http://www.nytimes.com/2008/02/11/education/11global.html?scp=5&sq=qatar+education+city&st=nyt on January 21, 2011.

48 Ibid.

49 "Answers from Charles E. Thorpe," *New York Times* Blog (February 11, 2008). Retrieved from http://news.blogs.nytimes.com/2008/02/11/answers-from-charles-e-thorpe/?scp=4&sq=qatar+education+city&st=nyt on January 21, 2011.

50 Ibid.

51 Ibid.

52 Ibid.

53 Virginia Commonwealth School of Arts, "Employment: Qatar Vacancies." Retrieved from http://www.vcu.edu/arts/test/VCUARTS/inside_vcu_arts/employment/qatar/chair_ides.shtml on October 28, 2011.

54 Qatar Foundation, "Why Education City: International Networks." Retrieved from http://www.qf.org.qa/output/page291.asp on January 20, 2011.

55 Ibid.

56 Wildavsky, *The Great Brain Race*, p. 43.

57 Ibid., p. 45.

58 Ibid., p. 44.

59 John Hechinger, "John Sexton's Global Campus Plans for NYU," *Business Week* (May 28, 2010). Retrieved from http://sg.finance.yahoo.com/news/John-Sextons-Global-Campus-bizwk-1159744304.html?x=0 on January 27, 2011.

60 New York University, "Global." Retrieved from http://www.nyu.edu/global.html#below on January 23, 2011.

61 Saadiyat Island Campus New York University, Abu Dhabi. Retrieved from http://nyuad.nyu.edu/about/locations/saadiyat.island.html on January 17, 2011.

62 Hechinger, "John Sexton."
63 Chris Bailey, "Sheikh Mansour: Profile," *Manchester Evening News* (September 22, 2008). Retrieved from http://menmedia.co.uk/manchestereveningnews/sport/foot ball/manchester_city/s/1068102_sheikh_mansour_profile on January 21, 2011.
64 Barney Gimbel, "The Richest City in the World," *Fortune* (March 12, 2007). Retrieved from http://money.cnn.com/magazines/fortune/fortune_archive/2007/03/19/8402357/ index.htm on January 21, 2011.
65 Bailey, "Sheikh Mansour."
66 Ibid.
67 Gimbel, "The Richest City in the World."
68 Bailey, "Sheikh Mansour."
69 "Executive Profile: Khaldoon Khalifa Al Mubarak," *Bloomberg Businessweek.* Retrieved from http://investing.businessweek.com/businessweek/research/stocks/private/person. asp?personId=22933351&privcapId=48893747&previousCapId=320105&previous Title=FIAT%20SPA on January 20, 2011.
70 Executive Affairs Authority, "Chairman of the Executive Affairs Authority." Retrieved from http://eaa.abudhabi.ae/Sites/EAA/Navigation/EN/chairman-executive-affairs-authority.html on January 23, 2011.
71 For a fascinating look at the development of corporatism in Singapore by its major leader see Lee Kuan Yew, *From the Third World to First: The Singapore Story: 1965–2000* (New York: HarperCollins, 2000).
72 World Bank, "The Global Schoolhouse" (June 13, 2008). Retrieved from http://psdblog.worldbank.org/psdblog/2008/06/the-global-sc-1.html on January 18, 2011.
73 Singapore Economic Development Board and the Education Services Division of the Singapore Tourism Board, "Singapore: The Global Schoolhouse" (undated). Retrieved from the International Institute of Education, http://www.iienetwork.org/page/116259/ on January 27, 2011.
74 Ibid.
75 Ibid.
76 Ibid.
77 Ibid.
78 Douglas Tseng, "Tisch Arts School's First Asian Campus Opens Doors Here," *Strait Times* (October 9, 2007). Retrieved from http://app.mfa.gov.sg/pr/read_content.asp? View,8432, on October 28, 2011.
79 Ibid.
80 "Leadership: Board of Directors," TischAsia. Retrieved from http://www.tischasia. nyu.edu.sg/object/tischasia_leadership.html on January 24, 2011.
81 Great Eastern. Retrieved from http://www.lifeisgreat.com.sg/en/jsp/products/index. jsp on January 28, 2011.
82 "OVERSEA-CHINESE BANKING CORP (OCBC:Singapore)," *Bloomberg Businessweek.* Retrieved from http://investing.businessweek.com/research/stocks/earn ings/earnings.asp?ticker=OCBC:SP on January 25, 2011.
83 "The Ascott Limited," *Bloomberg Businessweek* (January 27, 2011). Retrieved from http://investing.businessweek.com/research/stocks/private/snapshot.asp?privcapId=878 781 on January 30, 2011.
84 Capitaland, "About Us." Retrieved from http://www.capitaland.com/about/about. php on January 30, 2011.
85 Cathay Organization Pte Ltd, "About Cathy: About Us." Retrieved from http://www.cathay.com.sg/corporate.html on January 23, 2011.
86 UK's International Education Conference: Going Global 4, "World Potential; Making Education Meet the Challenge" (March 25, 2010). Retrieved from http://www.british council.org/goingglobal-gg4-opening-plenary.htm on January 27, 2011.

87 UK's International Education Conference: Going Global 4, "What Makes A Truly Global University" (March 25, 2010). Retrieved from http://www.britishcouncil. org/goingglobal-gg4-truly-global.htm on January 27, 2011.

88 UNESCO, "2009 World Conference on Higher Education: The New Dynamics of Higher Education and Research for Societal Change and Development" (Paris: UNESCO, 2009), pp. 3–4.

89 Cisco, "Together We Are the Human Network," viewed at http://together.cisco.com/? POSITION=SEM&COUNTRY_SITE=us&CAMPAIGN=HN&CREATIVE=HN-Together&REFERRING_ SITE=Google&KEYWORD=cisco# on February 1, 2011.

90 Cisco, "The Learning Society" viewed at http://www.cisco.com/web/strategy/edu cation/connected_learning_societies.html on January 30, 2011.

91 Ibid.

92 Cisco, "Connected Learning Societies," viewed at http://www.cisco.com/web/strategy/ education/connected_learning_societies.html on October 28, 2011.

93 Ibid.

Chapter 3

1 Soumitra Dutta and Irene Mia, (eds.), *The Global Information Technology Report 2010–2011: Transformations 2.0* (Geneva: World Economic Forum and INSEAD, 2011), p. 3.

2 National Education Technology Plan 2010, *Transforming American Education: Learning Powered by Technology* (Washington, D.C.: U.S. Office of Educational Technology, U.S. Department of Education, 2010), p. ix.

3 Sam Dillon, "Behind Grass-Roots School Advocacy, Bill Gates," *The New York Times* (May 21, 2011), p. 1.

4 Ibid.

5 Dutta and Mia, (eds.), *The Global Information Technology Report 2010–2011*, p. 6.

6 Ibid., p. 34.

7 Ibid., pp. 85–98.

8 Ibid., p. v.

9 Ibid.

10 Telefónica, "About Telefónica: Key Figures." Retrieved from http://www.telefonica. com/en/about_telefonica/html/magnitudes/magnitudes.shtml on April 25, 2011.

11 Telefónica, "About Telefónica: History." Retrieved from http://www.telefonica. com/en/about_telefonica/html/historia/index.shtml on April 25, 2011.

12 César Alierta, "The Promise of Technology" in Dutta and Mia, (eds.), *The Global Information Technology Report 2010–2011*, p. 61.

13 Evgeny Morozov, *The Net Delusion: The Dark Side of Internet Freedom* (New York: PublicAffairs, 2011).

14 Alierta, "The Promise of Technology," p. 61.

15 Ibid., p. 63.

16 Ibid., p. 62.

17 Soumitra Dutta, Irene Mia, and Thierry Geiger, "The Networked Readiness Index 2010: Celebrating 10 Years of Assessing Networked Readiness," in *The Global Information Technology Report 2010–2011*, p. 3.

18 Mikael Hagström, "Transformation 2.0 for an Effective Social Strategy," in *The Global Information Technology Report 2010–2011*, pp. 91–99.

19 SAS, "About." Retrieved from http://www.sas.com/ on April 26, 2011.

20 Hagström, "Transformation 2.0," p. 92.

21 Ibid.

22 Ibid.

23 SAS, "Analytics." Retrieved from http://www.sas.com/technologies/analytics/ on April 26, 2011.
24 SAS, "Education." Retrieved from http://www.sas.com/industry/education/index. html on April 26, 2011.
25 SAS, "SAS EVAAS for K-12: System Requirements." Retrieved from http://www. sas.com/govedu/edu/k12/evaas/index.html#s1=4 on April 23, 2011.
26 SAS, "SAS EVAAS for K-12." Retrieved from http://www.sas.com/govedu/edu/ k12/evaas/index.html#s1=1 on April 26, 2011.
27 Ibid.
28 Enrique Rueda-Sabater and John Garrity, "The Emerging Internet Economy: Looking a Decade Ahead" in *The Global Information Technology Report 2010–2011*, pp. 33–44.
29 Ibid., p. 34.
30 Ibid.
31 Cisco Systems, Inc., "Together We Are the Human Network: 2010 Annual Report" (San Jose, CA: Cisco Systems, Inc., 2010).
32 "About the Authors" in *The Global Information Technology Report 2010–2011*, pp. 399, 402.
33 Dutta and Mia, (eds.), *The Global Information Technology Report 2010–2011*, p. 6.
34 Jeff Kelly and Neil Blakesley, "Localization 2.0" in *The Global Information Technology Report 2010–2011*, pp. 85–90.
35 Ibid., p. 86.
36 Ibid.
37 "About the Authors," p. 400.
38 Ibid., p. 398.
39 BT Global Services, "About." Retrieved from http://www.globalservices.bt.com/ AboutusDetailsAction.do/About-us/about-bt-global-services/param/Record/about_ bt_global_services_about_bt_global_services_uk_en-gb/ts/1304086028469 on April 29, 2011.
40 Torbjörn Fredriksson, "The Growing Possibilities of Information and Communication Technologies for Reducing Poverty," in *The Global Information Technology Report 2010–2011*, pp. 69–77.
41 Ibid., p. 72.
42 Arne Duncan, "The Digital Transformation in Education: U.S. Secretary of Education Arne Duncan's Remarks at the State Educational Technology Directors Association Education Forum" (November 9, 2010). Retrieved from http://www.ed.gov/news/ speeches/%E2%80%9C-digital-transformation-education%E2%80%9D-us-secretary-education-arne-duncan on April 29, 2011.
43 Ibid.
44 Arne Duncan, "Statement on National Governors Association and State Education Chiefs Common Core Standards" (June 2, 2010). Retrieved from http://www.ed. gov/news/press-releases/statement-national-governors-association-and-state-education-chiefs-common-core on May 1, 2011.
45 National Education Technology Plan 2010, *Transforming American Education*, p. 22.
46 Ibid., p. 23.
47 Ibid., p. 37.
48 Ibid.
49 Ibid., p. 64.
50 Ibid., p. 63.
51 Duncan, "Statement on National Governors Association."
52 Duncan, "The Digital Transformation in Education."
53 U.S. Department of Education, "Karen Cator, Director of the Office of Educational Technology—Biography." Retrieved from http://www2.ed.gov/news/staff/bios/ cator.html on May 2, 2011.
54 Ibid.

55 U.S. Department of Education, "James H. Shelton III, Assistant Deputy Secretary for Innovation and Improvement—biography." Retreived from http://www2.ed.gov/news/staff/bios/shelton.html on May 2, 2011.
56 Stanford Center for Innovations in Learning, "Roy Pea." Retrieved from http://ctl.sri.com/people/displayPerson.jsp?Nick=rpea on October 28, 2011.
57 SRI, "About Us." Retrieved from http://www.sri.com/about/ on April 15, 2011.
58 TeachScape, "Board of Directors." Retrieved from http://www.teachscape.com/html/ts/nps/board_of_directors.html on April 15, 2011.
59 VIP Tone, "About." Retrieved from http://www.viptone.com/about.html on April 15, 2011.
60 Ibid.
61 Deloitte Center for the Edge. Retrieved from http://www.deloitte.com/centerforedge on May 2, 2011.
62 Gabriel Trip, "Jeb Bush Leads Broad Push for Education Change With 'Florida Formula'," *The New York Times* (April 26, 2011). Retrieved from http://www.nytimes.com/2011/04/27/education/27bush.html?ref=todayspaper on April 26, 2011.
63 The Walton Family Foundation, "K-12 Education Reform." Retrieved from http://www.waltonfamilyfoundation.org/educationreform on October 28, 2011.
64 The Broad Foundation, "About Us." Retrieved from http://www.broadfoundation.org/about_broads.html on May 5, 2011.
65 "The World's Billionaires #132 Eli Broad," *Forbes*. Retrieved from http://www.forbes.com/lists/2010/10/billionaires-2010_Eli-Broad_599L.html on June 11, 2011.
66 Ibid.
67 The Broad Center, "Record Number of Broad Residents Take on Local, State, Federal Roles Managing Education Reform." Retrieved from http://broadresidency.org/asset/0-tbr%20national%20press%20release.pdf on May 5, 2011.
68 Ibid.
69 Ibid.
70 Christina A. Samuels, "Critics Target Growing Army of Broad Leaders," *Education Week* (June 8, 2011). Retrieved from http://www.edweek.org/ew/articles/2011/06/08/33broad_ep.h30.html?tkn=ZUNFfSlHreM4Vp9j3zDdpovIbinGmnULufli&print=1 on June 11, 2011.
71 Ibid.
72 IQity, "Welcome to IQity." Retrieved from http://www.iq-ity.com/index.aspx on May 5, 2011.
73 Foundation for Excellence in Education, "Meet the Sponsors." Retrieved from http://www.excelined.org/Pages/Programs/Arts_for_Life/Meet_the_Sponsors.aspx on October 28, 2011.
74 Foundation for Excellence in Education, *Digital Learning Now*. Retrieved from http://www.excelined.org/docs/Digital%20Learning%20Now%20Report%20FINAL.pdf on October 28, 2011.
75 Ibid., p. 7.
76 Ibid., p. 5.
77 Pearson Foundation, "Home." Retrieved from http://www.pearsonfoundation.org/ on May 6, 2011.
78 Bill and Melinda Gates Foundation, "Gates Foundation Announces Portfolio of Innovative Grants to Develop New Teaching and Learning Tools that Support Teachers and Help Students" (April 27, 2011). Retrieved from http://www.gatesfoundation.org/press-releases/Pages/common-core-tools-110427.aspx on May 1, 2011.
79 Pearson, "Pearson at a Glance." Retrieved from http://www.pearson.com/about-us/pearson-at-a-glance/ on May 6, 2011.
80 Pearson, "Education." Retrieved from http://www.pearson.com/about-us/education/ on May 6, 2011.

81 Pearson Foundation, "Pearson Foundation Partners with Bill and Melinda Gates Foundation to Create Digital Learning Programs" (April 27, 2011). Retrieved from http://www.pearsonfoundation.org/pr/20110427-pf-partners-with-gates-foundation-to-create-digital-learning-programs.html on April 27, 2011.
82 Pearson, "Education: Around the Business." Retrieved from http://www.pearson.com/about-us/education/around-the-business/ on May 6, 2011.
83 Bill and Melinda Gates Foundation, "Gates Foundation Announces … "
84 Florida Virtual School, "About Us." Retrieved from http://www.flvs.net/areas/aboutus/Pages/default.aspx on May 9, 2011.
85 Eric Smith, "FLORIDA DEPARTMENT OF EDUCATION: Florida Virtual School as School Choice Option" (January 8, 2009). Retrieved from http://info.fldoe.org/docushare/dsweb/Get/Document-5250/dps-2009-07.pdf on October 18, 2011.
86 Ibid.
87 Reasoning Mind, "About Us." Retrieved from http://www.reasoningmind.org/?mv=5 on May 9, 2011.
88 Reasoning Mind, "Technology Sponsors." Retrieved from http://www.reasoningmind.org/index.php?mv=5&am=3 on May 9, 2011.
89 Digital Youth Network, "About Us." Retrieved from http://www.digitalyouthnetwork.org/1-about/pages/1-overview on May 9, 2011.
90 Institute of Play, "About." Retrieved from http://www.instituteofplay.org/about/ on May 9, 2011.
91 Quest Atlantis, "Welcome." Retrieved from http://atlantis.crlt.indiana.edu/site/view/Researchers#58 on May 9, 2011.
92 Bill and Melinda Gates Foundation, "Gates Foundation Announces … "
93 Michael Wines, "China Creates New Agency for Patrolling the Internet," *The New York Times* (May 4, 2011). Retrieved from http://www.nytimes.com/2011/05/05/world/asia/05china.html?_r=1&scp=1&sq=China%20creates%20new%20agency&st=cse on May 5, 2011.
94 "Internet Office for Healthy Web Development," *People's Daily Online* (May 6, 2011). Retrieved from http://english.people.com.cn/90001/90776/90882/7371893.html on May 10, 2011.
95 Ibid.
96 Ibid.
97 Morozov, *The Net Delusion*, p. 98.
98 Ibid., pp. 98–99.
99 Ibid., p. 99.

Chapter 4

1 James Paul Gee, *What Video Games Have To Teach Us About Learning and Literacy* (New York: Palgrave Macmillan, 2007).
2 Ibid., p. 215.
3 Katie Salen, "Toward an Ecology of Gaming," in Katie Salen (ed.), *The Ecology of Games: Connecting Youth, Games, and Learning* (Boston, MA: Massachusetts Institute of Technology, 2008), p. 2.
4 Jane McGonigal, *Reality is Broken: Why Games Make Us Better and How They Can Change The World* (New York: The Penguin Press, 2011), p. 14.
5 Gus Mastrapa, "White House: Ask What Game Developers Can Do For Your Country," *Wired* (March 11, 2010). Retrieved from http://www.wired.com/gamelife/2010/03/gdc-white-house/ on March 25, 2011.
6 Chad Raphael, Christine Bachen, Kathleen-M. Lynn, Jessica Baldwin-Philippi, and Kristen Mckee, "Games for Civic Learning: A Conceptual Framework and Agenda for Research and Design," *Games and Culture* 5 (2) 2010, p. 201.

7 Cory Ondrejka, "Education Unleashed: Participatory Culture, Education, and Innovation in Second Life," in Salen, (ed.), *The Ecology of Games*, p. 244.

8 Ibid.

9 Linden Lab, "About." Retrieved from http://lindenlab.com/about on February 8, 2011.

10 Gee, *What Video Games Have To Teach Us*, p. 2.

11 Mizuko Ito, *Engineering Play: A Cultural History of Children's Software* (Cambridge: Massachusetts Institute of Technology, 2009), pp. 29–36.

12 Steven Mintz, *Huck's Raft: A History of American Childhood* (Cambridge: Harvard University Press, 2004).

13 As quoted in Ito, *Engineering Play*, p. 30.

14 Ibid.

15 Ibid., p. 43.

16 Houghton Mifflin Harcourt, "Executive Leadership." Retrieved from http://www.hmhco.com/leadership.html on March 4, 2011.

17 The Learning Company. Retrieved from http://learningcompany.com/ on March 4, 2011.

18 Ibid.

19 The Learning Company, "History of Carmen Sandiego Brand." Retrieved from http://carmensandiego.com/hmh/site/carmen/home/articles?article=2560 on March 4, 2011.

20 Ibid.

21 Houghton Mifflin Harcourt, "Supplemental Schools." Retrieved from http://www.hmhinnovation.com/SUP-SS.php on March 4, 2011.

22 Ibid.

23 JumpStart, "Welcome to JumpStart." Retrieved from http://www.jumpstart.com/AboutUs/aboutus.aspx on March 4, 2011.

24 Ibid.

25 Knowledge Adventure, "Financing History." Retrieved from http://www.knowledgeadventure.com/CompanyInfo.htm on March 5, 2011.

26 Susan Haigh, "Cendant Ex-exec Gets 10 Years in Prison," *The San Diego Union Tribune* (August 4, 2005). Retrieved from http://www.signonsandiego.com/uniontrib/20050804/news_1b4cendant.html on March 7, 2011.

27 Vivendi, "Group." Retrieved from http://www.vivendi.com/vivendi/-Group on March 5, 2011.

28 Venture Investors, "About Us." Retrieved from http://www.ventureinvestors.com/about-us on March 8, 2011.

29 Telesoft, "About Us." Retrieved from http://www.telesoftvc.com/about_us/ on March 4, 2011.

30 Telesoft, "Arjun Gupta." Retrieved from http://www.telesoftvc.com/team_network/investment_team/data/1089224830_all.htm on March 4, 2011.

31 Azure Capital, "Paul Ferris." Retrieved from http://www.azurecap.com/team/team-member/Paul_Ferris on March 4, 2011.

32 Knowledge Adventure, "Management." Retrieved from http://www.knowledgeadventure.com/Management.htm on March 9, 2011.

33 JumpStart, "About Us." Retrieved from http://www.jumpstart.com/AboutUs/aboutus.aspx on March 10, 2011.

34 Ibid.

35 JumpStart, "Is It Safe?" Retrieved from http://www.jumpstart.com/Parents/Default.aspx on March 9, 2011.

36 Knowledge Adventure, "Learning through Online Games." Retrieved from http://www.knowledgeadventure.com/ on March 7, 2011.

37 Ibid.

38 Ibid.

39 Hilary Stout, "Toddlers' Favorite Toy: The iPhone," *The New York Times* (October 15, 2010). Retrieved from http://www.nytimes.com/2010/10/17/fashion/17TODDLERS. html?scp=1&sq=toddler+iphone&st=nyt on March 7, 2011.

40 JumpStart Preschool Magic of Learning 1. Retrieved from http://ax.itunes.apple. com/us/app/jumpstart-preschool-magic/id395058540 on March 7, 2011.

41 BlackBerry App World, "TVOKids Polka Dot Shorts." Retrieved from http:// appworld.BlackBerry.com/webstore/content/26663?lang=en on March 8, 2011.

42 Chris Kohler, "NPD December: $18 Billion Year For Game Industry," *Wired* (January 17, 2008). Retrieved from http://www.wired.com/gamelife/2008/01/npd-december-18/ on March 25, 2011.

43 McGonigal, *Reality is Broken*, p. 3.

44 Aphra Kerr, *The Business and Culture of Digital Games* (London: Sage Publications, 2006).

45 Ibid., p. 91.

46 Ibid., pp. 52–62.

47 Ibid., p. 55.

48 Ibid., pp. 55–56.

49 Kohler, "NPD December."

50 The NPD Group, Inc., "2009 U.S. Video Game Industry and PC Game Software Retail Sales Reach $20.2 Billion" (January 14, 2010). Retrieved from http://www. npd.com/press/releases/press_100114.html on March 25, 2011.

51 Ibid.

52 Stephen E. Siwek, *Video Games in the 21st Century: The 2010 Report* (Washington, D.C.: Education Software Association, 2010), p. 1.

53 Retrieved from http://www.theesa.com/contact/index.asp on March 25, 2011.

54 Entertainment Software Industry, "Industry Facts." Retrieved from http://www. theesa.com/facts/index.asp on March 25, 2011.

55 Entertainment Software Industry, "Public Policy: *Schwarzenegger v. EMA/Entertainment Software Association.*" Retrieved from http://www.theesa.com/policy/scotus.asp on March 25, 2011.

56 Clive Thomson, "Halo 3: How Microsoft Labs Invented a New Science of Play," *Wired* (August 21, 2007).

57 Ibid.

58 See McGonigal, *Reality is Broken*, pp. 66–67.

59 Michael Gazzinga, *Human: The Science Behind What Makes Your Brain Unique* (New York: Harper Perennial, 2008), pp. 99–105.

60 David Pogue, "A Parent's Struggle With a Child's iPad Addiction," *The New York Times* (February 24, 2011). Retrieved from http://pogue.blogs.nytimes.com/2011/02/ 24/a-parents-struggle-with-a-childs-ipad-addiction/?scp=1&sq=ipad%20addiction& st=cse on March 14, 2011.

61 For the reaction to the declaration that television was an "an educational wasteland" see Joel Spring, *The American School: 1642–2004 Sixth Edition* (New York: McGraw-Hill, 2005), pp. 394–403.

62 *Merriam-Webster's Collegiate Dictionary and Thesaurus, Eleventh Edition including Medical Desk Dictionary* (Innovative Knowledge Software, 2009).

63 Tara Parker-Pope, "An Ugly Toll of Technology: Impatience and Forgetfulness," *New York Times* (June 6, 2010). Retrieved from http://www.nytimes.com/2010/06/ 07/technology/07brainside.html?scp=1&sq=an%20ugly%20toll%20of%20technology& st=Search on March 14, 2011.

64 Pogue, "A Parent's Struggle With a Child's iPad Addiction."

65 Gary Small and Gigi Vorgan, *iBrain: Surviving the Technological Alteration of the Modern Mind* (New York: HarperCollins, 2008), p. 48.

66 Ibid.

67 Ibid., p. 50.
68 Ibid., p. 51.
69 Ibid.
70 Choe Sang-Hun, "South Korea Expands Aid for Internet Addiction," *The New York Times* (May 28, 2010). Retrieved from http://www.nytimes.com/2010/05/29/world/asia/29game.html?_r=1&scp=1&sq=South%20Korea%20expands%20aid%20for%20internet%20addiction&st=cse on March 2, 2011.
71 Ibid.
72 Dal Yong Jin and Florence Chee, "Age of New Media Empires: A Critical Interpretation of the Korean Online Game Industry," *Games and Culture* (January 2008), pp. 38–58.
73 Alex Golub and Kate Lingley, "'Just like the Qing Empire': Internet Addiction, MMOGs, and the Moral Crisis in Contemporary China," *Games and Culture* (January 2008), pp. 59–62.
74 Ibid., p. 62.
75 Ibid., p. 63.
76 Video Game Addiction: When Video Games Become More Than Just Games … . Retrieved from http://www.video-game-addiction.org/ on October 18, 2011.
77 Ibid.
78 Video Game Addiction, "Symptoms of Internet Computer Addiction Among Teens." Retrieved from http://www.video-game-addiction.org/symptoms-computer-addiction-teens.html on March 14, 2011.
79 "About," Netaddiction.com. Retrieved from http://www.netaddiction.com/index.php?option=com_content&view=article&id=72&Itemid=94 on March 14, 2011.
80 Netaddiction.com, "Are You An Obsessive Online Gamer?" Retrieved from http://www.netaddiction.com/index.php?option=com_content&view=article&id=80%3Agamer&catid=42%3Arecovery-resources&Itemid=88 on March 14, 2011.
81 Laura Widyanto and Mary McMurran, "The Psychometric Properties of the Internet Addiction Test," *CyberPsychology and Behavior* 7 (3), 2004.
82 Ibid., p. 1.
83 Netaddiction.com, "Internet Addiction Test." Retrieved from http://www.netaddiction.com/index.php?option=com_bfquiz&view=onepage&catid=46&Itemid=106 on October 28, 2011.
84 McGonigal, *Reality is Broken.*
85 Mihaly Csikszentmihalyi, *Flow: The Psychology of Optimal Experience* (New York: Harper Perennial, 1990), p. 71.
86 Ibid., p. 67.
87 McGonigal, *Reality is Broken*, p. 6.
88 Ibid., p. 9.
89 Ibid., p. 47.
90 Ibid., p. 43.
91 Ibid., p. 97.
92 Ibid., p. 99.
93 Ibid., p. 21.
94 Quest to Learn, "Mission." Retrieved from http://q2l.org/mission on April 17, 2011.
95 Ibid.
96 Quest to Learn, "Q2L Overview of Curriculum." Retrieved from http://q2l.org/kits/curriculum/Q2L_curric_overview.pdf on April 15, 2011.
97 Quest to Learn, "Our Approach to Technology." Retrieved from http://q2l.org/node/15 on April 15, 2011.
98 See Joel Spring, *The Politics of American Education* (New York: Routledge, 2011), pp. 118–50.

99 National Education Technology Plan 2010, *Transforming American Education: Learning Powered by Technology* (Washington, D.C.: U.S. Office of Educational Technology, U.S. Department of Education, 2010).

100 Ibid., p. xvii.

101 Ibid., p. 11.

102 Ibid., p. 21.

103 Ibid., p. 37.

104 Bill and Melinda Gates Foundation, "Grants." Retrieved from http://www.gates foundation.org/Grants-2010/Pages/New-York-University-OPP1019503.aspx on April 15, 2011.

105 Center for Highly Interactive Computing in Education, "Home." Retrieved from http://sitemaker.umich.edu/hice/home on April 16, 2011.

106 Center for Highly Interactive Computing in Education, "Funding." Retrieved from http://sitemaker.umich.edu/hice/funding on April 16, 2011.

107 Knowledge Networks On the Web, "About Know." Retrieved from http://know. umich.edu/aboutknow.asp on April 16, 2011.

108 Graduate School of Education, University of Pennsylvania, "Yasmin Kafai." Retrieved from http://www.gse.upenn.edu/~kafai/ on April 16, 2011.

109 Yasmin Kafai, "Projects." Retrieved from http://www.gse.upenn.edu/~kafai/projects/index.htm on April 16, 2011.

110 Merrilea Mayo, "Video Games: A Route to Large-Scale STEM Education?" *Science* (January 2, 2009), p. 79.

111 Ibid., p. 82.

112 Whyville.net, "Whyville for Sponsors." Retrieved from http://b.whyville.net/smmk/top/gatesInfo?topic=whyville_for_sponsors on April 16, 2011.

113 Ibid.

114 Chris Dede. Retrieved from http://isites.harvard.edu/icb/icb.do?keyword=chris_dede&pageid=icb.page361276 on April 17, 2011.

115 Virtual Performance Assessment: Using Immersive Technology to Assess Science Inquiry Learning, "About." Retrieved from http://vpa.gse.harvard.edu/about/ on April 17, 2011.

116 Ibid.

117 Virtual Performance Assessment: Using Immersive Technology to Assess Science Inquiry Learning, "Assessment #1: Save the Kelp!" Retrieved from http://vpa.gse. harvard.edu/media/assessment-1-save-the-kelp/ on April 17, 2011.

118 Virtual Performance Assessment: Using Immersive Technology to Assess Science Inquiry Learning, "About."

119 Ibid.

Chapter 5

1 Mark Bauerlein, *The Dumbest Generation: How the Digital Age Stupefies Young Americans and Jeopardizes Our Future* (New York: Jeremy P. Tarcher/Penguin, 2008) and Don Tapscott, *Grown Up Digital: How the Net Generation is Changing Your World* (New York: McGraw-Hill, 2009).

2 Marc Prensky, "Digital Natives, Digital Immigrants," *On the Horizon* (October 2001), pp. 1–6 and "Digital Natives, Digital Immigrants, Part II: Do They Really Think Differently?" *On the Horizon* (December 2001), pp. 1–6. Prensky's most recent publication continues the themes of these two articles: Marc Prensky, *Teaching Digital Natives: Partnering for Real Learning* (Thousand Oaks, CA: Corwin, 2010).

3 Michael Thomas (ed.), *Deconstructing Digital Natives: Young People, Technology and the New Literacies* (New York: Routledge, 2011).

4 Prensky, "Digital Natives, Digital Immigrants," p. 1.

5 Ibid.

6 Ibid.

7 Ibid., p. xix.

8 Prensky, *Teaching Digital Natives*, p. xix.

9 Hal Lancaster, untitled, *The Wall Street Journal* (October 6, 1998). Retrieved from http://www.marcprensky.com/about/Press-WSJournal.pdf on October 28, 2011.

10 Michael Meyer, "Just Don't Shoot the Client: How Do You Train Nintendo-generation Workers?" *Newsweek* (November 30, 1998). Retrieved from http://www.marcprensky.com/about/Press-Newsweek.pdf on October 28, 2011.

11 Games2train, "Current." Retrieved from http://www.games2train.com/site/html/current.html on May 21, 2011.

12 Spree Learning Games, "Games by Subjects." Retrieved from http://spreelearninggames.net/games/list/subjects on May 25, 2011.

13 Prensky, "Digital Natives, Digital Immigrants," p. 2.

14 Ibid.

15 Prensky, "Digital Natives, Digital Immigrants, Part II," p. 3.

16 Prensky, *Teaching Digital Natives*, p. 3.

17 Don Tapscott, *Growing Up Digital: The Rise of the Net Generation* (New York: McGraw-Hill, 1999).

18 Moxie Insight, "About Moxie Insight." Retrieved from http://moxieinsight.com/about/ on May 22, 2011.

19 Moxie Software, "About." Retrieved from http://moxiesoft.com/tal_about/management.aspx on May 22, 2011.

20 Tapscott, *Growing Up Digital*, p. 98.

21 Ibid., p. 108.

22 Prensky, *Teaching Digital Natives*, pp. 2–3.

23 Tapscott, *Growing Up Digital*, p. 133.

24 Larry Rosen, *Rewired: Understanding the iGeneration and the Way They Learn* (New York: Palgrave Macmillan, 2010), p. 201.

25 Ibid.

26 Ian Jukes, Ted McCain, and Lee Crockett, *Understanding the Digital Generation: Teaching and Learning in the New Digital Landscape* (Thousand Oaks, CA: Corwin, 2010), p. 9.

27 Rosen, *Rewired*, pp. 2–3.

28 Sue Bennett and Karl Maton, "Intellectual Field or Faith-based Religion: Moving on from the Idea of 'Digital Natives,'" in Thomas (ed.), *Deconstructing Digital Natives*, p. 172.

29 Michael Thomas, "Technology, Education, and the Discourse of the Digital Native: Between Evangelists and Dissenters," in Thomas (ed.), *Deconstructing Digital Natives*, p. 7.

30 Chris Jones, "Students, the Net Generation and Digital Natives," in Thomas (ed.), *Deconstructing Digital Natives*, p. 39.

31 Shakuntala Banaji, "Disempowering by Assumption: 'Digital Natives,' and the EU Civic Web Project," in Thomas (ed.), *Deconstructing Digital Natives*, p. 57.

32 Jones, "Students, the Net Generation and Digital Natives," p. 43.

33 Banaji, "Disempowering by Assumption," p. 53.

34 Gregor Kennedy and Terry Judd, "Beyond Google and the 'Satisficing' Searching of Digital Native," in Thomas (ed.), *Deconstructing Digital Natives*, p. 120.

35 Bennett and Maton, "Intellectual Field or Faith-based Religion," p. 172.

36 Matt Richtel, "Outdoors and Out of Reach, Studying the Brain," *The New York Times* (August 15, 2010). Retrieved from http://www.nytimes.com/2010/08/16/technology/16brain.html?ref=yourbrainoncomputers on February 1, 2011.

37 Ibid.

38 Ibid.
39 Matt Richtel, "Digital Devices Deprive Brain of Needed Downtime," *The New York Times* (August 24, 2010). Retrieved from http://www.nytimes.com/2010/08/25/technology/25brain.html?_r=1&ref=yourbrainoncomputers on March 3, 2011.
40 Ibid.
41 Ibid.
42 Matt Richtel, "Growing Up Digital, Wired for Distraction," *The New York Times* (November 21, 2010). Retrieved from http://www.nytimes.com/2010/11/21/technology/21brain.html?ref=yourbrainoncomputers on March 1, 2011.
43 Matt Richtel, "Attached to Technology and Paying a Price," *The New York Times* (June 6, 2010). Retrieved from http://www.nytimes.com/2010/06/07/technology/07brain.html?ref=yourbrainoncomputers on March 2, 2010.
44 Ibid.
45 Nicholas Carr, *The Shallows: What the Internet is Doing to Our Brains* (New York: W.W. Norton & Company, 2010).
46 Ibid., p. 115.
47 Ibid., pp. 115–16.
48 Ibid., p. 125.
49 Ibid.
50 Ibid., p. 194.
51 Gary Small and Gigi Vorgan, *iBrain: Surviving the Technological Alteration of the Modern Brain* (New York: HarperCollins, 2008), p. 66.
52 Sherry Turkle, *Alone Together: Why We Expect More from Technology and Less From Each Other* (New York: Basic Books, 2011), p. 227.
53 Ibid., p. 163
54 Rosen, *Rewired*, p. 201.
55 Small and Vorgan, *iBrain*, p. 123.
56 Ibid., p. 117.
57 Ibid.
58 Mizuko Ito, et al., *Living and Learning with New Media: Summary of Findings from the Digital Youth Project* (Cambridge, MA: Massachusetts Institute of Technology, 2008).
59 Ibid.
60 As reported in Turkle, *Alone Together*, p. xiv.
61 Mizuko Ito, et al., *Living and Learning with New Media,* Kindle, location 250–53.
62 See Bauerlein, *The Dumbest Generation*.
63 Turkle, *Alone Together*, p. x.
64 Sherry Turkle, *The Second Self: Computers and the Human Spirit* (Cambridge, MA: Massachusetts Institute of Technology, 1984).
65 See Michael Gazzaniga, *Human: The Science Behind What Makes Your Brain Unique* (New York: HarperCollins, 2008), pp. 79–203.
66 Turkle, *The Second Self*, p. 6.
67 Small and Vorgan, *iBrain*, pp. 115–48.
68 Ibid., p. 124.
69 Ibid., p. 133.
70 Ibid., p. 117.
71 Hugh Gusterson and Catherine Besteman, (eds.), *The Insecure American: How We Got Here and What We Should Do about It* (Los Angeles: University of California Press, 2009).
72 Turkle, *The Second Self*, p. 157.
73 Ibid., p. 200.
74 Ibid., p. 293.
75 Tapscott, *Growing Up Digital*, p. 54.

76 Nicholas Christakis and James Fowler, *The Surprising Power of Our Social Networks and How They Shape Our Lives* (New York: Little, Brown and Company, 2009), p. 290.
77 Ibid., p. 276.
78 Ibid., pp. 260–61.
79 Ibid., p. 260
80 Ibid., p. 300.
81 Felicia Wu Song, *Virtual Communities: Bowling Alone, Online Together* (New York: Peter Lang, 2009), pp. 100–20.
82 Robert Putnam, *Bowling Alone: The Collapse and Revival of American Community* (New York: Simon and Schuster, 2000).
83 Song, *Virtual Communities*, p. 16.
84 Ibid., p. 124.
85 Ibid.
86 Mark Bauerlein, *Whitman and the American Idiom* (Baton Rouge: University of Louisiana Press, 1991) and *Negrophobia: A Race Riot in Atlanta* (San Francisco: Encounter Books, 2001).
87 Quotes on front and back covers of Bauerlein, *The Dumbest Generation*.
88 Ibid., p. 234.
89 Ibid., pp. 15–26.
90 Ibid., p. 36.
91 Ibid., p. 77.
92 Ibid., pp. 149–50.
93 Ibid., p. 41.
94 Ibid., p. 95.
95 Ibid., pp. 120–24.
96 Ibid., p. 201.

Chapter 6

1 Brain D. Loader, "Introduction: Young Citizens in the Digital Age: Disaffected or Displaced?" in Brian Loader (ed.), *Young Citizens in the Digital Age: Political Engagement, Young People and New Media* (New York: Routledge, 2007), p. 8.
2 Milton L. Mueller, *Networks and States: The Global Politics of Internet Governance* (Cambridge, MA: The MIT Press, 2010), p. 5.
3 Ibid.
4 Ibid., pp. 5–6.
5 Ronald Deibert and Rafal Rohozinski, "Beyond Denial: Introducing Next-Generation Information Access Controls," in Ronald Deibert, John Palfrey, Rafal Rohozinski, and Jonathan Zittrain (eds.) *Access Controlled: The Shaping of Power, Rights, and Rule in Cyberspace* (Cambridge: The MIT Press, 2010), p. 9.
6 Evgeny Morozov, *The Net Delusion: The Dark Side of Internet Freedom* (New York: PublicAffairs, 2011), p. 82.
7 Regarding extreme nationalistic forms of education see Joel Spring, *Wheels in the Head: Educational Philosophies of Authority, Freedom, and Culture from Confucianism to Human Rights* (New York: Routledge, 2008), pp. 3–42.
8 See Joel Spring, *The American School: A Global Context From the Puritans to the Obama Era Eighth Edition* (New York: McGraw-Hill, 2011), pp. 386–420.
9 Shakuntala Banaji, David Buckingham, Liesbet van Zoonen, and Fadi Hirzalla, "CIVICWEB: Young People, the Internet and Civic Participation" (2009), p. 8. Retrieved from http://www.civicweb.eu/images/stories/reports/civicweb%20wp11% 20final.pdf on June 12, 2011.
10 Ibid.

11 The International Association for the Evaluation of Educational Achievement, "International Civic and Citizenship Education Study" (Amsterdam, The Netherlands: International Association for the Evaluation of Educational Achievement, 2010), p. 10.
12 Sonia Livingstone, Nick Couldry, and Time Markham, "Youthful Steps Toward Civic Participation," in Loader (ed.), *Young Citizens in the Digital Age,* pp. 21–33.
13 Gustavo S. Mesch and Stephen Coleman, "New Media and New Voters: Young People, the Internet and the 2005 UK Election Campaign," in Loader (ed.), *Young Citizens in the Digital Age,* pp. 35–67.
14 Joseph Kahne, Nam-Jin Lee, and Jessica Timpany Feezell, "The Civic and Political Significance of Online Participatory Cultures among Youth Transitioning to Adulthood," DMLcentral Working Papers, Youth & Participatory Politics (February 5, 2011). Retrieved from http://ypp.dmlcentral.net/publications on June 12, 2011.
15 Banaji, et al., "CIVICWEB," p. 4.
16 Ibid., p. 9.
17 Ibid., pp. 11–12.
18 Kahne, Lee, and Feezell, "Civic and Political Significance," p. 2.
19 Ibid., p. 21.
20 Roger Austin and John Anderson, *e-Schooling: Global Messages from a Small Island* (New York: Routledge, 2008), pp. 8–19.
21 Ibid., pp. 19–31.
22 Roger Austin, "Reconnecting Young People in Northern Ireland," in Loader (ed.), *Young Citizens in the Digital Age,* pp. 143–57.
23 Ibid., p. 149.
24 Ibid., p. 152.
25 Ethan Bronner, "Virtual Bridge Allows Strangers in Mideast to Seem Less Strange," *The New York Times* (July 9, 2011). Retrieved from http://www.nytimes.com/2011/07/10/world/middleeast/10mideast.html?_r=1&ref=world&pagewanted=print on July 10, 2011.
26 Ellen Middaugh and Joseph Kahne, "Online Localities: Implications for Democracy and Education," *Yearbook of the National Society for the Study of Education,* Volume 108, Number 1, 2009, p. 193.
27 Banaji, et al., "CIVICWEB," p. 4.
28 Jack Goldsmith and Tim Wu, *Who Controls the Internet: Illusions of a Borderless World* (New York: Oxford University Press, 2008), pp. 17–19.
29 Electron Frontier Foundation, "About." Retrieved from http://www.eff.org/about on July 7, 2011.
30 John Perry Barlow, "A Declaration of the Independence of Cyberspace" (February 1996). Retrieved from https://projects.eff.org/~barlow/Declaration-Final.html on July 7, 2011.
31 Ibid.
32 Ibid.
33 Ibid.
34 Ibid.
35 John M. Unsworth, "The Next Wave: Liberation Technology," *The Chronicle Review* (January 30, 2004). Retrieved from http://www3.isrl.illinois.edu/~unsworth/liberation.html on June 15, 2011.
36 Ibid.
37 Ibid.
38 Open Source Initiative, "The Open Source Definition." Retrieved from http://www.opensource.org/docs/osd on July 7, 2011.
39 TWiki, "TWiki – the Open Source Enterprise Wiki and Web 2.0 Application Platform." Retrieved from http://twiki.org/ on July 7, 2011.
40 Creative Commons, "About." Retrieved from http://creativecommons.org/about on July 7, 2011.

41 Ibid.
42 Ibid.
43 Larry Diamond, "Liberation Technology," *Journal of Democracy* (July 2010), p. 70.
44 Ibid., p. 78.
45 Voice of America, "Crowdmapping Arab Spring – Next Social Media Breakthrough?" (June 28, 2011). Retrieved from http://www.voanews.com/english/news/middle-east/ Crowdmapping-Arab-Spring-Next-Social-Media-Breakthrough–124662649.html on July 7, 2011.
46 Spring, *Wheels in the Head*, pp. 3–42.
47 On nationalistic and patriotic education see Spring, *The American School*, pp. 47–136.
48 Goldsmith and Wu, *Who Controls the Internet*, p. 98.
49 Ibid., pp. 98–100.
50 Ibid., p. 1.
51 Ibid., p. 3.
52 Ibid., p. 9.
53 Ronald Deibert, John Palfrey, Rafal Rohozinski, and Jonathan Zittrain (eds.), *Access Denied: The Practice and Policy of Global Internet Filtering* (Cambridge, MA: The MIT Press, 2008) and Ronald Deibert, John Palfrey, Rafal Rohozinski, and Jonathan Zittrain (eds.), *Access Controlled: The Shaping of Power, Rights, and Rule in Cyberspace* (Cambridge, MA: The MIT Press, 2010).
54 Morozov, *The Net Delusion*, p. 19.
55 Goldsmith and Wu, *Who Controls the Internet?*, p. 93.
56 Ibid., p. 93.
57 Cisco, "Together We Are the Human Network: 2010 Annual Report" (San Jose, CA: Cisco, 2010).
58 Ibid., p. 1.
59 Cisco, "Global Education Initiative." Retrieved from http://www.cisco.com/web/about/ ac227/ac222/society/socioeconomic_development_programs/global_education.html on July 9, 2011.
60 "Country Summaries" in Deibert, et al. (eds.), *Access Denied*, p. 310.
61 "MENA Overview" in Deibert, et al. (eds.), *Access Controlled*, p. 529.
62 Cisco, "Executive Summary," *Equipping Every Learner for the 21st Century: An Action Plan for Educational Transformation* (San Jose, CA: Cisco, 2008), p. 3.
63 Morozov, *The Net Delusion*, pp. 58–59.
64 Ronald Deibert and Rafal Rohozinski, "Control and Subversion in Russian Cyberspace," in Deibert, et al. (eds.), *Access Denied*, p. 20–21.
65 Ibid., pp. 20–27.
66 Ibid., pp. 538–42.
67 Jennifer Preston, "Anger and a Facebook Page That Gave It Voice," *The New York Times* (February 5, 2011). Retrieved from http://www.nytimes.com/2011/02/06/ world/middleeast/06face.html?_r=1&scp=1&sq=facebook%20and%20YouTube%20 fuel%20the%20Egyptian%20Protests&st=cse on July 10, 2011.
68 Ibid.
69 Ibid.
70 David D. Kirkpatrick and Jennifer Preston, "Egypt Releases Google Executive, Company Says," *The New York Times* (February 7, 2011). Retrieved from http:// www.nytimes.com/2011/02/08/world/middleeast/08google.html?scp=1&sq=Egypt %20releases%20Google%20executive,%20company%20says&st=cse on February 20, 2011.
71 Jenna Wortham, "Google Praises Executive's Role in Egypt Revolt," *The New York Times* (February 15, 2011). Retrieved from http://www.nytimes.com/2011/02/16/ world/middleeast/16google.html?sq=Egypt releases Google executive, company says&st= cse&scp=3&pagewanted=print on July 11, 2011.

72 James Glanz and John Markoff, "U.S. Underwrites Internet Detour Around Censors," *The New York Times* (June 12, 2011). Retrieved from http://www.nytimes.com/2011/06/12/world/12internet.html?_r=1&hp=&pagewanted=print on June 15, 2011.
73 Ibid.
74 "China" in Deibert, et al. (eds.), *Access Controlled*, p. 448.
75 Ibid.
76 Ibid., p. 455.
77 Ibid., pp. 457–58.
78 Ibid., p. 456.
79 Ibid., p. 459.
80 TRS Information Technology, "About." Retrieved from http://www.trs.com.cn/en/TRS/about/ on July 11, 2011.
81 Ibid.
82 TRS Information Technology, "TRS Text Taxonomy." Retrieved from http://www.trs.com.cn/en/pro/ckm/index.html on July 11, 2011.
83 Andrew Jacobs, "Chinese Student Takes Aim, Literally, at Internet Regulator," *The New York Times* (May 19, 2011). Retrieved from http://www.nytimes.com/2011/05/20/world/asia/20china.html?_r=1&scp=1&sq=Chinese%20students%20defense%20of%20internet%20freedom&st=cse on March 24, 2011.
84 Ibid.
85 Sharon Lafraniere and David Barboza, "China Tightens Censorship of Electronic Communications," *The New York Times* (March 21, 2011). Retrieved from http://www.nytimes.com/2011/03/22/world/asia/22china.html?_r=1&ref=todayspaper&pagewanted=print on April 2, 2011.
86 James Glanz and John Markoff, "Vast Hacking by a China Fearful of the Web," *WikiLeaks Archive – China's Battle With Google – NYTimes* (December 4, 2010). Retrieved from http://www.nytimes.com/2010/12/05/world/asia/05wikileaks-china.html?scp=1&sq=cables%20discuss%20vast%20hacking%20by%20a%20China&st=cse on December 20, 2010.
87 The Associated Press, "Facebook's CEO Visits China's Top Search Engine," *The New York Times* (December 20, 2010). Retrieved from http://latestchina.com/article/?rid=25765 on October 28, 2011.
88 David Barboza, "Microsoft to Partner With China's Leading Search Engine," *The New York Times* (July 4, 2011). Retrieved from http://www.nytimes.com/2011/07/05/technology/05microsoft.html?ref=business&pagewanted=print on July 12, 2011.
89 "Internet Office For Healthy Web Development," *People's Daily Online* (May 6, 2011). Retrieved from http://english.people.com.cn/90001/90776/90882/7371893.html on May 12, 2011.
90 Ibid.
91 Ibid.

Chapter 7

1 John Dewey and Evelyn Dewey, *Schools of Tomorrow* (New York: E.P. Dutton & Co. Inc., 1962).
2 Ibid., p. 226.
3 Ibid.
4 Center for Educational Research and Innovation, *Schooling for Tomorrow: Think Scenarios, Rethink Education* (Paris: OECD, 2006), p. 31.
5 Ibid., p. 36.
6 OECD, Schooling for Tomorrow: OECD Scenarios (2008), p. 6. Retrieved from http://www.oecd.org/document/57/0,3746,en_36702145_36702265_37191801_1_1_1_1,00.html on October 28, 2011.

7 Ibid., p. 7.
8 Ibid., p. 8.
9 John Dewey, "The School as Social Center," *National Education Association Proceedings* (1902) (Washington, DC: National Education Association, 1902), p. 381.
10 OECD, *The Starterpack: Futures Thinking in Action* (Undated), p. 39. Retrieved from http://www.oecd.org/document/33/0,3343,en_2649_35845581_38981601_1_1_1_1,00.html on July 19, 2011.
11 Ibid., p. 38.
12 Ibid.
13 Ibid.
14 Ivan Illich, *De-Schooling Society* (New York: Harper & Row, 1971).
15 See Joel Spring, *Wheels in the Head: Educational Philosophies of Authority, Freedom, and Culture from Confucianism to Human Rights Third Edition* (New York: Routledge, 2008), pp. 108–13.
16 OECD, *The Starterpack*, p. 43.
17 OECD, Schooling for Tomorrow: OECD Scenarios, p. 10.
18 OECD, *The Starterpack*, p. 44.
19 Ibid.
20 Friedrich Hayek, *The Road to Serfdom* (Chicago: University of Chicago Press, 1994).
21 Milton Friedman, *Capital and Freedom* (Chicago: University of Chicago Press, 1962), p. 89.
22 OECD, *The Starterpack*, p. 41.
23 Ibid.
24 Ibid.
25 Ibid., p. 42.
26 Jenny Anderson, "The Best School $75 Million Can Buy," *The New York Times* (July 8, 2011). Retrieved from http://www.nytimes.com/2011/07/10/nyregion/the-best-school-75-million-can-buy.html?_r=1&ref=education& pagewanted=print on July 8, 2011.
27 Ibid.
28 Avenues: The World School, "Second Language Fluency." Retrieved from http://www.avenues.org/second-language-fluency on July 23, 2011.
29 Avenues: The World School, "The World Course." Retrieved from http://www.avenues.org/global-vision-studies on July 23, 2011.
30 Avenues: The World School, "Global Preparedness." Retrieved from http://www.avenues.org/international-experience-global-orientation on July 23, 2011.
31 Anderson, "The Best School $75 Million Can Buy."
32 Avenues: The World School, "Technology." Retrieved from http://www.avenues.org/index.php?s=technology on July 24, 2011.
33 Florida Virtual School, "Global School." Retrieved from http://www.flvs.net/areas/elearning/Pages/U.S.%20and%20WORLDWIDE/GlobalSchool.aspx on July 23, 2011.
34 Ibid.
35 360Ed, "Florida Virtual School Chooses 360Ed as Global Service Partner" (January 14, 2009). Retrieved from http://www.360ed.com/site_media/uchi/pdf/360Ed%20FLVS%20Press%20Release.pdf on October 28, 2011.
36 360Ed, "Conspiracy Code." Retrieved from http://www.360ed.com/Products/Conspiracy-Code-American-History/ on July 24, 2011.
37 360Ed, "Educator Musing: McGraw-Hill and 360Ed Partnered to Create a Spark" (June 30, 2011). Retrieved from http://www.360ed.com/media/downloads/Classroom%202.0%20-%20Educator%20Musing.pdf on October 18 2011.
38 Ibid.
39 Florida Virtual School, "Global School."
40 Ibid.
41 University of Phoenix, "History." Retrieved from http://www.phoenix.edu/about_us/about_university_of_phoenix/history.html on July 23, 2011.

42 University of Phoenix, "Purpose." Retrieved from http://www.phoenix.edu/about_us/about_university_of_phoenix/mission_and_purpose.html on July 23, 2011.

43 See Diane Goldsmith, "Communication and Personality: Students' Attitudes to Online Learning," *Academic Quarterly Exchange* (Summer 2001). Retrieved from http://www.ctdlc/evaluation/humorpaper.pdf on July 23, 2011.

44 Robert Woods, Diane Badzinski, and Jason Baker, "Student Perceptions of Blended Learning in a Traditional Undergraduate Environment," in Anthony Picciano and Charles Dziuban (eds.), *Blended Learning: Research Perspectives* (Needham, MA: Sloan-C, 2007), p. 206.

45 Ibid., pp. 214–15.

46 Ibid., p. 203.

47 Jennifer Preston, "Social Media History Becomes a New Job Hurdle," *The New York Times* (July 20, 2011). Retrieved from http://www.nytimes.com/2011/07/21/technology/social-media-history-becomes-a-new-job-hurdle.html?_r=1&ref=todayspaper&pagewanted=print on July 21, 2011.

48 John Gleick, *The Information* (New York: Pantheon Books, 2011), p. 406.

49 Ibid., pp. 425–26.

50 Paul McDougall, "iPad Is Top Selling Tech Gadget Ever: Tablet-style Computers Are Flying Off Store Shelves almost as Fast as Apple Can Manufacture Them," *InformationWeek* (October 7, 2010). Retrieved from http://www.informationweek.com/news/storage/portable/227700347?printer_friendly=this-page on July 21, 2011.

51 Sam Grobart, "iPad Sales Times Announced," *The New York Times* (March 10, 2011). Retrieved from http://gadgetwise.blogs.nytimes.com/2011/03/10/ipad-sales-times-announced/?pagemode=print on July 21, 2011.

52 Winnie Hu, "Math That Moves: Schools Embrace the iPad," *The New York Times* (January 4, 2011). Retrieved from http://www.nytimes.com/2011/01/05/education/05tablets.html?sq=iPadschools&st=nyt&scp=1&pagewanted=print on July 22, 2011.

53 Ibid.

54 Ibid.

55 Ibid.

56 Ibid.

57 Kevin Kelly, *What Technology Wants* (New York: Viking Penguin, 2010).

58 Ibid., Kindle location 226–33.

59 Ibid., Kindle location 677–91.

60 Ibid., Kindle location 1146–53.

61 Simon Patten, *The New Basis of Civilization* (Cambridge, MA: Harvard University Press, 1968).

62 Ibid., p. 215.

63 Ibid., p. 141.

64 See Kelly Schrum, "Teena Means Business: Teenage Girls' Culture and 'Seventeen Magazine', 1944–50," in Sherrie Inness (ed.), *Delinquents & Debutantes: Twentieth Century American Girls' Cultures* (New York: New York University Press, 1998), pp. 130–55.

65 Ibid., p. 143.

66 Joel Spring, *Educating the Consumer-Citizen: A History of the Marriage of Schools, Advertising, and Media* (Mahwah, NJ: Lawrence Erlbaum Associates, 2003), pp. 5–6.

67 See Joel Spring, *American Education Fourteenth Edition* (New York: McGraw-Hill, 2010), pp. 224–37; Joel Spring, *The Politics of American Education* (New York: Routledge, 2011), pp. 150–60; and Joel Spring, *The American School: A Global Context from the Puritans to the Obama Era* (New York: McGraw-Hill, 2011), pp. 154–60, pp. 314–24, and pp. 364–83.

INDEX

Milken Institute Global Conference 35
mind, 4, 99; *see also* digital mind
Minnesota Education Computing
   Corporation (MECC) 76
Mintz, Steven 75
MIT, *see* Massachusetts Institute of
   Technology
MMOG, *see* Massively Multiplayer Online
   Games
mobile phones 50, 57–58; *see also* smart
   phones
Morozov, Evgeny 53, 70–71, 122, 133, 135
Moxie Insight 102
Mueller, Milton L. 122
multinationalization 40
multitasking 105–106: and ability to
   concentrate 102, 105, 107, 110; and
   ADD/ADHD 108, 119; effect on brain
   14–15, 99, 102, 105–106, 107
Murdoch, Rupert viii, 6–7, 15, 17

Nass, Clifford 105
national curriculum standards 94–95, 131,
   162; *see also* Common Core Standards
National Education Technology Plan 50,
   58–60; on use of digital games in
   schools 94; shadow elite of 61–63
nation-states 121–122
NCLB, *see* No Child Left Behind
Net Delusion, The 53, 70
Networks and States 122
New Basis of Civilization, The 159
New Teacher Project 51
New York City schools 3, 5–8; and ICT
   leaders 5–10; network connections
   15–19
New York University (NYU) 41–42,
   44–45
news, as entertainment 30
News Corporation 6–7, 8
Newton Learning 29
Next Generation Learning Challenges 69
N-gen (net generation) 100, 102; *see also*
   digital natives
Nintendo 82, 83
Nisbett, Richard 12–13
No Child Left Behind (NCLB): and
   truthiness 30; for-profit beneficiaries of
   27, 28–29, 33–34
nonverbal communication 108, 111, 154
Northern Ireland 125–126
North London Collegiate School 32–33
NYU, *see* New York University

Obama, Barack 94
Obama, Michelle 73
ODL, *see* open and distant learning
OECD, *see* Organization for Economic
   Development and Cooperation
Ondrejka, Cory 74
online communities 113–116, 119: and
   civic outcomes 125; as
   "superorganisms" 113–114; network
   theory 114; types of 115; *see also* social
   networks
online gaming: addiction to 87–89; and
   feeling of awe 92; educational 78,
   79–80; game design 91–92; social aspect
   of 91–92; *see also* gaming; video games
online instruction 2; and authoritarian
   education 156–157, 161–164; and class
   size requirements 65; and Common
   Core Standards 68–69; and ideological
   control 71, 72; and reducing costs
   65–66; attitudes towards 154–155;
   political and civic education 130–131;
   proposals for legal changes 65–66;
   reasons for supporting 155; replacing
   teachers with 60
open and distant learning (ODL) 49
Open Source Initiative 129
open source materials 128, 129
Ophir, Eyal 105
Oregon Trail 76, 77
Organization for Economic Development
   and Cooperation (OECD) 143–145,
   147–150
Oversea-Chinese Banking Corporation 47

Palestinians 126
Patten, Simon 159–160
Pea, Roy 62, 94
Pearson (company) 8, 66–67
Pearson Foundation 65; and Bill and
   Melinda Gates Foundation ix, 51, 61,
   66–67
Pearson School 35
performance state 30, 33
play 90
Polakow-Suransky, Shael 10, 15, 64
political activity 123–125
political consumerism 124
political education 121–141; and
   censorship 130–137; Internet as source
   of 140–141; online 130–131
political indoctrination 130, 148
Politics of American Education, The 33